WITHDRAWN

# House of Ideas

Before

and

After

# House of Ideas
## Creative Interior Designs

### Bill Baker

Macmillan Publishing Co., Inc.
NEW YORK
Collier Macmillan Publishers
LONDON

To my beloved children
Melanie
Wendell
Ron
Claudia
Cary

All art work, designs and photographs by the author, unless otherwise noted.

Macmillan Publishing Co., Inc.
866 Third Avenue, New York, N. Y. 10022
Collier-Macmillan Canada Ltd.

Library of Congress Cataloging in Publication Data

Baker, Bill.
House of ideas.

1. Dwellings—Remodeling.   2. Interior  decoration.
3. House furnishings.   I. Title.
TH4816.B33   643'.7   73-11734
ISBN 0-02-506280-8

First Printing 1974

Printed in the United States of America

# Contents

# House of Ideas

# Introduction

Ideally, proper design and creative decorating should be the result of a conscientious analysis of the time we live in and the person whose life the new creation is to enhance.

Ever since the start of civilization and probably even before, man has strived to put importance into his life's surroundings. Living quarters, whether it was a thousand, a hundred, or just ten years ago, proved unsatisfactory in time, and more than likely were changed to fit additional needs and requirements as well as newly acquired tastes.

Throughout history the creative movement nearly always had to be sanctioned by the leaders of society; therefore, good creative designers and inventors bearing a message of better things to come were neglected, ignored, and often scorned. Today finds little changed, while industry cries out for creative ideas and talents. Their calls remain unanswered for the most part. The true talent needed is often discouraged and unwilling to fight in a jungle where survival is only for the few who are able to hide behind walls of conformity.

This is really the most exciting era of America's youth. Today's children are more exuberant, creative, and talented than ever before in history. They are able to expand in many fields and are better able to apply themselves to creative projects. But the refined education of their senior years depends on the quality of the educators and the materials available to them.

Unfortunately, the craftsmen, all the way down the line, are so unconditioned to newer things that, even if a revolutionary change were to take place on the creative level after so many years of sameness, the better craftsmen—the spearheads of an already lacking industry—would still have to be reeducated.

Interior designing and decorating in its present limitations and abilities is certainly not a solution to the more complex structural needs. People themselves are often forced to look for guidance in better uses of space and new or even old appropriate products or approaches, and innovation through new products.

Were it not for a few creative pioneers who over the years have devoted much of their lives and income selflessly, nothing at all could have taken place to avoid a complete standstill in our search for more productive surroundings. It is necessary that we change our basic concept as to what is really important in better home living. And the sooner the better.

In this age, where by pushing one button, billions of dollars' worth of equipment is sent out into space photographing and televising perfect images, women still fall off the kitchen stool trying to reach that top shelf. Why?

I have twice in my life created a House of Ideas Theme. The first, finished in the mid-fifties, took place in a $20,000 development house. The do-it-yourself movement then was at its height and offered great benefits.

As sales promotion of tools and building products boomed into a multi-billion-dollar business, how-to books and magazines paid high fees for material suitable for the home-workshop-minded amateur.

I was well on my way in experimenting with a new way of living through built-ins, which was later used in one of my books.

This theme was to give birth to a new solution in space utilization in the home. Housekeeping was to become easier, space would be more efficiently used, and nearly every room in the house was to acquire a new look.

By building onto the wall, the new outer surface became a wood-paneled facing, giving the area a tailored finish. This enabled the homeowner or apartment dweller to hide unsightly and dust-catching cabinets while creating more efficient storage. For those who liked to entertain, an array of disappearing bars and gadgets provided surprises for the guests. This feature eventually came to have more appeal than the storage function.

The system was usually so calculated that, after figuring out the proper depth needed to hide the objects, an additional clearance of about 3 inches sufficed to give proper clearance for the bi-fold doors forming the new wall surface.

All this was possible through the proper use of existing hardware. Often the appraisal and projection of basic materials were different from the use intended by the manufacturers; sometimes this resulted in improvements.

The first House of Ideas featured such things as sewing machines and TV consoles sliding out of walls and guest beds folding down and out of walls, all to be out of sight when not in use. While these were still bulky and cumbersome, they formed the basis on which to build the improved versions that followed.

Several of these built-ins even found their way into commercial and institutional applications.

The basic materials used for these built-ins were nearly always plywood and hardware.

In the sixties the leading manufacturers of building products, headed by U.S. Plywood, sponsored the second and more successful House of Ideas.

While it was advisable to refer to and sometimes adapt previously tested applications, the goal of creating a more progressive exposé of different functions was actually the intention from the beginning.

Basically, most motions which are to conceal an area are based on a back and forth moving theory. Panels, drapes, and doors are obviously most qualified for such uses and since the basic projection was so simple, it was worthwhile to explore mechanization of these actions. Bicycle chains driven on slip-clutch sprockets connected to reversible motors, with limit switches precisely starting and stopping their actions, provide safe and successful solutions. There was, however, much more to be done to achieve the final dramatic results.

The reversible motor used for the mechanical drive is used also for automatic dimmers in theatres. Consequently, these motors were now engaged to change the light intensity while changing the physical appearance of the wall.

Depending on the ultimate purpose of a wall section, additional functions created never-ending surprises.

The AC power used to activate all the mechanics was transposed by a well-planned relay system operating on 12 volts, thus cutting down on wiring costs while using the same type of relays and timers used safely for the most complicated devices ranging from missiles to most

of Disneyland's wonders.

In such features as the "Living Wall," where further motions had to be tied in to the overall system, they became a part of the concert of movement. Each entity was properly timed to function without the need of any further attention other than pushing the starter button. This, in essence, transformed a decorative wall into a multifunctional entertainment center which, after running its preprogrammed course, reverted back to its original decorative wall.

Programmed motion which includes change of lighting can be very effectively put to the use of comfort and safety in a home.

Due to the nature of some of the items of interest, such as the one mentioned above, they cannot be visually illustrated as were the main features.

All the planning in the second House of Ideas was based on hypothetical living experiences. For instance, assuming a heavy snow or rain storm as a weather condition, the woman comes home in her car full of groceries, cleaning, etc. As she enters the driveway, which was cleared through a snow melting system, she pushes the transistor button in her car which opens the garage door. Suddenly the telephone rings. She picks up what she can from the car, proceeds to the pantry entrance, pushes the knee-touch plate mounted in the wall. The door slides open, she proceeds to the next door connecting the pantry with the kitchen, pushes another knee-touch plate, thus getting into the kitchen without the use of her hands, which, in this case, are holding heavy bundles.

In the kitchen, she sets down the packages and answers the phone. All this took three or four phone rings.

Ordinarily, this would leave three vital doors open, exposing the interior of the house to the bad weather. In this case, each door closes by itself about thirty seconds after the woman passes through. The main overhead lights in those areas also switch off. To do this, timers were connected to the mechanism of each of these doors. For safety, each door-driving device was installed with a slip-clutch, thus preventing accidents should anyone get caught in a closing door. In such a case the door would rumble against one's body until free to complete its cycle and close.

Burglary and holdups are increasing and present commercially available devices don't seem to effectively protect the person spending most of the day at home. Here is what was done in the House of Ideas.

A transistorized closed-circuit camera was installed above the soffit at house entrance with the aperture constructed to look like a downlight. This camera's connections were routed to the three most useful and lived-in areas via the ordinary television used there. This involved the portable set in the kitchen, a color TV below the big screen in the Living Wall, and another portable set in the teenage boy's room upstairs.

While the house was well provided with a most sophisticated audio intercom system, ranging from the front door through all the living areas, well into the patio and back yard, the visual protection often proved to be well worth its rather moderate expense.

The following demonstrates how this system would work: While home alone, Mrs. Trent answered a ring at the door through the audio intercom system, but became suspicious. It so happened that the portable TV set in the kitchen was on. Mrs. Trent activated the self-focusing remote camera by pressing a little button on the side of the TV. This cut out the program and clearly showed the front door area and the two callers on the TV screen. This gave Mrs. Trent a chance to call the police while stalling the callers.

To accomplish this a video separator was installed in each of the three TV sets. Once the switch button is pressed, normal TV reception is stopped and the remote camera at the entrance goes into action. In order to keep the cost to a minimum, the sound is picked up by the regular intercom which is located as is the telephone adjacent to the TV set.

To provide maximum safety within the home, especially when several young children are in the family, much thought was given for effective supervision. While important in any physical house layout, it was perhaps more so in this House of Ideas, due to its vast layout and

the upstairs bedrooms of the teenagers. This is where the pilot light's low-voltage light switch system came in very handy.

First, two master stations were selected: one in the kitchen and the other next to the night table in the master bedroom. In each case, these stations consisted of banks of switches which would light up when activated. This is where the main control function was supplied through interconnection of remote circuits. These master switch banks are usually placed next to the audio intercom and nearest the area where they are most convenient.

The master switch system is connected to every circuit—lights or wall receptacles. In the latter, we can expand upon TV or radio, which is plugged into any one of the circuit's receptacles. Of course, the electrical installation was so planned that proper separation of wiring sections would enable this to work without confusion.

While most people are aware of the benefits of a good intercom system, its proper use, or advantage, is often neglected. A good system can be so set up that one can eavesdrop on the children, hear them cough or turn and twist in bed—very helpful in the case of illness. Combined with a low-voltage safe switch system it is almost like being right there.

Many children may tend to abuse their bedtime privileges, especially if they are provided with their own radios, phonographs, and particularly TVs. Most of them actually fall asleep while listening to or watching TV. This, obviously, can result in a number of unpleasant consequences. The low-voltage pilot light switch system will prevent this.

With this system, once any unit requiring electricity is plugged in and turned on, it registers on the assigned switch on the master control panel. The assigned switch lights up. The same happens, of course, when the room lights are on.

In this house, certain bedtime hours were observed. While naturally they differed with the various ages of the children, they were often abused by the temptation which the well-equipped rooms offered. To curtail this, a look at the master switch plate would tell just who is doing what. The next move is to call the little ones in the particular area on the intercom system to ask them to turn the darn thing off and go to sleep.

Usually one of three things will happen: either they will obey or ask for a little more time or you hear them sleeping and breathing.

Unless the blasting of the radio or TV overpowers the observation of the latter, you usually get good and satisfying results.

If it is necessary to curtail the children's late entertainment, the switch is pushed off, thus cutting the circuit and, of course, whatever is connected to it. This can also be done to other areas, such as yards, and especially in basements or attics which often are neglected and turn out to be light-bill sources.

This House of Ideas was provided with a 2500 watt emergency power system (by the Automatic Switch Co.) which, controlled by an electronic "brain," did everything but talk. This system, powered by gasoline, had a 55 gallon barrel buried underground, far enough away from the living area of the house to avoid possible accidents.

The control system automatically activated the generator once a month for half an hour in order to exercise the mechanism.

If the electricity shuts off, in emergencies such as the East Coast black-out in 1964, the main power switch flips on, releasing enough power to light up several strategically placed night lights which provide sufficient lighting to walk around safely.

Other than that, there is enough power to keep all refrigerators, freezers, and heating circulators of the oil burner going. One kitchen circuit provided for coffee, hot soup, and other small necessities. The radio intercom was always going.

Adding a special pump and circuit to the hydronic heating and cooling system insured an adequate snow melting system in the winter which kept the main portion of the driveway mostly clear (except in heavy snowstorms). In the summer, the sophisticated cooling system controlled the temperature noiselessly and draftlessly.

For further safety, all strategic points of the ceiling in each area had a solenoid button unit, which, set for the appropriate area temperature, would sound off with bells and sirens inside and out should a flame or heat contact any of the buttons.

In addition, a smoke alarm system was installed in strategic areas. These units, looking like small decorative plastic containers, were mounted particularly at bedroom entrances. Their function was to sound off very loudly if smoke were to break the solenoid inside the container.

Other factors for better living control were ceiling exhaust fans mounted specially in the high areas of the cathedral ceiling, usually above the air-conditioning registers. These fans effectively extracted all stagnant air or smoke, which usually piles up in high ceiling pockets. The rest of the air circulation was well taken care of by the high mounted air-conditioning outlets and air returns. As heat rises and cool air drops, these supplies were installed accordingly.

For further living control, air purifying units were added to each of the three air-conditioning zones, thus keeping the air at a man's height as pure and moist as necessary.

For home cleaning, a very sophisticated vacuum system with wall outlets every 12 to 15 feet or less (the hose and attachments are to reach over 20 feet) was installed throughout the house, garage, attic, and basement areas. This system, rated for commercial use (many such installations are found in better hotels and motels), has a main tank facility, usually in the garage, which is at least 3 or 4 times as powerful as the best home vacuum cleaner. The tank capacity is sufficiently large to need to be emptied only once a month under normal use. The hose and attachments are very light and easy to maneuver around. As with this vacuum cleaner system, many of the other items and installations were also designed and manufactured primarily for commercial use. In order to have proper things for a better environment at home, the use of commercially designed manufacturer-oriented products is not only desirable but absolutely necessary.

There were many more installations and applications in the new House of Ideas which helped make those items mentioned useful and successful.

No single factor contributes as much weight in overall human comfort for those who live in these latitudes as a system that heats our homes. This house was equipped with the best engineered system possible.

Why rebuild a 100-year-old house rather than build from scratch?

By building a new home, inclusive of all these features, one would undoubtedly save considerably. However, it would be necessary to improvise the installation of the built-ins and all the rest of the features in order to effect any saving. To explain this properly, it would be necessary to explain what actually motivated the entire project, how and why it started, and how the many features actually were planned.

Like composing a piece of music, writing a poem, or painting a picture, none of which can be done by delimiting time, tone scale, amount of chords, or colors, this creation could not have been accomplished with restrictions.

This House of Ideas was created and not designed. It was made into designs and prints after its completion and tireless tests for the benefit of publication. Not to create all of this in an old house would have been defeating the objective.

The United States Plywood Corporation spearheaded this project from the start. Others, as listed on page 277, joined with unlimited help and enthusiasm.

The author acknowledges gratefully the help, guidance, and the financial support of some, and the nearly endless time for experimentation and final successful building of age-less mechanical devices by others. Without these contributions, none of this could have been as successful as it finally turned out.

Due to the continuous efforts of manufacturers to improve their products, you may find that some of the materials featured in this book are no longer available.

Your local building supply dealer will have no difficulty in recommending newer and, in some ways, better products developed by these same manufacturers.

With these products you can carry out all the ideas in this book for improving your house or apartment in a stylish, yet economical, way.

# Chapter 1
# Entrance Gallery and Staircase

Whether a home has an impressive entrance-way or merely a small greeting area, this space serves to introduce guests and friends to your home. It is a design "clue"—hinting at what is yet to come and setting a certain mood.

Because the central concept of the House of Ideas was innovation, this house demanded a very unusual and attractive entrance gallery. In fact, the final design stressed glamor and new ideas to a greater extent than might be expected in most homes.

The focal point of the entranceway is a sweeping, suspended staircase that dominates the area. The graceful handrails and modern plexiglass treads are supported from above on stainless steel cables. The translucent treads, which contribute to the illusion of weightless-ness, are each lighted individually to add still more drama, while providing added safety.

The problems encountered in building this entranceway are certainly worth exploring. Perhaps you'll find solutions to your own particular situation, no matter what the size or physical nature of your entranceway.

## Preparing the area

The center of this entrance gallery was originally an old kitchen and staircase area (Figure 2), the ceiling height of which was about 8 feet 7 inches. Height was important in order to achieve the desired dramatic effect, and this meant incorporating the area of an upstairs bedroom into the space allotted to the entranceway. All of the original partition walls and stairs were eliminated and the floor and the joists removed. In short, the entire area was opened up, leaving only the structural and bearing walls (Figures 4, 5, and 6).

Once the basic working area was cleared, the layout of the hallways and doors leading off the gallery and the new ceiling joists could be planned. The position of the staircase itself was determined by a lower wall leading to the living room area (see house plan, page 13).

## Tread size

The distance between the ground floor and top landing had to be divided so that the treads were no less than 7½ inches and no more than

Fig. 2.    Entranceway before being remodeled.

Fig. 3.    Remodeled staircase, from above.

Fig. 1.    (opposite page) House of Ideas staircase.

Figs. 4, 5, 6. Removal of old staircase and ceiling to create space for the entrance gallery.

8½ inches from the top surface of one step to the next. This requirement is easy to meet if there are no physical barriers, such as existing bearing walls. Where problems do exist, however, the solution is to build the staircase in two sections with a landing at a corner, approximately one-third of the way between the lower and the upper floors. This requires only straight stretches of stairs and meets the problem inexpensively without any compromise in the basic dimensions. Where limited space is a factor, staircases are often built with widely spaced stair treads, in some cases more than 9 inches apart (riser height). With 2-x-8-inch treads (which in net dimension are only 7½ inches deep), such a stairway is uncomfortable and dangerous.

In order to retain safe dimensions and create the desired appearance, the treads in this staircase were made 2½ inches deeper than necessary. The extra depth of one step was overlapped by the next. This extra depth proved a bonus from the construction point of view and it also acted as a safety feature.

### Tread material

The original plan had been to fabricate the stair treads of solid walnut and then suspend them on stainless steel rods. Later, when the center stringer (stair support) was being constructed, the idea of the steel suspension was retained, but modified. One-half-inch stainless steel wire rope cables were used instead of rods. Research into various stair materials revealed that the cost of plexiglass treads was only one-third higher than that of walnut treads. Plexiglass would not visually diminish the size of the entrance gallery nor would it compete with the wormy chestnut paneling that would cover all main walls in this area. And, it would give a strikingly dramatic first impression. Plexiglass treads were, therefore, used. Because plexiglass treads can be slippery and are vulnerable to scratches if left uncovered, the center 24 inches of each 42-inch-wide tread would be wrapped in latex foam rubber underlayment with Acrylan carpeting over it.

### Illuminating the treads

This carpeting made it possible to light the

staircase by inserting a miniature light bulb into a hole bored through the back of each tread. To accommodate the necessary wires, a 5⁄8-x-5⁄8-inch channel (later covered with ¼ inch solid wood veneer) was made in the top of the main stringer prior to installation of tread supports. Holes were bored into the tread supports to connect with the continuous channel. Low voltage wire was inserted through the bottom of the stringer and run into the main channel (Figure 7). Then, with a wire hook, 6-to-8-inch

Fig. 7.   Low-voltage wire being inserted into the pre-bored channels of the center stringer.

loops were pulled out through the holes in the tread supports.

Next, the tread supports were notched out in back, and small ½-x-1½-inch connector plates were inserted and screwed to the wood. Finally, the looped low voltage wire was cut and connected on each side of the small plates. Miniature sockets, made to receive 5⁄16-inch diameter elongated low voltage bulbs, were connected to these plates. When the bulb is inserted into the plexiglass tread, the entire perimeter emits a strong glowing light and the surface is illuminated evenly, though less intensely. This extremely decorative effect is possible in any transparent or translucent plastic material, since such materials carry rather than

reflect or absorb light no matter where it is injected.

The bulb area in the rear center of the tread is completely concealed on the underside by the wooden stringer tread support. On top it is hidden by the 6-inch-square stainless steel plate. Since the carpeting completely conceals the direct light source (the boring and the bulb itself), a small (2-x-2-inch) flap had to be cut into the carpet in the bulb area at the bottom back. This flap makes it easy to pull out the small assembly and change the bulb if and when necessary (a rating test, however, revealed that the life expectancy of these bulbs should be over ten years, especially if used with a Luxtrol dimmer, as in this case).

### Handrail supports

Before mounting the staircase-suspension cables to the attic construction, the handrail supports had to be slipped onto the cables. The only way to fasten the support in this type of construction is to slip it on the cable and lock it into position with either regular or, as in this case, Allen screws. Once this screw penetrates the wire rope cable, it will never budge. The rail height, and consequently the supports, are a maximum of 38 inches from the tread surface.

A solid and rather simple system of supports was devised by using two pipes, one inside the other. The narrower pipe covered the threaded cable and extended beyond the thicker one. A double-lock system to prevent slippage was the result.

### Handrail

The handrail presented a challenge in that its shape and material had to blend with the rest of the construction. All the hard, solid materials used so far needed the balance of some textural warmth. Wood was, therefore, the only logical answer for the handrail—and it would harmonize with the adjacent paneled wall.

After choosing the material, shape was the most immediate problem. Solid walnut pieces between 3 and 4 feet long were fabricated in the rough into a wedgelike shape. Tilting the wood rail by 30 degrees lent a more dramatic appearance and a more comfortable grip, al-

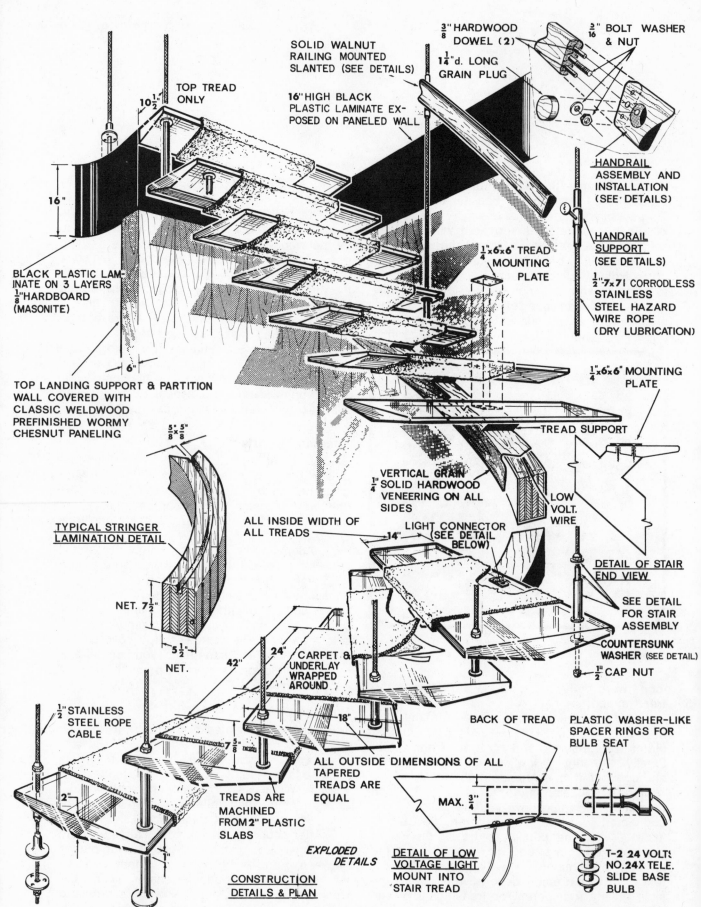

TOP TREAD ONLY

$10\frac{1}{2}$"

SOLID WALNUT RAILING MOUNTED SLANTED (SEE DETAILS)

16" HIGH BLACK PLASTIC LAMINATE EXPOSED ON PANELED WALL

$\frac{3}{8}$" HARDWOOD DOWEL (2)

$1\frac{1}{4}$"d. LONG GRAIN PLUG

$\frac{3}{16}$" BOLT WASHER & NUT

16"

HANDRAIL ASSEMBLY AND INSTALLATION (SEE DETAILS)

$1\frac{1}{4}$"x6x6" TREAD MOUNTING PLATE

HANDRAIL SUPPORT (SEE DETAILS)

BLACK PLASTIC LAMINATE ON 3 LAYERS $\frac{1}{8}$" HARDBOARD (MASONITE)

$\frac{1}{2}$"7x7I CORRODLESS STAINLESS STEEL HAZARD WIRE ROPE (DRY LUBRICATION)

6"

TOP LANDING SUPPORT & PARTITION WALL COVERED WITH CLASSIC WELDWOOD PREFINISHED WORMY CHESNUT PANELING

$\frac{5}{8}$" x $\frac{5}{8}$"

$1\frac{1}{4}$"x6x6" MOUNTING PLATE

TREAD SUPPORT

VERTICAL GRAIN $\frac{1}{4}$" SOLID HARDWOOD VENEERING ON ALL SIDES

LOW VOLT. WIRE

TYPICAL STRINGER LAMINATION DETAIL

ALL INSIDE WIDTH OF ALL TREADS

LIGHT CONNECTOR (SEE DETAIL BELOW)

DETAIL OF STAIR END VIEW

14"

NET. $7\frac{1}{2}$"

SEE DETAIL FOR STAIR ASSEMBLY

$5\frac{1}{2}$" NET.

COUNTERSUNK WASHER (SEE DETAIL)

$\frac{1}{2}$" CAP NUT

42"

24"

CARPET & UNDERLAY WRAPPED AROUND

$\frac{1}{2}$" STAINLESS STEEL ROPE CABLE

$7\frac{5}{8}$"

18"

BACK OF TREAD

PLASTIC WASHER-LIKE SPACER RINGS FOR BULB SEAT

2"

ALL OUTSIDE DIMENSIONS OF ALL TAPERED TREADS ARE EQUAL

TREADS ARE MACHINED FROM 2" PLASTIC SLABS

MAX. $\frac{3}{4}$"

EXPLODED DETAILS

CONSTRUCTION DETAILS & PLAN

DETAIL OF LOW VOLTAGE LIGHT MOUNT INTO STAIR TREAD

T-2 24 VOLTS NO.24X TELE. SLIDE BASE BULB

Fig. 8. Exploded detail of new staircase.

though it presented a difficult building maneuver.

Before the tilted rail was built, a half-round skeleton conforming to the stair plan was made. On this form (a slanted compound curve), the cut-out strips of wood are temporarily mounted. Once the pieces are cut, they are clamped or taped in place on the rail supports (which have been slipped onto every other cable).

The joint cuts can now be determined. The strips of wood are connected at each joint with two $\frac{3}{8}$-inch dowels and a $\frac{5}{16}$-inch fastener that is a bolt at one end and a screw at the other (see Figure 8). The fastener is screwed into one piece of the rail between the dowels, leaving the bolt end extending about 3 inches or enough to partially penetrate a 1¼-inch hole cut into the surface of the connecting section of handrail.

The handrail pieces are first dry-assembled without glue, to be sure the dowels fit properly. The machine bolt should penetrate enough so that a washer and nut can be fastened to it and tightened after tapping it slightly to the two surfaces. At this point, it is possible to tell whether or not the joint is perfect. Also check to see that the 30-degree slant continues up the rail without causing pulling or pushing on the suspension cables and without departing from the proper height. If adjustments are necessary, a disc sander can be very handy.

When a complete length of rail is in correct position, the joints can be glued. As the glue is applied and the bolts are fully tightened, each portion of the handrail is mounted to the stainless steel brackets before going on with the next joint. Take the assembled railing from the stainless steel supports to let the glue dry, and then glue a matching long grain plug into the 1¼-inch hole.

Next, sand all parts smooth and reposition the rail in 6- to 8-foot portions on the supports. This means sanding the other joints right on the suspension cables. Although the procedure is a bit troublesome, it is the only way to achieve a near-perfect job. The railing was finished with 2 light coats of deep-finish Firzite, a light rubbing with steel wool, and a final coat of paste wax.

**Stairway support**

The extent of the support for the stairway was determined by two factors: first, the *weight* of the wire rope cables, plexiglass treads, handrail, stainless steel pipe, spacers, nuts, bolts, couplings, etc., in addition to a person's weight on the staircase; second, the *location* of the stair structure in the core of the old house structure.

It was necessary to install a supporting reinforcement in the attic by strengthening and uniting the ceiling joists of the entrance gallery with the roof rafters. This was done by bracing and spiking 2-x-4s and 2-x-6s across the old ceiling joists in those areas where the steel cables were fastened. Additional bracing was provided by nailing 2-x-4s to the ceiling about every 3 feet.

Next came the installation of a mechanism that would take up the constantly increasing slack in the stainless steel wire rope cables (see Figures 9 and 11). One-half-inch threaded rods were welded to the ends of the cables. This allowed the placement of a ¼-x-3-x-3-inch steel plate with a ⅝-inch center hole through which the wire rope cable and the bolt were inserted. A ¾-inch o.d. inner pipe with the welded-on washer was slipped on. It also allowed attachment of a turnbuckle which can be twisted to loosen or tighten the stainless steel rope suspension cables, should it be necessary. On at least every third or fourth cable, a long threaded rod was screwed into the other end of the turnbuckle which was bent around the roof rafters for overall support.

Two precautions must be taken when using the method explained here. Although the threaded rod on the bottom is easily concealed by determining its exact length, the top length varies with each pair of cables, especially in an installation in an old house where the rafters are not consistent and the ceiling is often bowed.

Another factor to consider carefully is the reinforcement above the rafters. Here again we do not know where the 2-x-4 or 2-x-6 supports will be in relation to the staircase. In other words, if the supports for the carrying cables are in the center of the ceiling rather than near the bearing walls, cross supports made of short

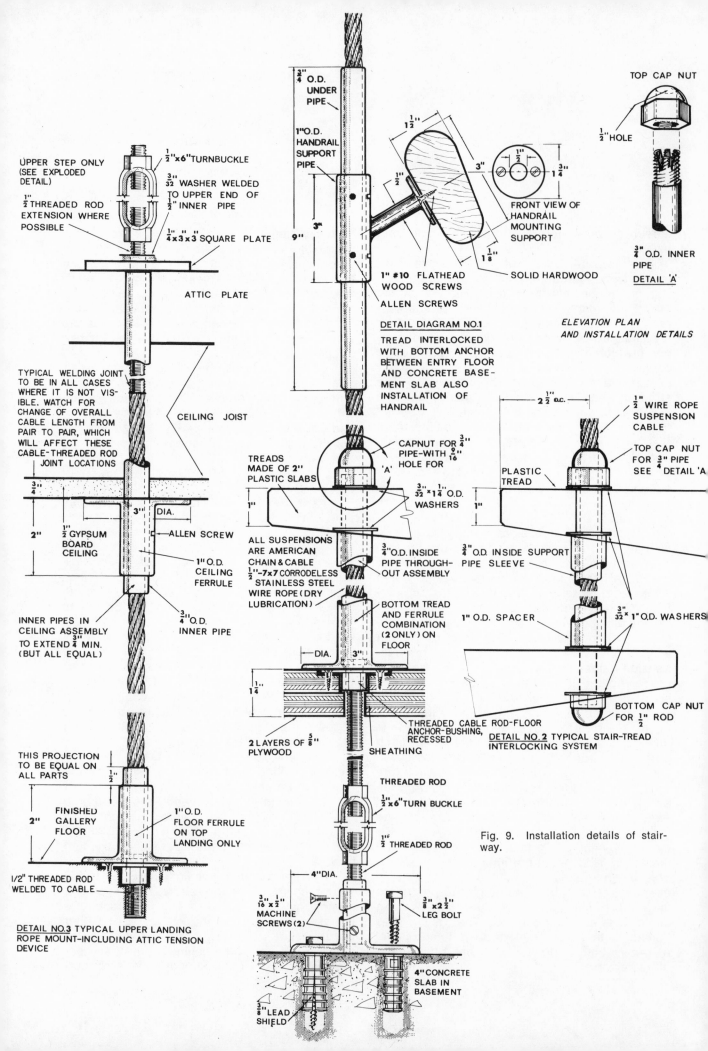

Fig. 9. Installation details of stairway.

blocks or strips and reaching at the most over two or three rafters are not adequate. These cables would exert great pull and the ceiling would bow down increasingly as tension was adjusted. Such a physically weak and unsightly installation can be avoided by running cross planks in the attic, long enough to get their support from the bearing walls. Here again, if the span is great enough to even slightly bend the cross supports, it may be necessary to put the cross supports on edge.

Fortunately, the suspension cables for this

## Cable length

A system was devised to fabricate each suspension cable individually (see Figures 9 and 11). The cable itself must be at least 1 inch within the upper ceiling and the welded-on ½-inch-diameter threaded rod must be long enough to penetrate all the necessary supports, with enough left over for the washer plate above all the wood bracing and for hand grip on the turnbuckle. The critical point is that each pair of cables is automatically different from every other due to the step incline. They may also

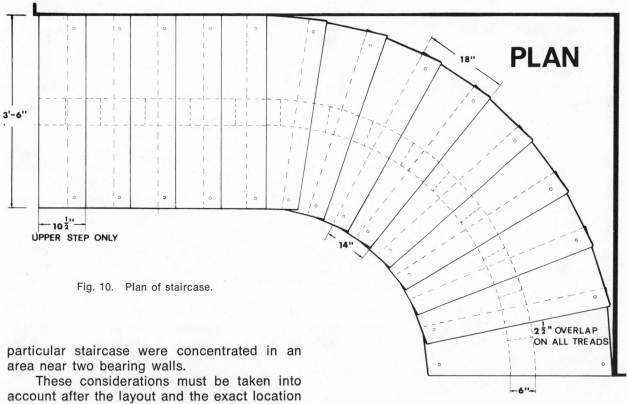

Fig. 10.   Plan of staircase.

particular staircase were concentrated in an area near two bearing walls.

These considerations must be taken into account after the layout and the exact location of the suspension cables are determined. Precaution must also be taken at the foot of the center stringer as well as the first pair of suspension cables which penetrate the first floor and fasten to the basement floor (see Figures 9 and 11).

differ from their own mates due to the change in the type of bracing above. Thus, individual measuring is essential prior to ordering the suspension cables.

Only after dropping the plumb onto a pre-marked plywood tread pattern and boring a 7/8-inch hole into the ceiling will you be able to determine the cut-off point of the cable, the welding joint of the threaded rod to the cable, and the necessary length of the threaded rod above the ceiling and on the bottom.

## Center stringer

The support construction outlined above was necessary because the center stringer would not be strong enough to carry the entire load of the stairway. Exposing it to the pressures and vibrations of daily use would be dangerous. Instead, the stringer served to stabilize, align, and anchor the treads. It also concealed the wire carrying the low voltage current which came out of the attic.

Because the success of the entire staircase is dependent on a correctly built center stringer, the task should be given to a professional. A stringer for a straight staircase, however, might be built by a skilled do-it-yourselfer.

Due to its compound curve, the center stringer in this case is a twisted piece of 6-x-8-inch wood which is constructed in staggered sections of 2-x-8-inch solid wood and with the aid of a tunnel-like frame structure, made with 2 templates. A top-view template shows the actual direction and shape of the center line of the staircase (Figure 10). The other template is an elevation showing the basic slant of the entire staircase which is laid out to receive the tread supports.

The tread supports will be spaced evenly and mounted to the top of the stringer. With the exception of 4 or 5 supports which are mounted in the extreme curve, they are the same on the top surface and absolutely square with the stringer. The top tread is 3½ inches narrower because the top tread support is partially inserted into the landing platform. The supports are approximately 5 inches high in front and 1⅝ inches high in back. Each straight tread is 14 by 42 inches; the top tread is 10½ by 42 inches. The treads around the curve are

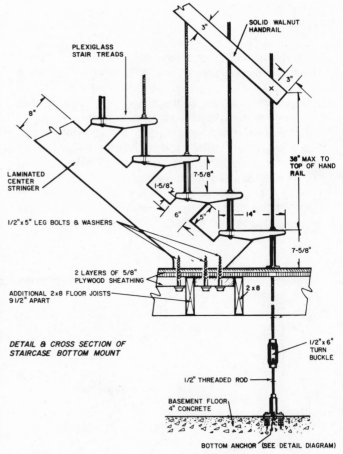

Fig. 11. Detail and cross section of staircase bottom mount.

14 inches at the visible center curve side.

The stringer is constructed of poplar or alder wood which is assembled in small ribs with joints staggered, using pieces 2 feet long or longer depending on the size of the curve. Glue is used for fastening. The stringer has to be cut from raw wood and brought to a perfectly smooth shape. Finish the stringer by attaching (with glue, screws, or dowels) the blocks to which the treads are mounted. The tread supports should be planed flush.

A solid wood veneer (walnut in this case) ¼- or ⁵⁄₁₆-inch maximum (less if curves are tight) is glued to the finished stringer construction. The grain of the veneer should run with the stringer length. Depending on the curves and compound twists, this veneer may also have to be pieced and most certainly will have to be steamed, water-soaked, preformed, and clamped to sustain the tension put on it when gluing it to the stringer construction. When the center stringer is completed, the wires are strung through and connected to the miniature connector plates in the back of each tread support. Leave sufficient wire on top to make the final electrical connection.

The final straight stretch of stairway consists of 5 straight treads. These will be mounted so that the center stringer is kept parallel to the right wall and a 1-inch margin is maintained between the right edge of the 5 even treads and the finished right wall.

The next step is to finish the edge of the top landing so it is at an exact 90 degree angle to the right wall. The top step will be flush with the finished upper landing edge. A "V" cut in this edge will serve to support the stringer. Therefore, all necessary provisions to receive the stringer and its fastening bolts and to prepare the route of the electric wire must be made first.

### Surrounding entranceway

Before permanently mounting the stringer, finish off the surface of the upper landing edge and all the surrounding floor, wall, and ceiling areas.

The ceilings are covered with ½-inch gypsum wall board and painted; the upper ceiling, a terra cotta color and the lower hall ceiling, white. The walls on the right side of the staircase are covered with prefinished wormy chestnut (architectural paneling) with black plastic laminate spacing between the sheets. The adjacent wall, where the staircase begins, is covered with 1-inch Moonstone ceramic tiles (Mosaic Tile) which are grouted with matching grout. The wall to the left of the staircase is covered with ⅝-inch-thick gypsum wall board and is painted terra cotta, matching the ceiling and some of the walls at the head of the stairs. Directly below the landing, the wall is covered with 18-inch-square slightly beveled (⅛ inch) antiqued ¼-inch plate glass mirrors (see Figure 1). This mirrored wall, opposite the family room, reflects a portion of the staircase, creat-

Figs. 12, 13. After installation of the center stringer, the second-floor landing area is covered with parquet floor panels.

ing an illusion of extreme depth, without the glare and diminishing effect an ordinary mirror would have created.

There is certainly much to learn from this exciting installation, and, surely, some of it is applicable to any remodeling job—whether it is an entrance gallery or another area. For instance, a common remodeling problem is contending with the fact that the standard sheet of prefinished paneling is 8 feet high. Because the total ceiling height in this entrance gallery was 17 feet, 8 inches, an ingenious wall cover-

Fig. 14.   Installation of prefinished paneling precedes installation of staircase.

Fig. 15.   Accent wall is covered with mosaic tile.

ing had to be devised. Piecing paneling will always result in an imperfect job because it is almost impossible to match grain and color in V-grooved paneling. The wall adjacent to the staircase illustrates the solution. On top of the first sheets of paneling, at the 8-foot level, a strip of black plastic laminate was installed, separating the lower section of paneling from that above it.

Because the 8-foot prefinished paneling would cover 80 per cent of the walls in the house, it was necessary to make all the walls uniform in height. To do this, all floors and ceilings (which were originally crooked and in bad shape) were furred out with wood shingles, strips, blocks, and plywood sheathing to produce a uniform 8-foot ½-inch room height throughout the house. Besides the aesthetic factor, this plan also cut down on the labor necessary to install the paneling.

Since no ceiling moldings were used, it was necessary to scribe the panels to the ceiling leaving only ⅝ inch to ¾ inch maximum space between the panels and the floor. This space was filled in with plywood scraps of the same thickness which were concealed by the base shoe (solid oak, finished to match, available from any lumber yard in a variety of woods —like a #8M Stop). Since the base shoe is about 1⅛ inch high and ½ inch thick, it creates a neat and inconspicuous finish. Where the base panel heating units are installed, the panels are fitted and the base moldings are butted to them.

On the mosaic tile wall, base moldings are unnecessary because the tiles are started at the floor level. On the mirrored wall, however, a 6-inch-high base, consisting of vertical V-grooved paneling with the base shoe, is installed (see Figure 1). A ¾-x-¾-inch matching solid wood strip at the bottom carrying the mirror weight, and a similar strip rabbeted out and mounted on top, increase the safety and aesthetic factors of this wall.

## Lighting

The lighting in a setting of this kind is certainly an important consideration. An ostentatious chandelier or lighting fixture could destroy the beauty and simplicity of its clean design and compete with the powerful staircase suspension system. The fixture shown has a slim and simple shape enriched by the addition of crystals. It adds a touch of luxury on a low budget and in no way interferes with the design or any portion of the decor. The electric current fed into the light is controlled by the same dimmer that controls the tread lights. The chandelier is hung on a very thin but very strong ⅛-inch stainless steel wire rope cable, with a thin low voltage transparent jacketed electric wire. When dimly lit, the chandelier appears to be floating.

Spotlights rather than flood bulbs carry over a warmth from the lesser lit to the more highly lit areas.

## Doors

To achieve maximum harmony with the walls, the doors in the area were mounted flush with no moldings. The finish of the 1¾-inch Weldwood solid core doors matched the adjacent paneling in almost all areas and the achitectural-type Royal Russwin door locks and Stanley cylindric butt hinges used on the doors became decorative assets to this area, as well as to the entire house.

## Windows and window treatment

The windows remained in the same general locations as in the old house, but they were modernized by the installation of Stanley aluminum weatherproof sashes. Although they conformed to the exterior on the second floor level, the sashes looked peculiar from the inside. To solve this problem, custom-made window shades were used. A heavy-duty window shade was laminated with drapery material and mounted to a heavy-duty spring roller. The bottom was scalloped and allowed to hang free 4 inches below the bottom wood strip of the shade. Since the shades cannot be reached by hand, a brass ring is attached and the shade is manipulated with a stick that has a brass hook on the end.

The long 3-pane window, with the 3 shorter panes below, had a special wood sash built for it. The window drapery was a fine, transparent, net-type material which served to enhance the sculptured beauty of the exterior block wall. This drapery is installed on a hardware device that holds permanent pleats, creating a tailored appearance when closed and folding to a small flat unit when opened.

## Flooring

The 9-foot circular carpeting is semipermanently secured to the floor because of the necessary cutouts at the staircase base. It is positioned so as to form a continuous spiral with the stair carpeting.

The vinyl flooring is Barcelona (by Amtico) similar to pebble stone and three-dimensional in texture. Because of the unusual nature of the remodeling project, the flooring had to be installed sooner than would normally be the case. It was, therefore, exposed to machines, saw horses, and boxes, but there are no signs of any damage. This vinyl flooring requires only damp mopping and vacuuming for maintenance. As in the choice of drapes and carpets, durability as well as strength and beauty were important considerations.

The final decorative touch was the addition of a hand-fabricated planter filled with ferns and other greenery which thrive under artificial light and the limited daylight available in the area.

This elegant new staircase and entrance gallery set the tone for the House of Ideas and, at the same time, they provide striking solutions to many remodeling problems.

Fig. 16. The remodeled staircase in all its glory.

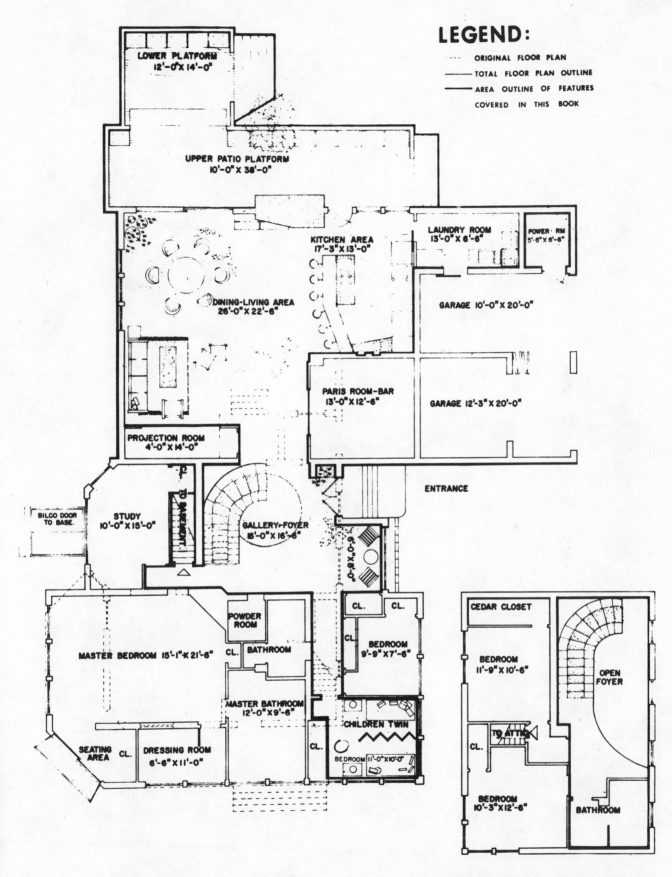

**LEGEND:**

- - - - ORIGINAL FLOOR PLAN
———— TOTAL FLOOR PLAN OUTLINE
▬▬▬▬ AREA OUTLINE OF FEATURES
COVERED IN THIS BOOK

LOWER PLATFORM
12'-0" X 14'-0"

UPPER PATIO PLATFORM
10'-0" X 38'-0"

KITCHEN AREA
17'-3" X 13'-0"

LAUNDRY ROOM
13'-0" X 6'-6"

POWER RM
5'-6" X 6'-6"

GARAGE 10'-0" X 20'-0"

DINING-LIVING AREA
26'-0" X 22'-6"

PARIS ROOM-BAR
13'-0" X 12'-6"

GARAGE 12'-3" X 20'-0"

PROJECTION ROOM
4'-0" X 14'-0"

ENTRANCE

BILCO DOOR
TO BASE.

CL.

TO BASEMENT

STUDY
10'-0" X 15'-0"

GALLERY-FOYER
18'-0" X 16'-6"

6'-0" X 6'-0"

CL.

CL.

CL.

POWDER
ROOM

BATHROOM

MASTER BEDROOM 15'-1" X 21'-6"

CL.

BEDROOM
9'-9" X 7'-6"

CEDAR CLOSET

BEDROOM
11'-9" X 10'-6"

OPEN
FOYER

MASTER BATHROOM
12'-0" X 9'-6"

CL.

CL.

TO ATTIC

SEATING
AREA

CL.

DRESSING ROOM
6'-6" X 11'-0"

CHILDREN TWIN

BEDROOM 11'-0" X 10'-0"

BEDROOM
10'-3" X 12'-6"

BATHROOM

# GROUND FLOOR PLAN

# SECOND FLOOR PLAN

Fig. 17. Floor plan of the house.

# Chapter 2
# Family and Living Areas

The inclusion of a family room in most recently built houses, and indeed, the addition of such rooms to many older homes, reflect a relatively recent phenomenon in our approach to living and to design. In general, this approach caters to a leisurely style of life with the accent on relaxation and enjoyment.

After World War II, there was a noticeable decrease in the formalities of life—the living room became much smaller and the dining room became a "dinette," usually incorporated into the living room. The "L" shape living-dining room arrangement is still very popular today.

The first of these changes took place in California, where a mild climate allowed experimentation with the usual separation of indoor and outdoor space. Altering the basic floor plan by moving the living room to the rear of the house opened up a number of design possibilities. One new Western trend was the lanai, a sort of sun room with louvered windows for walls, which was placed in the back of the house. Innovations like this one did much to change thinking on home design, especially homes in the middle income level.

As the public grew accustomed to new types of interior floor plans, the designers were busy changing overall house appearance and proportions, generally making them shallower and wider. This proportion, far superior from a design standpoint, was known as the "California ranch."

Within a short time, developers started to show their model homes with a focus on a large kitchen with indoor barbecue and lots of brick and quarry tiles. These kitchens often faced the front of the house, and featured a large serve-through counter to what had become the "family room." Reluctant to eliminate the formal living room entirely, builders placed it in the shallow part of the house, often facing both front and back.

The family room soon became a necessity in any new country home. Easterners added their own innovations, making the family room an all-purpose gathering center. When home improvement became a multi-billion-dollar business in the midfifties and early sixties, a great deal of the activity was in remodeling attics and basements for use as family rooms.

The aim was, and is still today, to centralize family living activities. Each area must completely and effectively adjust to the family, both as individuals and as a unit, and to their way of functioning. It must be a place where everyone can be content, and where they can entertain friends comfortably. To meet these criteria, the room has to be versatile and easy to maintain. This often means built-ins—with as few exposed horizontal surfaces as possible. Such a room must be capable of conversion from one use to another in the shortest possible time. It must lend itself to family gatherings, afford an opportunity for listening to music, watching TV, or just sitting and talking. It should also provide for showing films or slides with equipment that can quickly be tucked away.

The rooms described here illustrate two interesting approaches to the demand for comfortable and convenient family areas.

## The built-in family basement room

Many people wish to add room without having to build. In order to achieve this goal, most homeowners must utilize their basement space for family living. Sometimes the attic provides space for additional bedrooms.

The basement shown in Figure 1 illustrates the way in which one family dealt with their own basement area. It will serve as a guide to the solution of your own problems—whether you are concerned with space savings through built-ins or build-ons, or merely interested in easily solved problems such as building storage areas or compact bars.

When a room is small and narrow, there is very little one can do in the way of proper decorating. Placing most of the furniture against one wall will give the other a strange appearance. Using both walls will leave little room for passage.

The dimensions of this family room, on a half-floor of a development house, are 10 by 16 feet with a 7-foot, 4-inch ceiling. The problem here was to provide space for a diverse number of family activities. The need for a music center, a sewing center, and an emergency guest bed

Fig. 1. (opposite page) House of Ideas family room.

Fig. 2.

were apparent, and, although less important, an unusual bar would be considered an asset to the room.

Perhaps because of its basic design, few parts, and the fact that the wall it was to be built against had no heating connections, the bar was planned first. The only available solution for a moving bar was a tongue and groove interlocked wooden slide system as old as woodworking itself. This, in combination with casters mounted in two areas beneath the bar bottom, formed the basic points of movement.

All the other built-ins in this room are covered in their respective chapters: the built-in sewing center (page 163), stereo-TV theater (page 181), and emergency guest bed (page 71). Only the general concepts will be covered here.

At first, the baseboard heating convectors posed the greatest problem. Because 24 inches was about the amount of space the furniture would take up, the base was built out to that line and the entire heating installation was moved forward. When this room was completed, it did not look any narrower than similar rooms done without built-ins. In similar rooms furniture and equipment took up nearly the same 24 inches, affording only visual depth which was of little practical use.

Installing indirect cove lighting and painting the ceiling dark coral eliminated any feeling of a regimented technical installation. The unusual hourglass pattern on the ivory-coral vinyl terrazzo floor not only added color, but also gave the room a broader appearance. The silver-gray finished sandblasted fir paneling

Fig. 3.

became an integrated, but quiet partner in this concept of pleasing colors and textures.

Today, you can open a chosen set of doors and like magic a TV is ready to be pulled out into the room. Next to it, above an elaborate speaker system, and occupying half the height of the room, is a lazy susan storage unit holding several dozen records.

The disappearing emergency guest bed is installed next to the sewing center.

### An all-inclusive living area

To create a satisfactory family room, one must first analyze the family's habits. The result may be a highly individualized room such as the All-Inclusive Family Room in the House of Ideas (Figure 2) or a more traditional room, depending on the needs of the family.

The plan for the all-inclusive room included a kitchen directly adjacent to the dining and recreation area. When asked about doing the cooking in the middle of a family room, most people voiced approval of the idea, saying it would lift their morale and make the daily chores much easier. But how would this plan affect the rest of the room and what about the flow of normal family functions?

Obviously, a kitchen and a formal dining area within such a multifunction complex created a problem; specifically, exposure of pots and dishes after dinner. The solution here is the laundry/pantry, equipped with an efficient sink and large counter area to serve such purposes (see pages 142–143).

During the day the rather formal sitting area is in plain view, but after dark any of the areas can be "shut off" by proper lighting control. Lighting is critical to the success of the all-inclusive living area, making it possible to camouflage certain areas by strongly outlining more desirable ones. Proper choice and placement of fixtures, aiming of light beams, and correct control of light value consistency are all important. This system had to be coupled with duplication and often triplication of light switch placement. Because ordinary 110-volt switches would have turned the wall sections into control panels, a low voltage system was used for the switches, requiring only bell wires leading from the transformers (above the ceiling) to the multi-switch plates. Because the switch plates contain from 1 to 12 individual independent switches, fewer switch units are required and they are smaller and more attractive than normal wall switches. Furthermore, they are absolutely safe and shockproof, as well as luminous when activated.

The placement of the concealed Living Wall (page 190) and the Continental Bar (page 222) is such that either or both ran be used at the same time without interfering with the other.

Fig. 4. Looking toward kitchen from living area.

Fig. 5. Looking from kitchen into living area.

# Chapter 3
# Fireplaces

The role of the fireplace is different today from what it was years ago. Fireplaces were no longer necessary to provide heat for cooking or warmth, until the recent energy crisis. They do, however, have a certain intangible function, making an attractive addition to any room and providing a comforting and welcome sight.

A good fireplace should be amply constructed and deep enough to hold a large fire safely. A good flue with enough space between it and the screen is another important safety feature. Also, a fireplace should not be a source of work requiring constant attention and frequent cleaning.

Actually, fireplace clean-up systems have improved tremendously. Trap lids are often built into each back corner of the hearth. These lead to an empty channel provided by the contractor during construction. This type of clean-out trap is explained in detail on page 23.

Only after checking to see that your fireplace is safe and in good working order, should you begin to think about selecting decorative hardware and accessories.

## The all-inclusive fireplace
In the all-inclusive living area of the House of Ideas (page 16), the fireplace structure is primarily a basic wing of what is a large multi-function family room (Figure 1). As such it can be considered much more than a fireplace. In this house, the fireplace serves a decorative function. It presents a wall of special stonework lighted from above by theatrical Kliegl spot-wallwasher-combination fixtures. When the rest of the family living area is sustained by mood lighting, which was made possible by proper planning and separation of switches, the featured fireplace appears especially majestic.

This magnificent structure was built without any prepared drawing. By carefully anchoring the heavy stones to the basic brick structure, an interwebbed structural support was created. This support system would determine whether or not cantilevering the fireplace mantel sections would be feasible.

Why is cantilevering important, considering the extra expense and the additional work?

Because it creates a visual division of parts or sections and complements the fire screen which usually appears as an ordinary wire mesh. It also broadens the appearance of the fireplace and enhances the design. Because it creates sharp and bold outlines, a cantilevered structure is perhaps the best type for any contemporary design.

The hardware for this fireplace was made of stainless steel installed by means of 4 bolts in tapped (prethreaded) holes in the supporting steel lintel. The double-flue system was constructed of 8-x-12-inch ceramic pipes. The other important factors are the proper route of the flue and the proper depth and placement of the hearth which was built of 2-inch-thick slate slabs and selected real used brick. Even the top of the chimney and the type of smoke stack finish has a lot to do with the success of a fireplace.

To make a fireplace really worthwhile, it should be planned for summer as well as winter use. In this case, two barbecues were built in— one regular charcoal burning unit on the outside and an electric Charco Broiler, Baker's Pride, on the inside.

Although not constructed with this fireplace, another idea might be a nonconnected hearth on the outside and a barbecue pit (6 feet by 9 inches) all the way across the outside shoulder (ledge) instead of the present slate top. By covering it with a custom stainless steel grill and top, the pit would be suitable for cooking "big ranch style." Such a venture would be inexpensive during original construction.

While most of the materials used here were readily available products, the unusual stones were not. Designers sometimes ask the client if he is interested in having outstanding feature stones, and if so, they tell him where to find enough pieces to create some individual touch of interest.

## Old fireplaces
*Before doing any remodeling,* check the fireplace system for safety. Before this particular fireplace was remodeled, it did not have a flue and the mortar between the bricks had crumbled, creating dangerous cavities. The

Fig. 1.    (opposite page) House of Ideas fireplace.

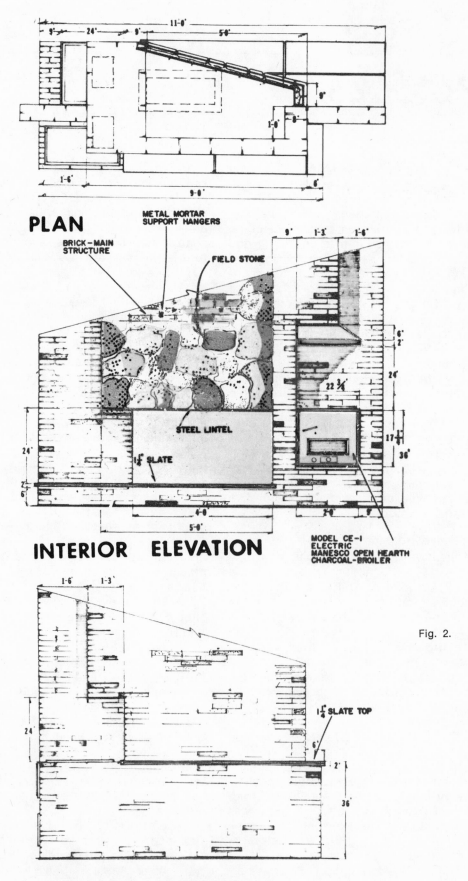

**PLAN**

BRICK—MAIN
STRUCTURE

METAL MORTAR
SUPPORT HANGERS

FIELD STONE

STEEL LINTEL

$1\frac{1}{2}$ SLATE

$22\frac{3}{4}$

**INTERIOR  ELEVATION**

MODEL CE-1
ELECTRIC
MANESCO OPEN HEARTH
CHARCOAL-BROILER

$1\frac{1}{2}$ SLATE TOP

**EXTERIOR  ELEVATION**

Fig. 2.

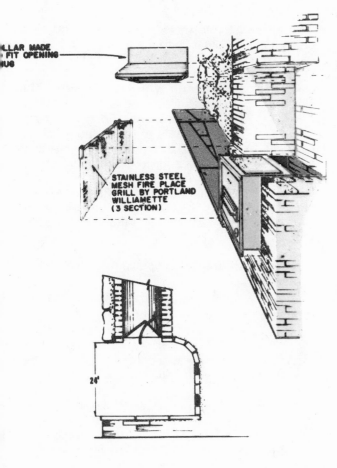

STAINLESS STEEL
MESH FIRE PLACE
GRILL BY PORTLAND
WILLIAMETTE
(3 SECTION)

24'

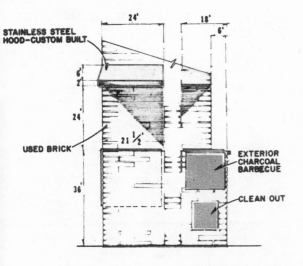

STAINLESS STEEL
HOOD-CUSTOM BUILT

USED BRICK

EXTERIOR
CHARCOAL
BARBECUE

CLEAN OUT

## SIDE VIEW & SECTION

makeshift work that had been done on it many years before had not lasted and the result was a hazardous situation. Always check chimney stacks during the season when fireplaces are in use. Even when there are flues in the stacks, settling in time may cause them to separate, allowing sparks to escape.

*Remedying a faulty fireplace.* If a fireplace does not have a proper flue exhaust, insert one in the existing stack by tearing down the accessible portion—usually ranging from the attic floor all the way up. Where cracked flues allow flames to escape, the best thing to do is to put several layers of mortar around the exposed chimney. Then cover the entire surrounding area with any approved surface method. But, always keep the fires in such a structure low and not very hot. A fire alarm system with a solenoid detector in the stack area as well as near the fireplace structure would be mandatory in such a situation.

### Fireplaces as decoration

A faulty old fireplace (or even a badly built new one) must not be used under any circumstances. The precautions recommended here provide protection in case someone does use the fireplace. Because removing a fireplace is expensive and invariably results in a leaky roof, it is best to use the old fireplace as a purely decorative structure.

### The master bedroom fireplace

Although an old fireplace can be charming and fortuitous in any room, a sparse modern system of decoration might require remodeling the old fireplace, as was the case in this master bedroom of the House of Ideas.

The mantel and the stack were framed in from floor to ceiling with 2-x-3-inch furring strips and ¾-inch fir plywood sheathing applied to it to attain a solid base (Figure 4). To avoid any accidental mishaps, a layer of Glasweld topped with several layers of fiberglass insulation was stuffed into that area before sealing.

Three sections of ¾-inch Weldwood walnut plywood paneling or lumber core with carefully matching grain were fitted to the mantel structure. They were installed 4 inches apart

Fig. 3. Before: original structure after removing the lath and plaster.

Fig. 4. The new framing is done with 2-x-3-inch construction fir.

Fig. 5. After applying ¼-inch fir sheathing to framing, 4-inch spacer strips are temporarily tacked on and ¾-inch walnut plywood is carefully fitted and scribed to ceiling. Visible edges are covered with Weldwood wood trim. The finished panels are finally mounted with glue and a few 6-penny finishing nails. Nails are countersunk ⅛ inch, puttied and sanded; then the smooth surface is treated with Watco satin oil and dark satin wax. The marble mantel is built first, then the inside floor is covered with slate; finally, the select marble front is cemented in place.

with glue and fine nails countersunk and then finished to a mat surface. The two 4-inch gaps were later covered with ¹⁄₁₆-inch stainless steel strips held on by contact cement.

The marble hearth was installed next. The slab, which had been a table top, fit the area perfectly. Fortunately, enough 6-inch-wide marble scraps were available to frame the fireplace opening. A specially designed and fabricated stainless steel grill and a modernistic metal sculpture mounted in the center of the mantel provided the finishing details. A Kliegl 2146 precision wallwasher aimed at the completed fireplace (Figure 6) achieved just the right dramatic touch.

### Changing a traditional fireplace into a classic modern

Everyone has his own ideas as to how a remodeling job should be properly organized. Usually, however, the delicate items are taken care of last, especially if they are costly. The fireplace mantel, like a piece of art, should be selected only after completion of the area which it is to enhance.

In this particular case, the room had nearly 100 feet of wall area. It would have been foolhardy to make such a large area complement the fireplace area which totaled only about 6 feet. Though this is not so every time, it is almost always safe to assume that no one single portion of an area should ever be selected as the basic theme for designing a large and multifunction area.

The original fireplace in the Designer's Dream Room was a rather opulent, Victorian marble structure. This mantel had to be removed in order to achieve a solution befitting the overall projected redesign of the area.

The mantel of the new fireplace is made of ¾-inch matching grain Brazilian rosewood plywood with 4 equally spaced 3-inch-wide x ⅝-inch thick feature strips inserted. These strips are of Indian rosewood with hand-carved, inlaid, diamond-shaped pieces of ivory. Because this material imported from India comes in 30-x-20-inch slabs, the 3-inch strips had to be carefully sliced off, vertically, in order to retain the continuity and symmetry. To further expand on the

Fig. 6. (opposite page).

attempt to create a more dramatic mantel, the following selections of additional techniques made the feature unusually outstanding. The inlaid ivory strips were ⅛-inch thinner than the ¾-inch Brazilian rosewood which predominatly covered the fireplace area, creating a bi-level exposure. In addition to that, ⅛-inch-wide pewter strips mounted to each side of the inlaid areas extending ⅛ inch beyond the rosewood plywood surface accentuated the dramatic appearance.

The fireplace opening was framed with 4-inch-wide x 1-inch-thick very light shade travertine marble extending beyond the outer structure of the mantel. The resulting structure now blends perfectly with the surrounding features. When the Kliegl pin light projected its streak-like downward illumination, the results of this technique were tremendous.

The fireplace in Figure 8 is a continuation of three fireplaces, one above the other. The basic support structure could be tied into one continuous entity ranging from this spot in the basement to the main fireplace in the living room above, to the master bedroom on the second floor, and finally to the chimney. However, separate flues from each fireplace built parallel, with about 4 inches between each for concrete insulation and support, ended 3 inches above the chimney cap. This, of course, turned out to be a rather wide but decorative stack extending beyond the slate roof.

The owner of this house originally intended this basement fireplace for use as a family recreation room, which it eventually became. The surface of the fireplace area ranging over the entire wall was covered with 1-x-1-foot precast blocks of concrete and marble dust with marble chips embedded and ground and polished to a smooth surface. Several shades of beige and brown marble chips made this a very appealing site. (See Figure 9.)

Fig. 7. Fireplace from the Designer's Dream Family Room (converted from a traditional to a classic modern).

Fig. 8. Fireplace in a basement (before remodeling).

Fig. 9. Basement fireplace remodeled.

Fig. 1.   Children's Double Roo

# Chapter 4
# Children's World

Planning and decorating a room for a child can and should be a pleasant task. Since a major portion of a child's life from infancy through adolescence will be spent here, the child's room becomes largely his world and he will identify with it even if he is sharing the room with a brother or sister. The decor and proper function of such a room, therefore, become significant.

Equally impressive is the advice of modern psychologists who urge us to create for our children an atmosphere that is secure and relaxed—an area that provides for their personal privacy and allows for their individual differences, yet harmonizes with their developing personalities.

Add to all this an awareness of how quickly children grow. Then consider the necessity of maintaining reasonable budget limitations, and the decoration of a child's room, intended as a pleasurable project, can become a somewhat overwhelming problem.

Were such a project assigned to a good decorator, he would probably surprise you by asking your child's opinion of various color schemes, being clearly aware that the child is going to be the principal inhabitant of the room. The sophistication of the child's answers may surprise you even more. Whatever the age of the child, consider his needs *and* his opinions.

It is a practical idea to decorate the room as if it were intended for an older child, even if it is not. Children grow quickly and their tastes and desires change just as rapidly. One suggestion might be paneling, either real wood or the new and excellent reproductions. The walls can then be decorated with decal cut-outs to match the age level and interests of the child. Available in most hardware and paint stores, these decals vary in size from 12 to 18 inches and come in a wide selection of colors and motifs. An imaginative arrangement on the walls can produce a highly appealing effect.

The most dramatic change in decorating will probably come when the crib is exchanged for the youth or full-sized bed. At this point, the infant's equipment is removed and replaced with the necessary bedroom furniture such as bed, dresser or cabinets, and wall shelves to hold the youngster's books, toys, and personal treasures. This type of decorating, which keeps up with the child's age and interests, achieves an attractive, well-planned, but inexpensive and never outdated redecorating program.

One of the basic rules in good decorating is to choose a durable, top-quality floor covering that will be a permanent installation, not requiring major expense each time redecoration of the room is being considered. In the House of Ideas, the floors were covered with fine hardwood parquet, coated with vinyl. These floors do not require waxing; they are simply vacuumed or damp-mopped. In this way an attractive surface is preserved while keeping maintenance down to a minimum in a high traffic area.

Later, as the child grows and the decor becomes more adult, the use of an area rug, change in curtains and accessories, and the use of such furnishing as wall desks and built-in dressers provide effective redecorating. As the family grows larger and the rooms seem to grow smaller, such examples as the Children's Double Room may provide a happy solution to a familiar problem.

## Children's Double Room

Space always seems to be at a premium, and although a separate room for each child would be the optimum situation, this is sometimes impossible. The Children's Double Room (Figure 1 and Figure 3) provides an exciting solution to the space problem.

When more than one child is to share a room, we are faced with more than just a practical change. If the children are too small to understand the finer points of sharing a room, it might become difficult to keep them in line. On the other hand, if they are at an age where they might be sensitive about what they have to share, then it is up to the parents to see that there is no cause for any resentment. This room is especially designed to prevent conflict by providing all the advantages of privacy.

Both halves of the room are identical in every detail. Each child has a bed, a combination desk-dresser, and a wall-mounted night table. In fact, everything down to the smallest detail, such as the lamps, was carefully planned this way. A partition wall folds back to create space for play during the day and pulls out again at bedtime allowing for privacy. A large closet with built-in drawers provides complete storage and hanging space (Figure 4).

The whole design of this room makes it easier for both the children and their parents to keep the room clean and orderly. The small number of pictures helps keep maintenance to a minimum. The Swedish oak flooring is sealed with a plastic coating which does away with the need for waxing. Similarly, the walls require little care. Only the ceiling, a powder-peach color, may have to be repainted every 5 to 7

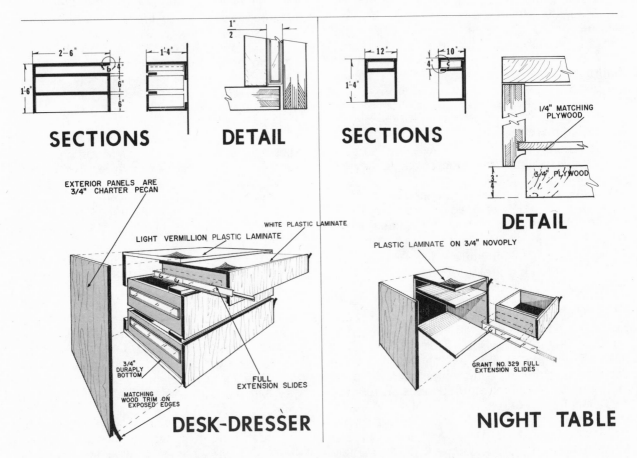

SECTIONS        DETAIL        SECTIONS        DETAIL

EXTERIOR PANELS ARE 3/4" CHARTER PECAN

WHITE PLASTIC LAMINATE

LIGHT VERMILLION PLASTIC LAMINATE

PLASTIC LAMINATE ON 3/4" NOVOPLY

3/4" DURAPLY BOTTOM

FULL EXTENSION SLIDES

MATCHING WOOD TRIM ON EXPOSED EDGES

GRANT NO. 329 FULL EXTENSION SLIDES

1/4" MATCHING PLYWOOD

3/4" PLYWOOD

DESK-DRESSER        NIGHT TABLE

CHILDREN'S BEDROOM BUILT-INS

Fig. 2.

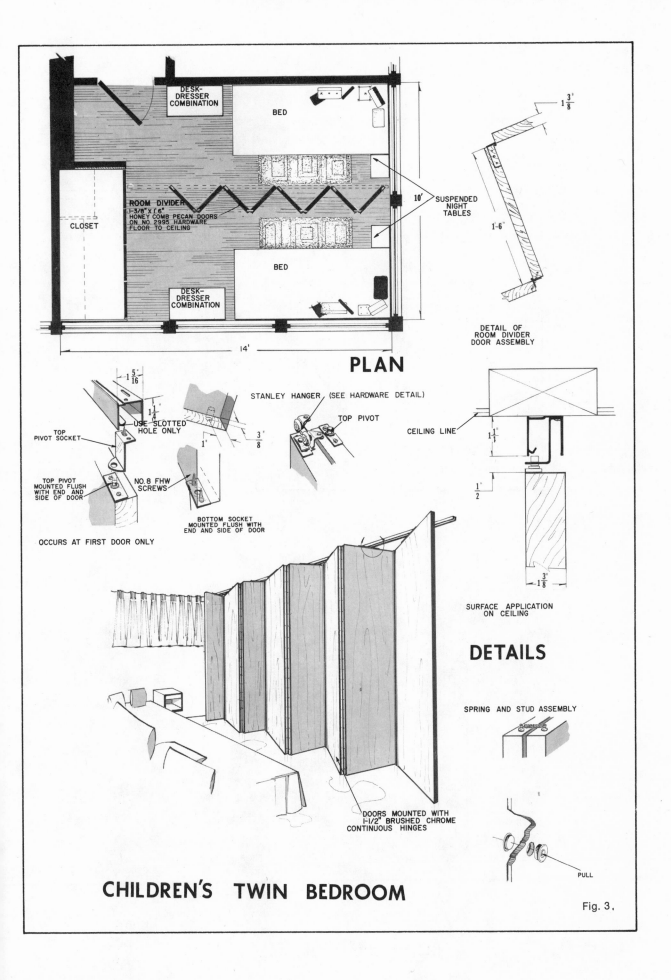

DESK-DRESSER COMBINATION

BED

ROOM DIVIDER
1-3/8" X 1'6"
HONEY COMB PECAN DOORS
ON NO. 2995 HARDWARE
FLOOR TO CEILING

CLOSET

BED

DESK-DRESSER COMBINATION

14'

10'

SUSPENDED NIGHT TABLES

PLAN

$1\frac{3}{8}$"

$1'-6"$

DETAIL OF
ROOM DIVIDER
DOOR ASSEMBLY

$1\frac{5}{16}$"

$1\frac{1}{4}$"

USE SLOTTED HOLE ONLY

$\frac{3}{8}$"

$1$"

STANLEY HANGER (SEE HARDWARE DETAIL)

TOP PIVOT

CEILING LINE

$1\frac{1}{4}$"

$\frac{1}{2}$"

$1\frac{3}{8}$"

TOP PIVOT SOCKET

TOP PIVOT MOUNTED FLUSH WITH END AND SIDE OF DOOR

NO. 8 FHW SCREWS

BOTTOM SOCKET MOUNTED FLUSH WITH END AND SIDE OF DOOR

OCCURS AT FIRST DOOR ONLY

SURFACE APPLICATION ON CEILING

DETAILS

SPRING AND STUD ASSEMBLY

PULL

DOORS MOUNTED WITH 1-1/2" BRUSHED CHROME CONTINUOUS HINGES

# CHILDREN'S TWIN BEDROOM

Fig. 3.

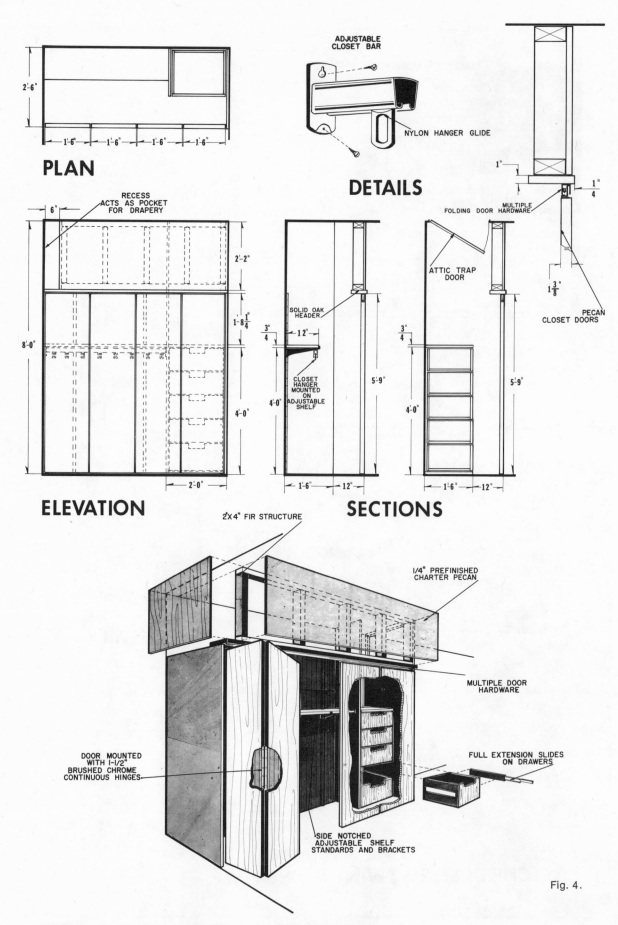

**PLAN**

2'-6"

1'-6"  1'-6"  1'-6"  1'-6"

**DETAILS**

ADJUSTABLE
CLOSET BAR

NYLON HANGER GLIDE

1"

1"
4

FOLDING DOOR
HARDWARE

MULTIPLE
DOOR HARDWARE

1 3"
8

PECAN
CLOSET DOORS

**ELEVATION**

RECESS
ACTS AS POCKET
FOR DRAPERY

6'

2'-2"

1'-8 1"
4

8'-0"

4'-0"

2'-0"

**SECTIONS**

SOLID OAK
HEADER

3"
4

1 2"

CLOSET
HANGER
MOUNTED
ON
ADJUSTABLE
SHELF

4'-0"

5'-9"

1'-6"   12"

ATTIC TRAP
DOOR

3"
4

4'-0"

5'-9"

1'-6"   12"

2"X 4" FIR STRUCTURE

1/4" PREFINISHED
CHARTER PECAN

MULTIPLE DOOR
HARDWARE

DOOR MOUNTED
WITH 1-1/2"
BRUSHED CHROME
CONTINUOUS HINGES

FULL EXTENSION SLIDES
ON DRAWERS

SIDE NOTCHED
ADJUSTABLE SHELF
STANDARDS AND BRACKETS

Fig. 4.

# CLOSET WITH BUILT-IN DRAWERS

years. Aluminum sashes (available in different types), which are used throughout the house, require practically no maintenance. Vacuum cleaner outlets are located conveniently near every room.

The colorful and practical decor consists of Charter Pecan prefinished paneling, yellow drapes, colorful bedspreads and cushions, and area rugs.

### A small room for a boy and a guest

It is really surprising what can be done in a very small space. The area of this particular room (Figures 5 to 11) was 7½ by 9 feet, perhaps one of the smallest areas ever made into a combination playroom, study, and bedroom

for two.

The combination desk-dressers in the Children's Double Room (page 28) are identical in design to the combination dresser beneath the left end of the desk (Figures 6 and 7). In fact, this, as well as the wall-hung night table and the set of drawers at the other end of the desk, was built at the same time and of the same materials (Charter Pecan and a semigloss orange plastic laminate on top surfaces), which cut down expenses considerably.

Since materials and tools are readily available today, budget-conscious homeowners could build custom pieces such as these at home. (See Figures 8, 9 and 10.) For those not mechanically inclined, it would even pay to

Fig. 5.   Left: main bed with trundle guest bed, pushed in.

Fig. 6.   Right: combination desk unit with additional pull-out work surface.

Fig. 7. Trundle bed pulled out, leaving ample space for desk unit and passage.

hire a neighborhood carpenter or cabinet maker to do the majority of the work right on the spot.

The two desk units are screwed to the plastic laminate-covered top which holds the entire assembly together. The structure is mounted to the wall studs (usually 16 inches apart on center) using 2-inch screws through ¾-x-3-inch plywood backmounting strips which are part of the cabinet back structure. To eliminate legs, the unit is mounted to the wall, 10 inches from the floor. Surprisingly enough, only 5 screws are needed to support this big unit; as a corner unit, the combination creates much of its own bracing.

The upper shelves are installed with adjustable brushed chrome hardware screwed into studs. The shelves are 8-inch slices of ¾-inch pecan plywood sheet. Covering all visible edges with matching wood trim makes the shelves appear as though they were solid wood, while matching the surrounding plywood in color and texture. Even though shelves like these are intended primarily to hold books, it is desirable to cut and install them in a random fashion. While losing some storage area, this type of staggered shelf mounting makes a decorative wall, rather than repetitious storage area.

The bed itself is a real space-saver (Figure 9). It is built like all the other beds in the House of Ideas—a ¾-inch Novoply (chipboard) mattress base and a 3¾-inch plywood frame to sustain the mattress. The trundle guest bed (made like the one in the Teenage Boy's Room, page 42) and an 18-inch end cabinet built to its left with drawers and shelves turned out to be real room stretchers. Because the trundle bed clears the wall desk unit by 1 foot when it is rolled out completely, there is room for traffic.

All the materials and colors in this room are exactly the same as those used in the Children's Double Room (page 28), as is the lighting. There is a good reading spot in the ceiling above the pillow of each bed. It is run on low voltage, achieved by power relays mounted in the attic area directly above, as are all light controls in the rooms. The general ceiling lights are R-1 Emerson flush ceiling fixtures using R-30 bulbs (75W). Because they are distributed with a three light maximum on each circuit, more than one circuit and switch was usually required. In this room there are only two controls: one for the three general lights, and the other for the reading spot. Aside from these lights, a "lampette" is used for close reading and working at the pullout desk.

The two adjustable windows, the fine heating and cooling systems, and the reliable safety systems present in all of the other rooms, were, of course, included in this room as well.

### A girl's room built around a wall

When creating a room, a designer usually analyzes the characteristics and habits of its occupant-to-be. In this case, it was a pre-teenage girl, who wanted her own record player

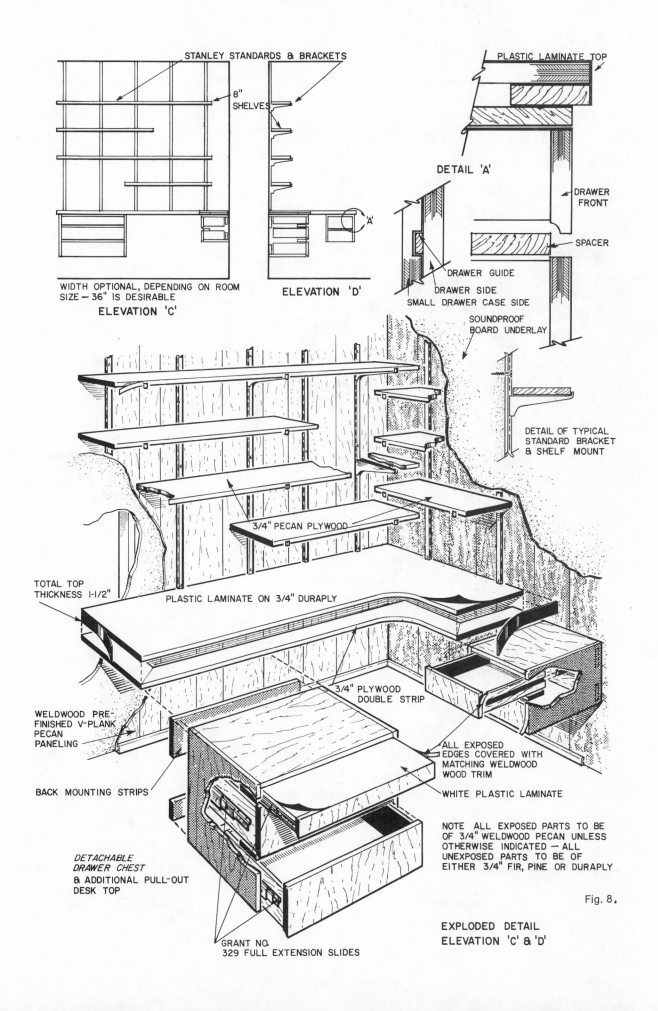

STANLEY STANDARDS & BRACKETS

8"
SHELVES

WIDTH OPTIONAL, DEPENDING ON ROOM
SIZE — 36" IS DESIRABLE

ELEVATION 'C'

ELEVATION 'D'

PLASTIC LAMINATE TOP

DETAIL 'A'

DRAWER
FRONT

SPACER

DRAWER GUIDE

DRAWER SIDE
SMALL DRAWER CASE SIDE

SOUNDPROOF
BOARD UNDERLAY

DETAIL OF TYPICAL
STANDARD BRACKET
& SHELF MOUNT

3/4" PECAN PLYWOOD

TOTAL TOP
THICKNESS 1-1/2"

PLASTIC LAMINATE ON 3/4" DURAPLY

3/4" PLYWOOD
DOUBLE STRIP

WELDWOOD PRE-
FINISHED V-PLANK
PECAN
PANELING

ALL EXPOSED
EDGES COVERED WITH
MATCHING WELDWOOD
WOOD TRIM

BACK MOUNTING STRIPS

WHITE PLASTIC LAMINATE

NOTE ALL EXPOSED PARTS TO BE
OF 3/4" WELDWOOD PECAN UNLESS
OTHERWISE INDICATED — ALL
UNEXPOSED PARTS TO BE OF
EITHER 3/4" FIR, PINE OR DURAPLY

DETACHABLE
DRAWER CHEST
& ADDITIONAL PULL-OUT
DESK TOP

Fig. 8.

GRANT NO.
329 FULL EXTENSION SLIDES

EXPLODED DETAIL
ELEVATION 'C' & 'D'

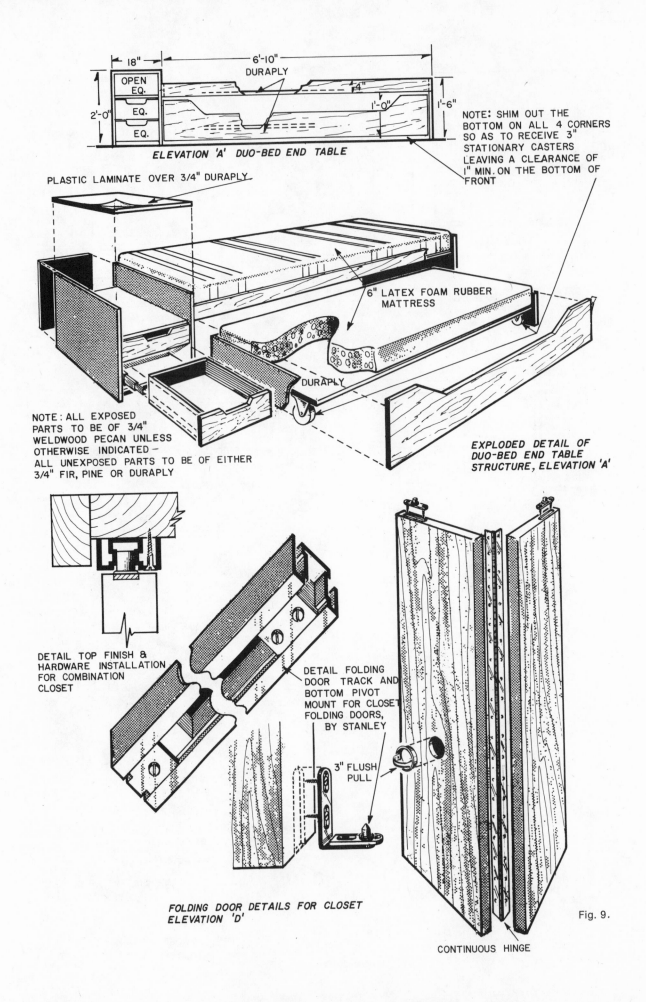

18"

6'-10"
DURAPLY

OPEN
EQ.

2'-0"

EQ.

EQ.

4"

1'-0"

1'-6"

ELEVATION 'A' DUO-BED END TABLE

NOTE: SHIM OUT THE BOTTOM ON ALL 4 CORNERS SO AS TO RECEIVE 3" STATIONARY CASTERS LEAVING A CLEARANCE OF I" MIN. ON THE BOTTOM OF FRONT

PLASTIC LAMINATE OVER 3/4" DURAPLY

6" LATEX FOAM RUBBER MATTRESS

DURAPLY

NOTE: ALL EXPOSED PARTS TO BE OF 3/4" WELDWOOD PECAN UNLESS OTHERWISE INDICATED — ALL UNEXPOSED PARTS TO BE OF EITHER 3/4" FIR, PINE OR DURAPLY

EXPLODED DETAIL OF DUO-BED END TABLE STRUCTURE, ELEVATION 'A'

DETAIL TOP FINISH & HARDWARE INSTALLATION FOR COMBINATION CLOSET

DETAIL FOLDING DOOR TRACK AND BOTTOM PIVOT MOUNT FOR CLOSET FOLDING DOORS, BY STANLEY

3" FLUSH PULL

FOLDING DOOR DETAILS FOR CLOSET ELEVATION 'D'

CONTINUOUS HINGE

Fig. 9.

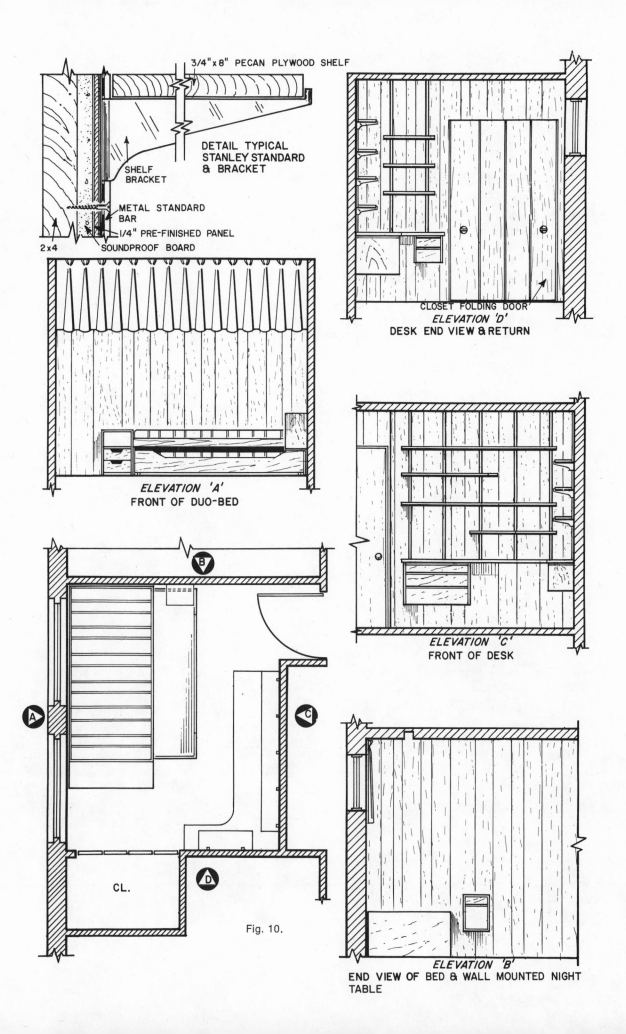

3/4" x 8" PECAN PLYWOOD SHELF

DETAIL TYPICAL
STANLEY STANDARD
& BRACKET

SHELF
BRACKET

METAL STANDARD
BAR

1/4" PRE-FINISHED PANEL

SOUNDPROOF BOARD

2 x 4

CLOSET FOLDING DOOR
*ELEVATION 'D'*
DESK END VIEW & RETURN

*ELEVATION 'A'*
FRONT OF DUO-BED

*ELEVATION 'C'*
FRONT OF DESK

CL.

Fig. 10.

*ELEVATION 'B'*
END VIEW OF BED & WALL MOUNTED NIGHT
TABLE

and needed book shelves and a desk aside from her basic requirements—a bed, dresser, and night tables. It seemed that these needs could best be served by the creation of a multifunction center (Figure 11). This decision was confirmed by the limited size of the room and budget considerations. By building against the wall with a window, it was possible to create a fluffy airiness with curtains, scalloped valances, and brilliant lighting.

The multipurpose wall unit has gray glazed louver doors which match an existing commercial French provincial bed and dresser set and further brighten the room. The unit (Figures 13, 14, and 15) contains storage for several dozen books, records, toys, school supplies, and current work; tuck-away storage for valuables; room on the upper units for nostalgic mementos, record player, hideaway TV, tuner amplifier, and built-in speakers; and a desk with shallow pencil drawers. The whole area is very efficiently lighted with direct and indirect lighting.

Because there are no horizontal planes (aside from the desk top), the room is very easy to keep neat. Everything is versatile, sliding out easily for use and disappearing into the wall when not in use.

## Tailored room for a teenage girl

When a girl becomes a teenager, her requirements suddenly become more demanding and certainly more discriminating. Indeed, the important creative innovations in the room in Figure 16 invariably reflected the character of the 16-year-old girl who would live in it because

Fig. 11.   A girl's room built around a wall.

Fig. 12. "Before" photo.

she participated directly in the decorating decisions.

This room was an interesting challenge because it was to be installed in an attic. The design plan outline was taken from dimensions appropriated from the structural prints, for the room had not yet been built. The carpenters literally "raised the roof" to reshape the house, giving it much needed additional space. Because this was an attic room of a house located in an area where summer and winter temperatures reached extremes, there could be no compromise in insulation (Figures 17 and 18), wall covering, and good carpeting. The extension of the existing heating and cooling systems was of course part of the structural job of building the room.

Since there was only a limited area available, the only design solution was to put storage built-ins in the lower rafter areas and to create multifunctional units like the vanity combination night table-desk extension which is part of the chest of drawers. This wall-hung unit, which is cantilevered to sustain a feeling of lightness, is extremely desirable for such an area.

The tailored look rather than a frilly one was dictated not only by the girl's preferences, but also by space limitations which demanded a versatile design that could be achieved only by such built-in facilities.

The glass display case was specially requested by the young lady to display her swim-

Fig. 13. Heavy record storage and general storage. Drawers are mounted on Grant #325 full extension slides. The lighter ones are mounted on Grant #329 full extension slides.

Fig. 14. Over the record storage area is the record player drawer. The TV above, mounted on a sliding platform, can be pulled out and turned in any direction, as a ¾-inch plywood top below it is installed on a metal lazy susan.

Fig. 15. After sliding all units in, the entire section is covered by decorative folding louver doors installed on Grant bifold hardware.

Fig. 16.   Cantilevered wall-hung unit.

ming trophies and knickknacks. To justify this important piece of cabinetry, which stands out in a rather wide streamlined area, other functions were incorporated into this unit. It was given the importance it deserved by using it as a source for mood light. The right side of the case was built with a double-sided shaft with "deluxe warm white" fluorescent tubes on the inside. This creates a direct light beam toward the shelves on the inside, and by indirect means, like a vertical cornice, projects indirect lighting against the right portion of the wall and out to the mirror. In addition, the case is

illuminated from a light box built on the top. Both of these interior case light sources are covered with opaque glass for even and soft diffusion. This lighting system is on one circuit as well as on a separate switch which enables the girl to use only this source while watching TV.

The lighting is broken up into four possibilities, including two general room overhead light source groups. The light switch controls are at the room entrance as well as at the bedside.

Colorful drapes, upholstery, and pillows maintain a soft and pleasant feeling in this part of the room. The opposite wall contains a very

Fig. 17.   Breakthrough from old attic to built-on section.

Fig. 18.   Typical new section and old partition ahead. Note the insulation: fiberglass wrapped and sealed with aluminum foil.

versatile closet which has bi-fold doors, and a very efficient clothes storage setup. It is covered on all walls with cedar closet lining for moth protection.

There is also a very comfortable upholstered chair in the left corner which can be converted into a guest bed by simply lifting the back of the seat.

Although this room was designed for a 16-year-old, it would serve her needs and those of the rest of the family for many years to come.

### The teenage boy's room

Just as with the teenage girl's room, the 15-year-old boy for whom this room was planned had a hand in some of the decisions. His needs too had to be taken into consideration. For instance, a simple desk top on which to do his homework was no longer adequate. He needed room for books and research materials. Storage for lots of records as well as room for stereo equipment were also requirements. He also wanted a large upholstered chair where he could read and practice his guitar as well as a wall of built-ins for well-organized storage of mementos. The plan had to include adequate sleeping accommodations for overnight guests as well as a combination train board (see page 47).

Although the features in this teenage room (Figure 19) look very expensive, they are all homemade (except the adjustable desk set—a Herman Miller product—which was quite reasonable). With the help of the plans shown here, the home handyman or the neighborhood carpenter can build these rather costly looking furnishings on a fairly low budget.

In selecting this adjustable combination wall set, one of the criteria was versatility—it must grow with the boy. There are various adjustable modular wall sets, but this particular system, shown in Figure 21, was appealing because it has a sort of modern elegance which would contribute to the overall success of the room. By slightly altering the installation of the adjustable wall-mounted hardware, and by inserting sound-deadening boards behind the prefinished walnut paneling, we achieved a

Fig. 19.

flush-mounted installation, a cleaner and richer appearance due to the paneling, and a sound-proof room because the installation was on the partition wall. The Rittenhouse AM-FM intercom unit, a telephone jack, and outlets for the TV and stereo system were built into the area.

The bed (Figure 21 and Figure 27), like all the beds in the house, is essentially a ¾-inch plywood or particle board (Novoply) mattress base. A double layer of ¾-inch plywood was used for the end panels, as well as the front strip (total 1½-inch thickness). The back strip

remained, to be a single layer (¾-inch). The front strip is only 3¾ inches high (¾ inch to cover the mattress platform and the remaining 3 inches to extend above to retain the mattress). The 1½-inch-thick ends and the ¾-inch back also extend 3 inches above the bed platform, uniform all around; they also extend to the floor, sustaining the entire unit firmly. Total height of the bed ends is 16¾ inches, leaving a clearance of 13 inches beneath the bed platform. The trundle guest bed drawer has a 12-inch front, 6-inch sides and back, all of ¾-inch ply-

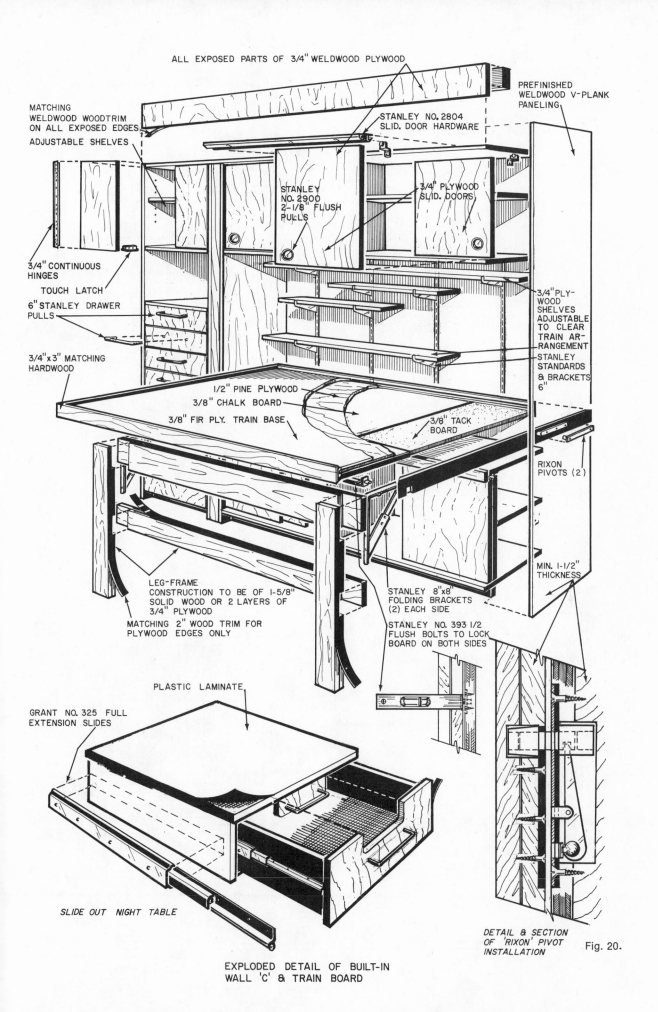

ALL EXPOSED PARTS OF 3/4" WELDWOOD PLYWOOD

PREFINISHED WELDWOOD V-PLANK PANELING

STANLEY NO. 2804 SLID. DOOR HARDWARE

MATCHING WELDWOOD WOODTRIM ON ALL EXPOSED EDGES

ADJUSTABLE SHELVES

STANLEY NO. 2900 2-1/8" FLUSH PULLS

3/4" PLYWOOD SLID. DOORS

3/4" CONTINUOUS HINGES

TOUCH LATCH

6" STANLEY DRAWER PULLS

3/4" x 3" MATCHING HARDWOOD

3/4" PLYWOOD SHELVES ADJUSTABLE TO CLEAR TRAIN ARRANGEMENT

STANLEY STANDARDS & BRACKETS 6"

1/2" PINE PLYWOOD

3/8" CHALK BOARD

3/8" FIR PLY. TRAIN BASE

3/8" TACK BOARD

RIXON PIVOTS (2)

LEG-FRAME CONSTRUCTION TO BE OF 1-5/8" SOLID WOOD OR 2 LAYERS OF 3/4" PLYWOOD

MATCHING 2" WOOD TRIM FOR PLYWOOD EDGES ONLY

STANLEY 8" x 8" FOLDING BRACKETS (2) EACH SIDE

STANLEY NO. 393 1/2 FLUSH BOLTS TO LOCK BOARD ON BOTH SIDES

MIN. 1-1/2" THICKNESS

PLASTIC LAMINATE

GRANT NO. 325 FULL EXTENSION SLIDES

*SLIDE OUT NIGHT TABLE*

*DETAIL & SECTION OF 'RIXON' PIVOT INSTALLATION*

Fig. 20.

EXPLODED DETAIL OF BUILT-IN WALL 'C' & TRAIN BOARD

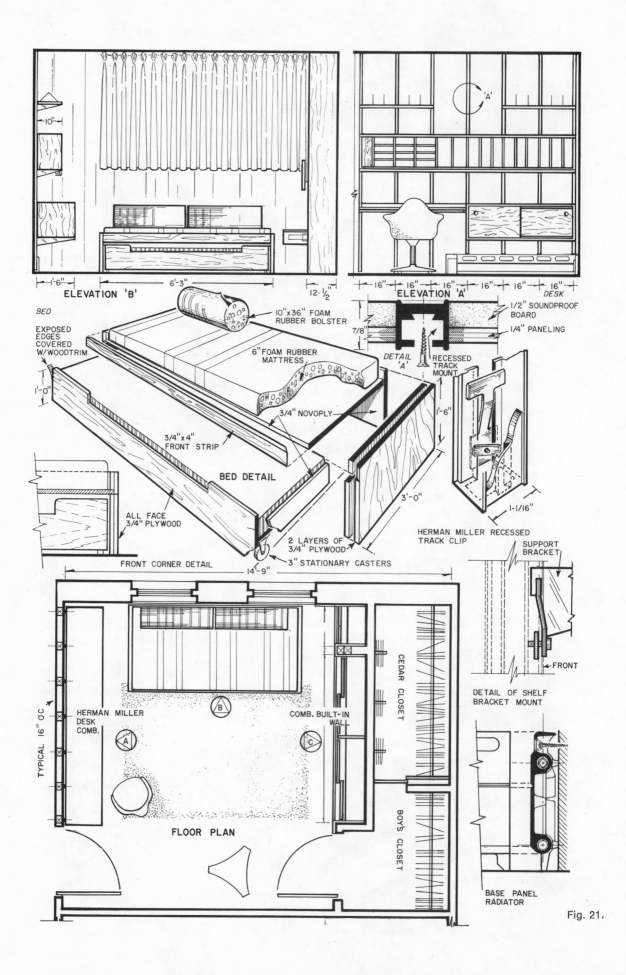

ELEVATION 'B'

1'-6"  6'-3"  12-1/2"

ELEVATION 'A'

16" 16" 16" 16" 16" 16"  DESK

BED

EXPOSED EDGES COVERED W/WOODTRIM

1'-0"

3/4"x4" FRONT STRIP

10"x36" FOAM RUBBER BOLSTER

6" FOAM RUBBER MATTRESS

3/4" NOVOPLY

BED DETAIL

DETAIL 'A'

7/8"

RECESSED TRACK MOUNT

1/2" SOUNDPROOF BOARD

1/4" PANELING

1'-6"

3'-0"

1-1/16"

HERMAN MILLER RECESSED TRACK CLIP

ALL FACE 3/4" PLYWOOD

FRONT CORNER DETAIL

2 LAYERS OF 3/4" PLYWOOD

3" STATIONARY CASTERS

SUPPORT BRACKET

FRONT

DETAIL OF SHELF BRACKET MOUNT

14'-9"

TYPICAL 16" O'C

HERMAN MILLER DESK COMB.

A

B

C

COMB. BUILT-IN WALL

CEDAR CLOSET

BOY'S CLOSET

FLOOR PLAN

BASE PANEL RADIATOR

Fig. 21.

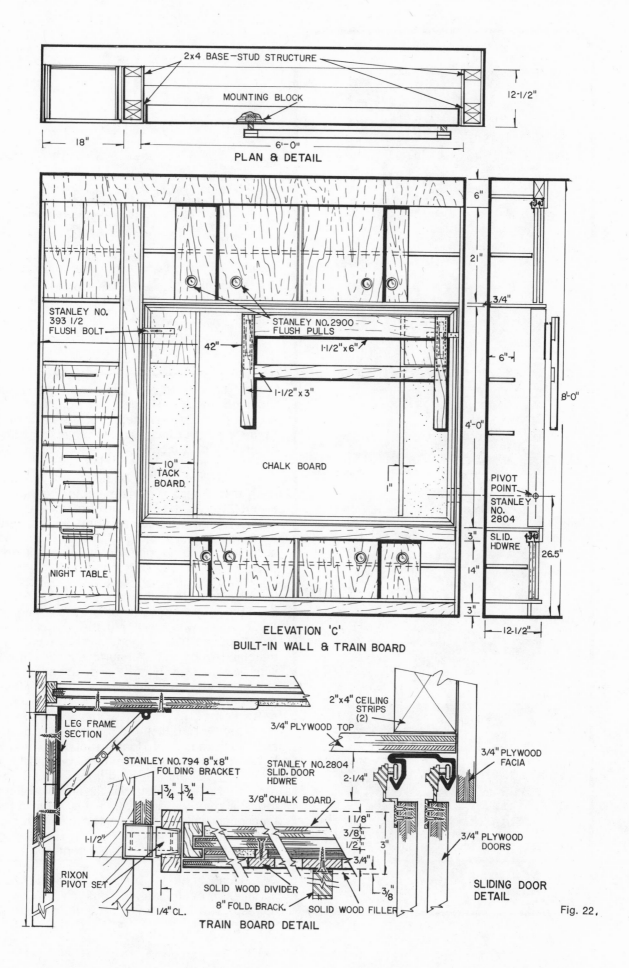

2x4 BASE—STUD STRUCTURE

MOUNTING BLOCK

12-1/2"

18"

6'-0"

PLAN & DETAIL

6"

21"

3/4"

STANLEY NO. 393 1/2 FLUSH BOLT

STANLEY NO. 2900 FLUSH PULLS

42"

1-1/2" x 6"

6"

8'-0"

1-1/2" x 3"

4'-0"

CHALK BOARD

10" TACK BOARD

1"

PIVOT POINT
STANLEY NO. 2804

SLID. HDWRE

3"

26.5"

NIGHT TABLE

14"

3"

ELEVATION 'C'
BUILT-IN WALL & TRAIN BOARD

12-1/2"

LEG FRAME SECTION

2"x4" CEILING STRIPS (2)

3/4" PLYWOOD TOP

3/4" PLYWOOD FACIA

STANLEY NO. 794 8"x8" FOLDING BRACKET

STANLEY NO. 2804 SLID. DOOR HDWRE

3/4" 3/4"

2-1/4"

3/8" CHALK BOARD

1-1/2"

1 1/8"
3/8"
1/2"

3"

3/4" PLYWOOD DOORS

3/4"

RIXON PIVOT SET

1/4" CL.

SOLID WOOD DIVIDER

8" FOLD. BRACK.

SOLID WOOD FILLER

3/8"

SLIDING DOOR DETAIL

TRAIN BOARD DETAIL

Fig. 22.

Fig. 23. After screwing the vertical metal support bars to wall (16 inches on center), and after mounting between them sound-deadening boards, ¼-inch prefinished panels are carefully fitted and installed, using panel adhesive and 1-inch #18 brads.

Fig. 24. Side wall paneling is also installed over the sound-deadening board, scribing panels to ceiling.

Fig. 25. Shelf supports are screwed to each end of each item as per instructions. The support brackets are next fastened in the channels to receive all accessories level at their planned areas.

Fig. 26. Being very versatile, this Herman Miller desk wall system was chosen to be used as shown.

wood. The ¾-inch Novoply mattress support is mounted about 2¼ inches up from the bottom edges, as the overall height of the hard rubber (non-swivel) flat-base mount casters should be about 2½ to 3 inches maximum. The slide-out trundle front must have a clearance of ¼ inch on top, ½ inch on the bottom, and ¼ inch on each end. These dimensions and the available size of the casters will govern the necessary recess of the mattress platform on the bottom of all such installations, especially where an area rug or high pile carpet might tend to obstruct the pulling out of the bed.

The top mattress is standard 6-x-39-x-76-inch Koylon. The bottom mattress is also of 6-x-34-x-72-inch Koylon foam rubber and both are covered with regular mattress ticking.

Exposed wood edges were covered with matching wood trim. All surfaces were finished with "deep finish" Firzite, and rubbed with fine steel wool and Butcher's Wax. One-inch furniture glides were placed in each corner for protection.

The two 10-inch-diameter round bolsters are also made of foam rubber. They are covered in the same material as is used for the drapes—gold with terra cotta red stripes.

The built-in wall in the far end of the room forms a partition separating this room from a family cedar closet which was put here because the room had plenty of space. Besides ample storage space, this wall contains a fold-down train table (for details, see page 43).

Because of the built-ins, most horizontal surfaces are eliminated, thus simplifying the upkeep. The drawers in the built-in also elim-

Fig. 27. All movable components in their places.

Fig. 28. To clear chalkboard, the folding legs are locked into horizontal position.

Fig. 29. Trundle bed, pulled out.

Fig. 30. Trainboard platform folded out and down, supported by locked leg frame.

inate the need for the usual chest or two, again cutting down on upkeep as well as giving a clean, uncluttered appearance, important and unusual in a boy's room.

The colors are mostly earthy reds and terra cotta. Even the ceiling is painted terra cotta, which tends to wrap the room in a comfortable warmth.

Other features, such as the Mohawk rug, the walnut parquet floor, and the room's only touch of blue in the Coconut chair make this a success both decoratively and practically.

### A world in a room for two boys and a friend

The room shown in Figures 31, 32, 33, 34, and 38, which was exactly 10½ by 13 feet, was designed to accommodate two young boys (with room for a guest). Not only were sleeping accommodations provided, but work and play areas as well. Also included were a chalk board which folds down and becomes a train city (see page 50), a disappearing record player, and lots of toy, book, and record storage.

There are 8 large drawers for clothing and, of course, a wall closet which is covered with cedar closet lining. Because of the size of the room, bunkbeds (with a trundle bed) were called for. Above the bunkbeds is a storage unit to hold winter blankets. There is even a 12-inch unit at the end of the chest of drawers with a KV slide-out rack for belts, neckties, etc. Lighting is above the cabinets and at each bed.

The wood used is Sen (oriental ash). To finish or blend plywood or solid wood with any paneling, see instructions and recommendations in Chapter 14, page 265. The coral surfaces, which are of semi-gloss plastic laminate, cover the desk top, each alternate drawer front, and the vertical bunkbed supports. Plastic laminate is nearly indestructible, as is the Sen plywood and the wall paneling after proper finishing. The beds are ¾-inch Novoply (chipboard) with 6-inch-thick latex foam rubber mattresses.

See Figures 33 and 34, the bunkbed unit and wall-hung storage unit. More people increasingly require more living space. This is gradually dwindling away from us. Perhaps those

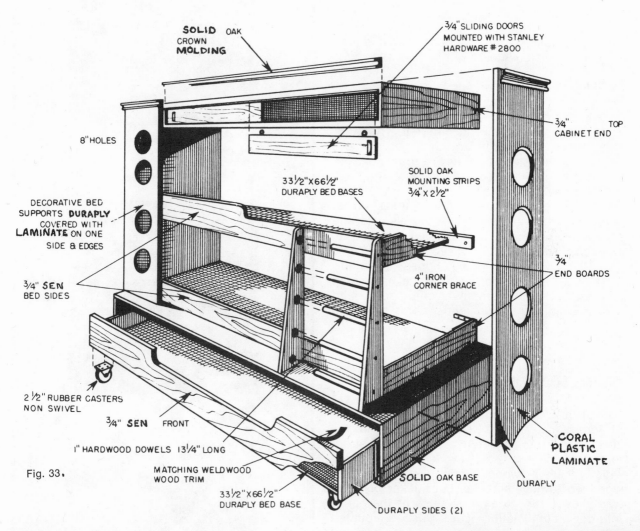

SOLID OAK CROWN MOLDING

¾" SLIDING DOORS MOUNTED WITH STANLEY HARDWARE #2800

8" HOLES

¾" TOP CABINET END

33½"x66½" DURAPLY BED BASES

SOLID OAK MOUNTING STRIPS ¾" x 2½"

DECORATIVE BED SUPPORTS DURAPLY COVERED WITH LAMINATE ON ONE SIDE & EDGES

¾" SEN BED SIDES

4" IRON CORNER BRACE

¾" END BOARDS

2½" RUBBER CASTERS NON SWIVEL

¾" SEN FRONT

1" HARDWOOD DOWELS 13¼" LONG

Fig. 33.

MATCHING WELDWOOD WOOD TRIM

33½"x66½" DURAPLY BED BASE

SOLID OAK BASE

DURAPLY

CORAL PLASTIC LAMINATE

DURAPLY SIDES (2)

(on opposite page)

Fig. 31.  In addition to the 2 fixed beds, a trundle bed on the bottom makes it 3. Also, top storage for additional blankets uses every inch available.

Fig. 32.  In addition to adequate desk space, this unit contains book and record storage, adjustable TV, hi-fi, covered record player and a tilt-out toy storage bin.

Fig. 34.  Cantilevered chest of drawers with narrow end cabinet, containing a slide-out belt and tie rack.

with larger families may well consider this idea for their living solution.

### Train tables

A boy's room is usually conventional and basically satisfactory but sometimes parents want to do something a little bit different. The combination units on the following pages will delight any youngster—and they're practical, too.

A boy needn't keep his favorite train set hidden away in the basement to be brought out only at Christmas and other special times. In these features, train tables, desks, storage space and more are consolidated into single, multipurpose units.

Although such units may appear to require a lot of work, they do not. A home handyman or a neighborhood carpenter could easily build one in a couple of weekends. On a minimum wall of 8 feet such a unit would give a boy's room greatly increased utility—and the boy much happiness.

### Teenage boy's train combination

Such a train combination was built at the far end of the Teenage Boy's Room of the House of Ideas (see Figure 30). As shown in the illustrations, the skeleton of the entire structure is basically 2-x-4s which are covered with ¾-inch plywood. Ordinarily, thinner plywood would have sufficed, but thicker plywood was chosen for strength because of the heavy fold-down combination board which is mounted with Rixon swinging door hardware mortised and recessed into the plywood sides.

As shown in the details, the overall construction is extremely basic and simple. The fold-down board is a three-layer sandwiched platform with a ¾-x-3-inch hardwood border.

Exact size of storage areas is immaterial, as the sliding door panels are always fitted after the unit is correctly installed and finished. The doors are hung with sliding door hardware which comes packed with instructions explaining exactly the necessary allowances.

All drawers are mounted with Grant Pulley full-extension No. 329 slides which again are furnished with simple-to-follow installation diagrams and instructions. For heavier loads, use No. 335 slides.

Fig. 35. Rixon pivots are recessed and fastened firmly to receive train board.

Fig. 36. Legs must snap into position before the board is lowered.

Fig. 37. Train board in a folded-out position.

### Folding train city

The train setup in Figure 38 was installed in the room referred to as "A World for Two Boys and a Friend," page 50. The entire layout covers an area of 8 by 8 feet. This particular wall is divided into a 30-inch solidly built panel. This panel consists of two 2-x-4s, the ¾-inch solid hardwood edge and a well-built supporting framing, all of which is covered in front with ¼-inch Sen plywood paneling. The wall-hung chest which is 24 inches deep is partially supported by this panel, leaving a 6-inch clearance between the drawers and train board. A 5½-foot section is used for the board.

Although done on a strict budget and in a room that had to serve two and possibly three boys, it achieved its purpose by affording vital

storage space and at the same time provided an enjoyable train layout.

The exposed wood is Sen, an oriental ash of a light gray-beige hue. If you are cramped for space and want to do something like this on a low budget, this particular setup is a good solution.

### The "O" combination wall

The installation in Figures 45, 46, and 47 is in a room that was originally the garage. It was first transformed into a playroom, and then it became a room for an older boy. The object was to provide a play and work area which could be shared by two brothers (10 and 7 years old). Actually, it succeeds in doing even more, giving the boys an attractive setting and

Fig. 38.

Fig. 39. The entire function of the ultimate design is drawn onto the top surface of the board, and tracks are temporarily placed within the outlines.

Fig. 40. Lead wires are connected to the wiring on the bottom and pushed through holes bored through the top at strategic points according to the layout.

Fig. 41. Once all tracks are secured, ¾-inch plywood cutouts (for tunnel structure) are fastened with glue and thin screws.

Fig. 42. A layer of ¼-inch pliable synthetic foam rubber is stapled over the tunnel area, thus creating an elevated level.

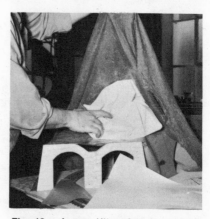

Fig. 43. A gauzélike cloth is soaked in liquid adhesive and then put over crinkled paper to achieve a paste with which to form a mountainlike shape.

Fig. 44. The cloth dries quickly, and shaping it is simple. After it stiffens, artificial moss patches are spotted and fastened with glue. Switch connections are installed here to coordinate the automatic motion of objects. Finally, buildings, stations, pumps, and automatic lighting are installed and connected.

Fig. 45.

providing a series of design ideas conducive to study as well as relaxation or play.

The center unit, a suspended wall-mounted structure, houses the desk and book storage. It includes drawers and vertical shelves for paper, envelopes, and all the paraphernalia required by a young student. It also provides adequate record storage.

Occupying almost half of the wall unit is a tightly condensed combination "music center." Starting from the bottom in Figure 46, this section includes an amplified record player and AM-FM radio, then a slide-out platform for the TV, and, on top, a dual speaker setup carrying one 5-inch midrange speaker and a tweeter on each side of the panel. While rather cramped into this small area, it will reproduce stereo fairly well.

The entire unit can be completely closed off behind a pair of bi-fold doors. Thus it will stay clean longer and always look neat.

Fig. 46.

Framing the case are dual green slate boards, especially appropriate for two boys. The rest of the unit is covered with tack board, which comes in handy for displaying school work. The top shelf is for toys. In its closed position, the unit is remarkably neat and decorative, as well as useful. Most surprising is the fact that it takes only 18 inches of floor space from the width of the room.

By lifting the top plywood strip (which then snaps into place), two flush bolts are exposed. Sliding them aside allows the entire front to be pulled down. For safety's sake, the bolts are positioned out of the children's reach, so they will need help in lowering the unit.

When it is extended, the unit becomes a

Fig. 47.

circle which opens up new possibilities for train board layout and operation (the "O" installation is designed for the large-scale Lionel train sets). Actually, the "O" gives an illusion of having a much larger stretch of track than there actually is.

Storage is provided for all the equipment used, and there is space to add more shelves.

The unit is made of oak plywood surrounded by prefinished V-plank oak paneling. Although it is a permanent part of the room's structure, it can be removed easily and quickly should the time ever come when it is no longer needed.

No matter what type unit you choose, it will bring a world of happiness to the children.

# Chapter 5
# Master Bedrooms

It has been said that bedrooms reflect the characteristics of the women who use them. Although it is true that bedrooms are decorated and furnished with feminine influence, this does not necessarily mean lots of frills and lace; these touches enhance only certain styles and distinct periods. Since the bedroom is a private room, personal taste and satisfaction are always the first considerations.

Unfortunately, most commercially manufactured bedroom sets will not provide the individuality so desirable in a bedroom. Since this is one room where mixed furniture style assemblage is not only possible, but also desirable, good taste is most important.

The selection of the proper bed is the key to the success of the entire room. Other than a comfortable bed, about which there can be no compromise, all else is good storage and decoration, expressive of personal taste. In the following features, ¾-inch-thick Novoply (chipboard) slabs were used for all the beds, although size and bed base construction differed slightly as did the unusual headboards.

## A lavish master bedroom

The proof of a room's success is determined by the reactions of the people who have lived in it for a couple of years. As we have said, any design must depend on a careful analysis of its occupants' characters, the times in which they live, and what they want out of the room. Other decisions such as style or period are important, but secondary. While pertinent to the ultimate success of the room, these points are hardly as important as a good bed with an equally comfortable headboard, and a place to sit if you choose to spend a winter day or a rainy Sunday in the room.

The bedroom shown in Figures 1 and 2

Fig. 2

Fig. 1. (opposite page) House of Ideas master bedroom.

was built primarily for comfort, as a place to sleep or watch television or listen to music. It had been the living room and balcony of a 100-year-old house—unified now into the master bedroom and dressing room. A combination of design techniques and available technology makes this room the most lavish in the House of Ideas—perhaps overwhelmingly so at first glance. Nevertheless, this room fulfilled every expectation and proved to be a very successful experiment in safe, comfortable, and beautiful living.

Because of its soundproof construction (achieved by using Barrett sound-deadening board on the walls), the room was very quiet. But certain technological innovations allowed the enjoyment of living in a completely soundproof room without worry. To one side of the headboard were a number of low-voltage master control switches. When the wiring had been installed, all of the house's low-voltage wires (such as bell wires) were brought through a shaft in the headboard behind these switches so they could be connected there. Since these special low-voltage switches have pilot lights on them, you can tell at a glance just what lights are on in the house. In fact, the pilot lights even indicate which TV sets are on. If a child falls asleep leaving the TV or the lights on, these can be turned off remotely through the switchboard (one of two master controls).

Having the fire alarm bell and smoke alarm buzzer as well as their control board right outside the bedroom door was another precaution. In an emergency, they could be heard at once. Pinpointing the location where the ceiling alarm sensor has gone off is easy because lighted markers on the control board indicate the location of the activated alarm button (these buttons are installed in every area of the house).

The carpeted headboard wall (Figures 3 through 5) provides a unique decorating effect and it makes a comfortable backrest as well. Carpeting was chosen over upholstery material because it is rich and plush and cleans more easily. Even dusting is simple—just run the vacuum cleaner over the wall! The oyster white dense cut pile carpet, which is installed over a 2-inch-thick latex foam rubber padding, is

Fig. 3. Curved headboard is constructed of 2-x-3-inch vertical fir pieces mounted to 2-x-12-inch fir top and bottom plates, cut to a curve in the front only.

Fig. 4. Two-inch foam rubber padding is fastened to the plywood base, then covered with a final layer of carpet. Installation of the carpet should be taut and plumb. Curve of bed platform against headboard wall is carefully scribed and cut to fit.

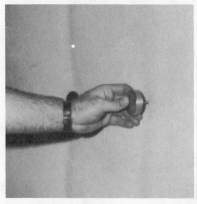

Fig. 5. Installing screw-in 2-inch stainless steel disk-buttons to prenailed resets to create a tufted surface.

Fig. 6. Setting antique wall mirrors is done with numbered ¼-inch thick by approximately 12-x-12-inch pieces in order to achieve a continuous pattern.

Fig. 7. Four-inch wide plywood strips are mounted, recessed (2 inches) between each chest.

Fig. 8. The basic multiunit suspended chest is built right on the site. After the unit is self-contained in its basic structure, 2-inch No. 10 screws are put into each wall stud through upper and bottom back support strips.

Fig. 9. Assembly of bottle drawer rack of refreshment bar.

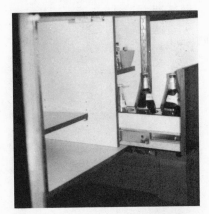

Fig. 10. Completed bar covered inside with white plastic laminate.

Fig. 11. Assembly of TV elevator mechanism, which is to fit into the first chest unit.

Fig. 12. TV elevator platforms (one fixed, and the top movable) are installed and balanced in the cabinet.

Fig. 13. Finished TV elevator in action. After button is pushed, lid opens and TV turns on before moving up.

Fig. 14. As TV reaches top, it turns toward bed.

made of Caprolan, a synthetic fiber material (by Allied Chemical Fiber Division). The high loop carpeting on the floor is made of the same fiber and is underlaid with the thickest available foam rubber waffled sheets. Result: it's like walking on clouds.

The remaining walls are covered with walnut paneling and fogged (antiqued) mirrors (Figure 6). The mirrors were carefully placed— one bank opposite the end of the bed and the other over the continuous counter. This counter, incidentally, proved to contain more storage area than was needed, so a small refreshment bar at the near end of the counter, big enough to hold four bottles, several glasses, and a 1½-cubic-foot refrigerator (see Figures 9 and 10, and Figure 15), was added. At the far end of the counter is another of those better living dreams. Just push a button next to the headboard: the lid opens and up comes the color TV set, already turned on. At its fullest elevation, the set slowly turns to face the bed (see Figures 12 though 14). As all this is happening, lights in that general area dim down to a 25 percent (or less if desired) glow.

The drapes are operated by efficient Judd motors, rather than being part of the low-voltage electronic relay system that was used in the Family Living Area (see page 16).

With deep earthy colors, leaning strongly toward terra cotta, taking command over the mood of this room, it was desirable to balance the color scheme by expanding on the use of the oyster white of the headboard. The most logical solution was to continue this color onto the bedspread, also a product of Caprolan fiber which was custom sewn and lined for sturdiness. Now the decorative strength of the rather large bed became even more emphatic.

In strong contrast to the oyster white in that area were the dark walnut cabinets and the terra cotta drapes and carpet. To balance and spread the contrast, the marble used for the counter top is an imported Italian Cremo which softened the strikingly strong effect of the bed. And to call attention to the existence of the beautifully simple fireplace (see page 25), marble was used there as well. The colors of the room are reflected in strategically placed antique mirrors.

Lighting was the final area of importance to be considered. If properly and knowledgeably applied, light is a powerful decorating aid creating color and mood (see Chapter 14). This master bedroom required eight circuits or separate light sources for various purposes. Reading light was provided by installing Kliegl No. 2145 fixtures over each side of the headboard. By framing in the lights with adjustable blinder shields inside the fixture, which is actually made for picture frame lighting, one person can read at night without disturbing the other. Conversation lights had to be soft enough to complement the area they were serving, but strong enough to light the surroundings. This was achieved by using Kliegl No. 2146 (wallwasher) fixtures, spaced far enough apart at the headboard cover to produce slender pyramidical shapes. Single fixtures were placed at the sliding glass door, over the vanity table, and in the center of the fireplace against the modern sculpture (see Chapter 3). While the 100W bulbs used in these fixtures illuminate through a projection lens so as to magnify and pinpoint their luminous output, the effect is a reflected mixture of soft tones picked up from the basic colors in those areas. There are also three different cycles of sharp downlights (Emerson) which by proper use of R-30 spotlight bulbs (75W) create approximately 36-inch-diameter spots on the floor in three general areas (very effective in this large room).

The wall area adjacent to and on the right of the stereo console is actually a bearing pillar. It was put there to sustain the steel flitch plate supporting the entire upper house in that section, and replacing the bearing wall which formerly supported it. This wall section is made entirely of concrete blocks (mortar-filled). It divides the man's closet around the corner as well as the woman's closet in the dressing room. Covering this 36-inch-wide wall was of utmost importance. For one thing, it is opposite the entrance. Secondly, being covered with smoked antiqued mirrors, it became the reflector of the bed. These mirrors, which were of the same finish throughout the house, had a unique appearance, in that the ingredients used for the process of antiquing were a mixture of antique brass and silver. A variable shade of warm gray background make the overall aging factor a truly artistic achievement. Finally, by creating a light shaft as a source of indirect lighting, the wall became a dramatic pace breaker. This was achieved by overlapping the front surface by 6 inches to gain enough area for 16-inch incandescent slimline bulbs behind a ¼-inch acrylic plastic diffuser plate mounted floor-to-ceiling. A Superior Electric automatic Luxtrol dimmer, when turned on, builds this circuit up to about 80 percent of its full strength. Turned off, it is just like the TV-light combination mechanism which is controlled by the same type dimming system. This is advantageous when getting into bed after turning off the lights, or when leaving the room, as it stays lighted long enough to help you avoid stumbling in the dark.

A rather limited amount of furniture was used in this room. The night tables were built like suspended discs so they would not compete with the graceful majesty of the master bed. This was successfully achieved by building 20-inch-diameter discs, 6 inches thick, and installing a 10-inch-wide, 3-inch-high invisible drawer in each. The four ⅜-x-1½-inch stainless steel legs seem to hold the walnut discs suspended 24 inches in midair, just as they project most favorably.

One final important innovation was added for convenience and safety: a video intercom system was incorporated by installing a small separator unit in the remote-controlled color TV set. Not only can you talk to anyone at the front door through the Emerson AM-FM intercom system, but you can also see the caller by simply pressing a button that interrupts the program on the TV screen. A remote closed-circuit camera at the front door is connected to this system. Releasing the button quickly brings back the program.

Several of the features included in this lavish master bedroom wouldn't normally be part of an economical building and decorating scheme. Again, the needs of the occupant will always dictate what is necessary and what isn't. But any of the many innovations which combine here to produce a very lavish room could be

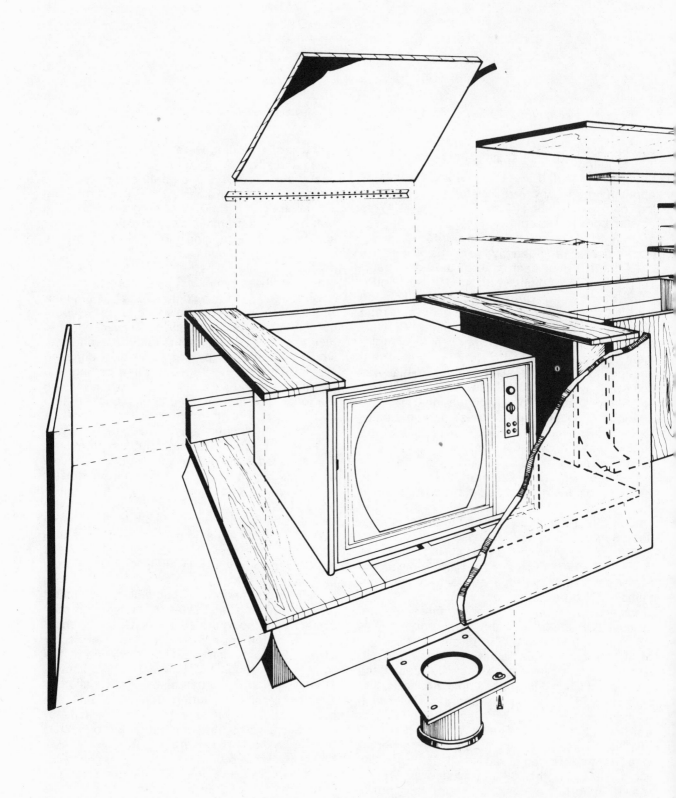

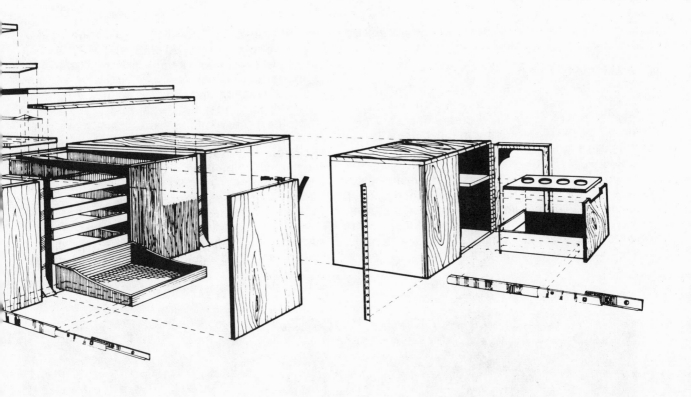

Fig. 15.

used on a different scale to make any master bedroom safer or more comfortable.

## A tailored bedroom

The lavish bedroom in the previous feature was created with a definite freedom of movement, availability of space, and certainly a very generous budget. Different circumstances in the room in Figures 17 and 18 dictated a different objective.

Although the room wasn't large and there wasn't very much storage space, it had enough basic area to be comfortable and functional as well as dramatic in appearance. Because there were only two small windows in the entire room, and these spread far apart, the challenge to create something interesting was even greater.

The problem here was to provide large amounts of storage space in a new, unusual-looking room while avoiding the static appearance storage units tend to create. By hanging drapery all across one wall, and partly across the other, the windows were visually enlarged. Antiqued (fogged) mirrors were placed on the head-on wall to give visual depth. The two closets were built on a slant in order to break up the monotony of the four walls, using fine walnut panels and louver doors to offset the strong use of drapery on the other walls.

Aside from the need for good reading light, dramatic lighting is most desirable in a master bedroom. Mood lights for watching TV, listen-

Fig. 16. Built-in vanity with lighting from within; bed unit with tilting headboards providing extra storage. Lighting source is within overhead section.

Fig. 17. Suspended chest of drawers with antiqued mirror panes divided by a cornice, providing illumination to both sides.

ing to music, or reading were installed in the built-in wall above the bed's headboard. The headboard cabinet contained two reclining upholstered supports for leaning back while watching TV or reading, making this rather large bed versatile as well as comfortable.

Besides serving an important function, the vanity, illuminated from within like the headboard wall, created a dramatic point of interest on an inactive wall.

Building all other storage cabinets into the wall produced storage space equal to that usually found only in much larger rooms. To guarantee massive storage without disturbing the pleasant surroundings, the main storage area was made an integral part of the decor. The 15-drawer, cantilevered dresser provided a vital and powerful counter top as well. This dresser, the mirrors installed above it, and the illuminated divider soffit in the center of the mirrors, aiming indirect lighting to both sides, became the focal points of the room.

The tendency of prefinished wood paneling to overwhelm a small area was overcome through the use of proper color, fabric texture,

Fig. 19. The attic in preparation.

Fig. 20. An attempted use of an area in the attic's front section was wasted except for the plumbing.

Fig. 18

Fig. 21. After proper insulation has been installed, outside walls are finished off with cedar closet lining, as are partitions for clothes closets.

Fig. 22. Bed with tilting headboard and built-on multi-purpose night table (right headboard end).

Fig. 23. Headboard, reclined.

Fig. 24. Refreshment bar.

Fig. 25. Planter divider with acrylic panels and uplights.

and the interchangeable and controllable lighting. Too much trivial softness might have destroyed the strength of the clean lines that were created.

### A plush bedroom in the attic

The surprise arrival of twins born to a financially comfortable family forced the owners to make one of two decisions: either expand or move. Since they lived in a desirable neighborhood, and liked their home and their friends, they decided to stay—and expand. Unfortunately, however, the small property did not allow them to add on to the existing house.

Because they had an unusually large and high attic, they converted it into a complete living area. Divided by a floor-to-ceiling illuminated planter 6 feet wide (see Figure 25), the entrance lounge was separated from the new master bedroom. They once tried to use the portion in front of the attic for the maid, but it did not work.

The family's living habits set the pace for most decisions. As theatrical people, they sought the most unusual. Because they had an extremely large wardrobe, closets and more storage than usual for an area like this had to be incorporated into the room. Their desire was pinpointed: to have a living bedroom with all the essentials hidden (except the bed) and some other attractions. Lighting was perhaps the biggest challenge in this windowless 36-foot-long room. .

To start, all rafters had to be reinforced in order to support the drop ceiling in the center. This item became perhaps the most important decision. As the roof and consequently the rafter line came to a peak, creating a 9-foot-wide drop frame was important. Made of 1-x-6-inch lumber on the peripheral edges and 1-x-4-inch webbing in the center, covered with 1-x-1-foot acoustical tile, this drop ceiling was suspended with horizontal crossbracing above and metal hangers mounted around them and down to the ceiling webbing (1-x-4-inch). Leads for air heating and cooling already existed in the house. Another zone control and a double thermostat covered the new attic extension. Because of hot summers and cold winters, all possible areas had to be well insulated. The ducts were installed directly above the drop ceiling, and convectors beyond the foot of the bed provided a comfortable room temperature. To finish off the area it was necessary to first build out the peripheral areas. Nearly 75 percent of this space became hanging storage, as well as drawers ranging from 2-inch depth (for jewelry or men's accessories) to 8-inch depth (for sweaters and the like). But all of it was behind folding doors, which when closed formed a wall covered with prefinished planked Accent Weldwood walnut paneling. Only one interruption, a refreshment bar (see Figure 24), offset the area just enough to retain the classic effect.

This bar was covered partially with random color 1-x-1-inch ceramic tile (silver-gold-beige and offwhite) and prefinished paneling. In back of the bar a fogged antique mirror sliding door covered the ample storage reachable from the front of the bar, adding depth in that area.

There was additional storage for a portable

TV and even skis.

The vanity table was a very luxurious setting in the small room adjacent to the bathroom (not shown).

The headboard cabinet mounted to their own kingsize bed truly was an interesting feature in itself. When opened, each end cabinet door swung out with a complete night table with a drawer and even a built-in telephone. A small bookcase to only one side provided the bold departure from monotonous symmetry while serving its purpose in that area.

Actually, to look at this room without the important consideration of the designed lighting would be rather disappointing. Which proves the importance of designing with lighting in mind.

To begin with, one circuit (each circuit has a switch at the entrance and at the bedside—in the night table) covered all indirect lights as follows: the soffits on both sides of the drop ceiling, and 4 Kliegl "up light" fixtures behind the headboard cabinet and up the silk drape backdrop. Further indirect lighting comes from under the bar apron and there are 2 up lights behind the bar. A light glow comes out of the white opal glass drop ceiling of the bar insert and of course the planter. All this alone creates an indescribable feeling of drama.

For direct lighting there are 2 Kliegl pin lights over each pillow for reading. Only 4 more flush down-lights further down in the ceiling and 1 behind the drape complete the designed lighting plan.

A commercial stereo with remote control in the antelounge can be controlled from the bed—as can most anything else. There is an intercom built into the headboard. The upholstered headboards are reclinable for reading or watching TV, while at the same time providing limited storage for extra blankets and pillows behind them.

"What a way to live; it's like a Turkish delight" was their remark after having used the room for well over a year.

# Chapter 6
# Emergency Sleeping for Guests

As technology advances, it is paradoxical that our homes seem to grow smaller and smaller. At one time, an extra room was a must for every house. However, as taxes and the price of land and labor skyrocketed, people began to tailor their homes to their exact needs and no more. The guest, consequently, had to move in with one of the children or sleep on the couch or a sofabed. The solution is the installation of built-in disappearing beds. They provide the sensible answer in a world in which family and guests are only hours away by jet and visits become more and more frequent.

The original disappearing bed (in the first House of Ideas) was a simple do-it-yourself project, the prototype of what is used today. The bed is made of plywood and requires only a few square feet of wall space with 12 inches maximum depth and very little in materials and labor. Its design is versatile and varied enough to be projected into many different settings and situations. In view of its low cost and space-saving features, the built-in bed is here to stay.

## Built-in foldaway guest room

The bed in Figure 1 consists of a 6-inch-thick foam rubber mattress placed on top of a ¾-inch Novoply base. The base is hinged to a ¾-inch plywood support platform within the built-in enclosure, leaving a 1-inch clearance on each side of the mattress base.

As shown in the chapter on family living, page 15, and because of the available depth, it was expedient to utilize the space fully by building a headboard cabinet. The cabinet is anchored against the two side panels and the back by screwing it to the wall studs with 2½-inch screws through the back mounting strips. The design allows enough clearance for an upholstered and adjustable headboard of appreciable size (see Figure 4).

A metal bracket, especially designed to lift out and down, is mounted to the headboard (Figures 2 and 3). In this way, the upholstered headboard panel can be converted from an attractive decorative item to a sturdy reclining backrest. Another advantage is that the headboard can be lifted up and the 7-inch-deep headboard cabinet unit used as vital storage for

Fig. 2. Installation of lift-out-and-down bracket for upholstered headboard.

Fig. 3. Bracket is mounted to headboard unit.

Fig. 4. Bed platform moves into enclosure after leg support is folded down.

Fig. 1. (opposite page) Foldaway guest room.

pillows and light bedding. The shelf above this storage is for books and the ledge of the entire headboard unit can be used for a clock or a radio.

The sliding door cabinet, installed 18 inches above the headboard cabinet, has adjustable shelves in which to store clothing or incidentals. The 7-inch-deep cabinet system, therefore, provides adequate storage as well as an anchor base for the foldable bed base and mattress.

When folded up, the headboard cabinet, the bed structure, and the mattress require only 16 inches of overall depth, including the necessary clearance. Even though an overall dimension of 24 inches was used in order to conform with the adjacent built-in wall, this emergency guest bed could be accommodated in an overall depth of just 20 inches, including the bi-fold exterior doors covering the bed structure and ample clearance.

To keep the mattress from sliding off the ¾-inch Novoply base, a ¾-x-3-inch border was mounted around the two sides and the front edge of the platform flush with the bottom surface. To keep the mattress from falling off when it is folded up and put away, sew a 2-inch border with eyelets every 6 inches to the front edge of the mattress. Then mount lock pins to the plywood base in line with the eyelets, much as is done on convertible car tops. Another way is to use 2 "seatbelts" 4 feet apart, starting 18 inches from the front end.

To lock the entire platform into place when it is in an upright position, an old-fashioned wood gate-lock (Figure 7) will suffice. Or, use a 6-to-8-inch surface sliding bolt.

In the down position, the height of the bed is 16 inches (measured from the floor to the top of the mattress). To start with, the bottom of the wall unit itself (¾ inch) had to be 8½ inches from the floor in order to clear the base panel heater convector element. The support platform (¾ inch) is mounted on top of this and the bed is mounted with a 2-inch continuous hinge (piano hinge) all the way across. The folding leg, which is cut to height and made of 2 thicknesses of ¾-inch plywood, is installed with 2 Stanley (8-x-8-inch) folding brackets (Figures 5 and 6).

Fig. 5. Hinge-bracket (8-x-8 inch) is mounted to bed base to fold the leg panel.

Fig. 6. To unlock the hinge bracket, push the center cross brace upward. Before lifting bed back into place, hinge bracket safety support is snapped back. Installing bed properly ensures all-around clearance.

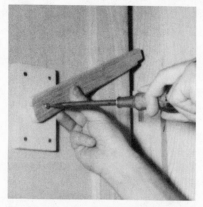

Fig. 7. A shop-made wooden latch will suffice to keep bed secure.

EXPLODED DETAIL OF BUILT–IN FOLDAWAY GUEST ROOM

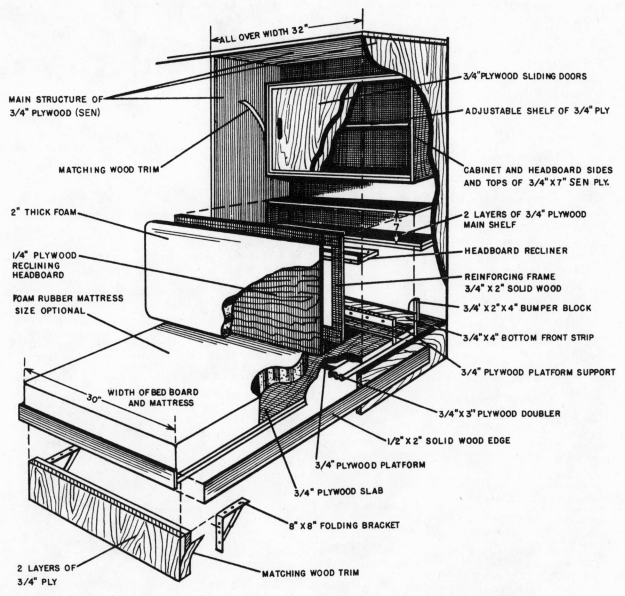

ALL OVER WIDTH 32"

3/4"PLYWOOD SLIDING DOORS

MAIN STRUCTURE OF 3/4" PLYWOOD (SEN)

ADJUSTABLE SHELF OF 3/4" PLY

MATCHING WOOD TRIM

CABINET AND HEADBOARD SIDES AND TOPS OF 3/4" X 7" SEN PLY.

2" THICK FOAM

2 LAYERS OF 3/4" PLYWOOD MAIN SHELF

1/4" PLYWOOD RECLINING HEADBOARD

HEADBOARD RECLINER

FOAM RUBBER MATTRESS SIZE OPTIONAL

REINFORCING FRAME 3/4" X 2" SOLID WOOD

3/4" X 2" X 4" BUMPER BLOCK

3/4" X 4" BOTTOM FRONT STRIP

3/4" PLYWOOD PLATFORM SUPPORT

WIDTH OF BED BOARD AND MATTRESS

30"

3/4" X 3" PLYWOOD DOUBLER

1/2" X 2" SOLID WOOD EDGE

3/4" PLYWOOD PLATFORM

3/4" PLYWOOD SLAB

8" X 8" FOLDING BRACKET

2 LAYERS OF 3/4" PLY

MATCHING WOOD TRIM

Fig. 8.

Fig. 10

The material used for the entire inside of the built-in bedroom is Sen plywood (oriental ash). For best finishing guidance and suggestions for materials, see Chapter 14, page 265.

A good way to quickly make up the bed is to use snap-on sheets and properly fitted oversheets. Use standard mattress size, about 6 inches thick (foam rubber).

The folding doors covering the built-in bed are ¾-inch Novoply (chipboard) covered with ¼-inch sandblasted fir paneling, to be finished after installation, or ¼-inch prefinished gray Shenandoah Revere, which is similar but requires less work. To avoid warping, the panels are only spot-glued and nailed with ¾-inch #16 brads. Each panel is cut to equal size and the two 4-inch horizontal feature spaces between the panels are painted with matte sandalwood latex paint.

Stanley bi-fold door hardware is used. To install it follow manufacturer's instructions. All sizes herein are adjustable, with the exception of the mattress and its platform, which should be standard if possible.

## Built-in foldaway double guest room

Built much in the order and with the same basic material as the built-in foldaway guest room, this

Fig. 11

Fig. 9

Fig. 12

has added advantages in that it is for two and has this nice combination center unit (Figures 9–12).

## Built-in beds in dressing room and library

In the House of Ideas, there are disappearing beds in both the dressing room and the library. The dressing room bed (Figure 22 and Figures 13–15) is used primarily in cases of illness, so as to avoid discomfort in the double bed. It can also be used to have a sick child close by, or a close family guest if necessary. It was placed in the dressing room because the room had a limited function anyway, and the bed takes up only 1 foot of wall space depth. The material used here is ¾-inch Novoply covered with ¼-inch prefinished Accent walnut paneling, spot-glued and nailed with 1-inch #18 brads

through the grooves if at all possible. Sink nails ¹⁄₁₆ of an inch and putty holes using matching Weldwood Blend Sticks—available at any hardware store or lumber yard. For further instructions consult the entire chapter as well as step-by-step pictures and detailed diagram. All the features in this chapter are essentially built in the same technique, using the same hardware basically needed for the function of these built-in beds. It would be possible to use any one of these features to suit any need.

The library unit (Figures 18–21) provided for afternoon naps (to avoid using the master bed) and easily accommodated guests as well.

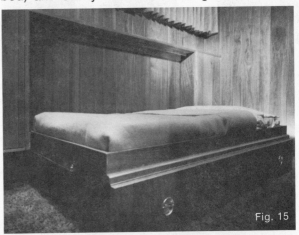
Fig. 15

Fig. 13

Fig. 14

Fig. 9. This built-in foldaway bed is built on the same order as is the built-in folding guest room bed. It differs only in that there are two identical beds divided in the center by a 3-foot built-in unit with sliding doors, covering shelf storage on top. The wood used here is Sen-ply (oriental ash), satin finished. Covering this area is ¼-inch Surfwood or prefinished Shenandoah (Revere Gray) paneling applied to the closed Novoply (¾-inch) folding doors.

Fig. 10. With open doors.

Fig. 11. With beds down, note indirect lighting above cornice and downlights in each bed compartment for reading. Behind headboards is storage for the pillow and extra blankets.

Fig. 12. Close-up shows that one of the pull-out drawers of the lower center unit is actually a night-table top covered with blending plastic laminate.

Fig. 13. Note the mortised recessed bolt holding the bed in place, accessible only when leg assembly is up.

Fig. 14. The flush front construction is achieved by building up the area below the folding leg.

Fig. 15. Bed in open position. Conventional automobile seatbelts are used to hold mattress and bedding in place.

Fig. 18. It was possible to include an emergency bed within a multipurpose wall in the library. The wall here is closed. This paneling is Accent walnut.

Fig. 19. After the leg assembly is lifted, pulling loose the lock bolt, bed can be lowered.

Fig. 20. Ample storage for pillows and blankets, too.

Fig. 21. Entire built-in combination library wall in open position.

Fig. 16. Stanley spring bracket collapses by pushing it into the indentation, thus allowing the folding leg support to close flush. Notice the flush lock bolt which holds the entire pull-out bed locked in place on each side.

Fig. 17. Installation of Rixon pivot. Two layers of ¾-inch plywood are minimum requirement for a safe hold. This, in essence, works on the same principle as do the trainboards.

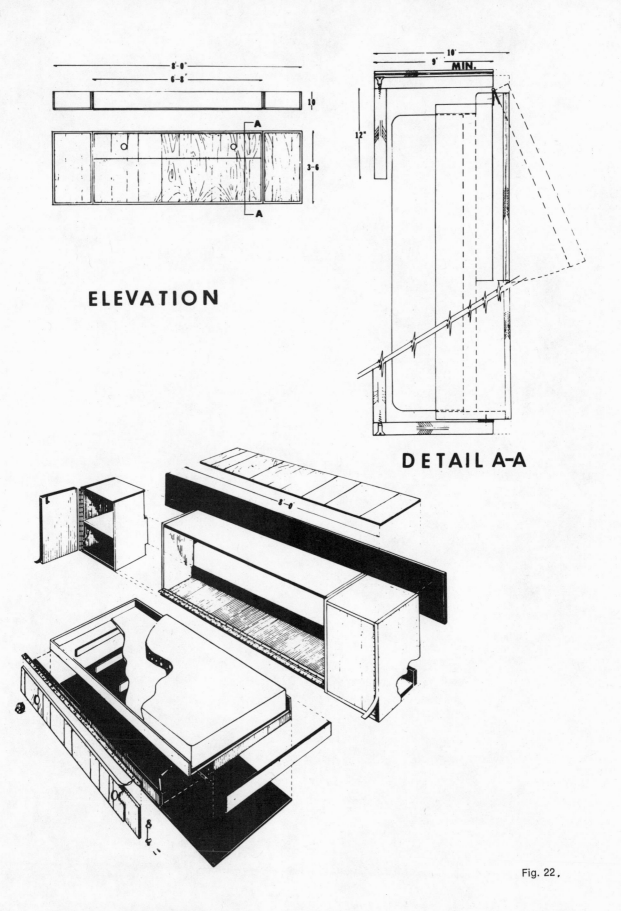

ELEVATION

DETAIL A-A

BUILT-IN BED

Fig. 22.

# Chapter 7
# Best Bathrooms

Many homeowners feel that money spent on improving the bathroom is somewhat wasted since the room is seen primarily by members of the family (except in the case of a powder room). But there are many arguments in favor of better and more functional bathrooms, one of which is that they do not require a much larger budget to arrive at more desirable results.

## Cost factors

The largest expenses in building a bathroom are the cost of plumbing, the basic fixtures, and the tile work (tiles on the walls, around the tub or shower, and on the floor may be required by the building codes in the area). If you are just making improvements (perhaps new fixtures in an existing bathroom), the cost may be surprisingly low.

Of course, further improvements (covering an entire wall with ceramic tiles, for example) or the use of better quality materials will be more expensive, but even this is slight when the cost is amortized over, say, a period of seven years. Even so-called luxury items such as good electric heating, a steam bath attachment, a combination infrared and exhaust fan are not really budget-breakers. Again, the basics mentioned above account for about 75 percent of the cost of bathroom construction. Naturally, such a statement must be relative, particularly when one considers what is available in today's decorator supply market. You can certainly spend more by purchasing gold-plated faucet sets or other objets d'art which are primarily optional decorative accessories.

Most people have never had the experience of comparing a simple adequate bathroom with one that is well-designed, well-equipped, and easy to maintain. It is fair to state that a change to a finer bathroom can mean an improved outlook on life. Your day will start and end on a happier note—after all, this is the place where you do most of your grooming, even if your home includes a separate dressing room.

## Special problems

As with so many home improvements, most of us do not seek a solution to a problem bathroom unless a need for improvement is really pressing. Often, it is only when a major repair is required that such matters are even considered. However, once the initial impetus has been applied, there is much that can be done.

While the average homemaker has fair judgment in most decorating situations, there are more than the usual problems involved in bathroom planning. Special knowledge and understanding, somewhat comparable to that involved in kitchen planning, are required. Correct placement and replacement of fixtures and equipment is essential if the entire effort is to be worthwhile. Both the exposed and concealed elements of a bathroom are important.

As with all rooms in the house, the bathroom must be traffic-oriented. The number of people using the room and the people themselves (young, elderly, handicapped, etc.) determine some important basics. The number of bathrooms in the home, or on the same floor, and the size of the budget are also factors in determining the size of each one.

Unless both budget and space availability are no object, one must first ascertain what is the right bathroom for the given family, based on the materials, equipment, and fixtures available. Only after listing all the necessary and desirable items can a budget and design study of the project be done.

## Wall and floor treatment

If it is possible within the limits of the budget, a completely tiled tub area is suggested, especially in those baths used by children. A further practical—as well as decorative—aspect is the creation of a feature wall where suitable. Vinylgard paneling (by U.S. Plywood) is available in several color tones and fine wood grains. It is primarily suggested for heavy traffic areas and is ideal for nonwet bathroom walls. Its tough vinyl coating is highly resistant to scratching and staining.

The floors, whether tile or marble block, should be the overall support of the room—decoratively as well as structurally. Proper design here is most important. Also important, especially in second-floor bathrooms, is waterproofing of all joints and floors. In fact, good

Fig. 1.  (opposite page) House of Ideas family bathroom.

and thorough flashing prior to pouring the concrete bed is mandatory in upstairs bathrooms.

## Fixtures

A good bathroom should have a shower stall in addition to a shower in the tub—only a lack of space should affect this rule. Solid enclosures (such as those shown in the featured bathrooms) with either ¼-inch glass or plastic panes are far superior to shower curtains (which are recommended only in tub enclosures for children). A solid enclosure keeps water heat and condensed steam where it belongs, rather than allowing it to escape all over the bathroom causing additional wear to areas outside the tub section. Solid enclosures give an impressive appearance to the room—and hide a dirty tub when cleaning has to be delayed. Most important, an enclosure allows use of the bathroom by two people at the same time without sacrificing privacy. Finally, considering the budget, a projected maintenance cost study would probably indicate that a good solid enclosure will outlast several sets of curtains and will certainly be a minimal price factor when figured over a period of several years.

Thermasol is a steam-producing unit available in various sizes and capacities. It can be installed in a home bathroom for less than the price of a few dozen public Turkish bath tickets. The pleasures of owning such an inexpensive luxury are immeasurable. And, since it is out of sight, it does not become a factor in the decor of the room. A safety timer control is included on the unit. Such a unit should be carefully selected with the advice of a good plumber. It can be installed even in a finished bathroom with a minimum amount of wall breakage and repair.

By their very nature, bathrooms tend to have a cluttered appearance at times. Conceal-All built-in utility fittings such as toilet tissue holders, medicine cabinets, and disappearing toothbrush holder/glass holder/soap dispensers, etc., are available in such finishes as chrome, brushed chrome, brass, copper, and the like. Such fittings are perfect for organizing the inevitable clutter, yet they are relatively rare in modern bathrooms. Made by Marchand, Inc.,

of New York, these fittings are among the few truly new decor novelties for bathrooms and a leader in design and quality.

With regard to the major fixtures for the bathroom, there are several leading companies in the field. American Standard is the most experienced producer of quality bathroom fixtures. As well as being the pioneers, they are also the manufacturers of the unusual, clinically approved Neo-Health Toilette used in the Family Bath feature. This toilet, which includes a cleaning spray, is actually sculpted and formed to fit the anatomy.

You surely need not be wealthy in order to have an exhaust fan connected to the bathroom ceiling, or as available, to have a multicombination ceiling unit by Emerson (Chromalox) providing light, heating, exhaust, and even a provision for an ultraviolet bulb for tanning, as shown in the following featured bathrooms. It is more a matter of being discriminating and practical. The same is true for the lighting inside your shower or tub enclosure, and for good area rugs on the floor or well-placed holders for decorative towels.

Certainly, good vanity and cabinet planning will be a big part of the bathroom design. A number of other bathroom improvement ideas, detailed in the following pages, will be justifiable expenditures helping to make your life a little bit nicer and more comfortable.

## Family bath

When only one bathroom must serve several people, it is advisable to double up on fixtures such as showers and washbowls. This will represent savings on the plumbing bill, an item of expense to be watched with particular care.

The House of Ideas bathroom in Figures 1–4 was originally so clinically designed that it lacked both beauty and charm. It did, however, have a selection of fixtures of finest quality and a custom-designed Acme marble "Versailles" vanity. Unfortunately, the matching mosaic tile and blending marblechip Misa on the floor, immaculate and attractive as they were, lent an air of utilitarianism. The only thing to do was to carefully plan a flowing pattern of color in items yet to be selected. Strong orange

Fig. 2. A most complete custom vanity installation with decorated Ovalyn lavatories and custom-made gold-plated fittings and handles. Best accessories will conceal all units and good lighting.

Fig. 3. Area showing arrangement of the less active wall, containing the built-in electric wall heater, towel rack and electric shoe shiner, and the Buckingham tub, with shower and mixer dial. For children's safety, a curtain was used instead of a solid tub enclosure.

Fig. 4. A view into the most complete shower stall, including bench (left) and Conceal-All soap-grab. Not seen is the Aquarian adjustable shower head, single lever dial mixer valve, and below, a steam bath valve. All enclosed by Keystone stainless steel shower door, translucent and with adjustable louvers on top.

Fig. 5. Old studs and rafters are furred out to be straight and even. Next, lamp fixture frames are mounted and wired.

Fig. 6. Plumbing is installed next, carefully spotting tub and shower mixing valves (single lever faucet with temperature control), as well as drain and vent pipes.

Fig. 7. Shower door is framed out after rough cement coat application.

Fig. 8. After tile installation, the shower door is installed.

Fig. 9. Adjustable frame as well as shower door metal hanger allows for late adjustment.

Fig. 10. Mica floor blocks are installed last, starting equally spaced from the center.

and terra cotta colors were chosen. Towels are a good means of color expression, but since they are sometimes put away or being laundered, it is advisable to repeat the color elsewhere. In this case, it was done in two round bath rugs and again in the bathtub curtains, which are striped in alternating shades of red and gold.

The entire area was softened by the use of delicate and enduring decorative panels around the oval sinks and the beige marble top of the vanity. The ceiling was painted red-orange to match the towels, rugs, and curtains. The ceiling color reflecting onto the floor changed the gray hue of the Misa tiles to beige. Also, changing the vanity moldings to a matching orange-red lifted the entire color scheme. In the end a rather clinical bathroom had been turned into a decorative success.

Although aesthetics are undoubtedly very important when designing a bathroom, efficiency must be the primary consideration.

Budget and space permitting, a well-functioning shower stall should be no less than 3 by 3 feet in dimension, with an additional 1-foot-deep tiled ledge about 28 to 32 inches from the floor for seating during a steam bath. In the House of Ideas the bench was actually framed in when building the walls of the shower (opposite the steam bath valve), and was completely tiled with copper flashing underneath and "bull-nose" tiles on the edges. With this type of design, a facility steam bath can be quite a pleasurable experience.

Other features include a Keystone shower door with an upper louver opening for ventilation, and an Aquarian bath/shower control with diverter spout showerhead by American Standard. Also built in for extra safety are the soap grip, an extra wall grip, nonskid tiles on the floor, and a concealed overhead light (150W). All combine to make a perfect shower structure.

A 5½-foot Buckingham tub, the largest on the market, was also used and because it has a stepped front apron, preventing the construction of an enclosure, a curtain was necessary (Figure 3). For future necessity, another shower-head was installed in the tub area.

Even though this was an inside bathroom (without window), which would not get cold, a Chromalox-FWH electric heater and blower was installed in the wall. For exhaust, a combination infrared lamp heater, blower, and exhaust fan of the same make was installed in the ceiling.

The Neo-Health toilet bowl (Figure 3) is unique in that the seat is molded to the shape of the body. (The American Bidet Company also makes a contoured seat structure, which has a warm-water spray and a fan for drying; this seat will fit any toilet.)

A number of brushed chrome built-in Conceal-All units were installed to prevent the room from getting messed up easily and to make cleaning easier.

This bathroom turned out to be functional, pretty, and reasonable in price.

### Children's twin bathroom

Because the bathroom in Figure 12 was shared by a boy and a girl in their teens, it was especially designed to avoid interferences and struggles for priority.

The basic problem in remodeling the old bathroom was the separation of the sexes, which dictated building a partition and doubling up on the necessary fixtures.

The existing bathroom was carefully analyzed to determine how rerouting would affect the structure and the budget. Because it was a corner room, moving a window was fairly simple. Next, new bathroom fixtures had to be positioned. Although the bathroom was not very spacious to begin with, it was advisable to divide the room into three separate areas (see plan, Figure 14), and to select the smallest, most compact fixtures available.

The selection of a Restal corner tub guided the basic partition location. An additional 6-inch tile rim on the three sides of the tub provided a useful ledge, but also gained an important 12 inches for the necessary toilet (knee) clearance.

Although you cannot create space where there is none, you can certainly gain a lot of it by properly utilizing every inch there is. Perimeter placement of equipment, appliances, and fixtures is the best solution for space saving,

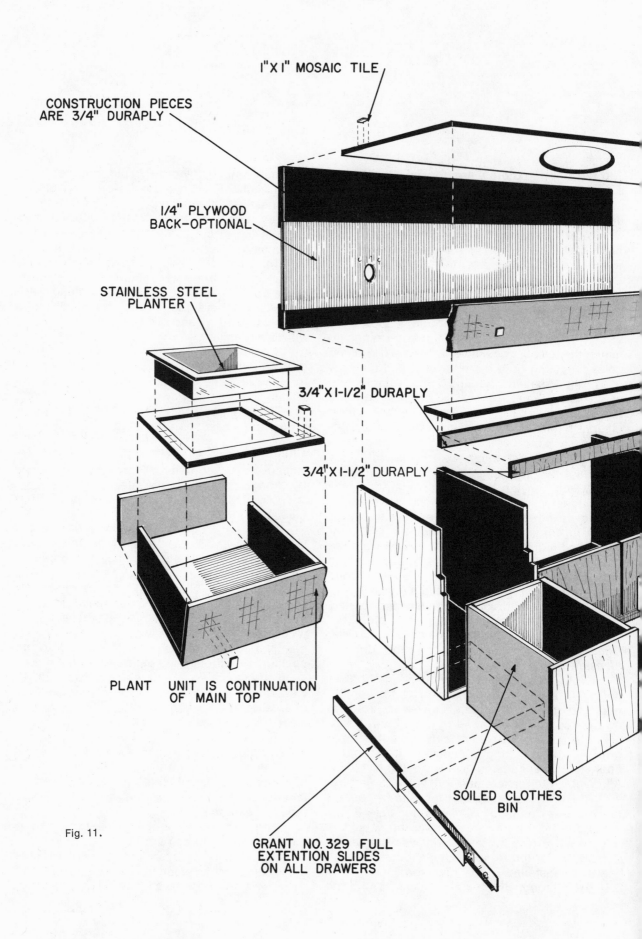

I" X I" MOSAIC TILE

CONSTRUCTION PIECES
ARE 3/4" DURAPLY

1/4" PLYWOOD
BACK—OPTIONAL

STAINLESS STEEL
PLANTER

3/4" X I-1/2" DURAPLY

3/4" X I-1/2" DURAPLY

PLANT UNIT IS CONTINUATION
OF MAIN TOP

SOILED CLOTHES
BIN

Fig. 11.

GRANT NO. 329 FULL
EXTENTION SLIDES
ON ALL DRAWERS

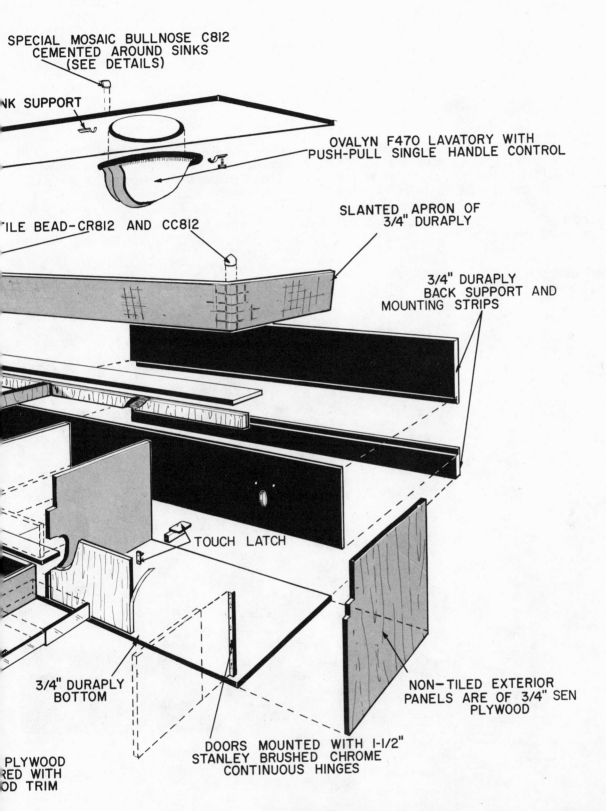

SPECIAL MOSAIC BULLNOSE C812
CEMENTED AROUND SINKS
(SEE DETAILS)

NK SUPPORT

OVALYN F470 LAVATORY WITH
PUSH-PULL SINGLE HANDLE CONTROL

TILE BEAD-CR812 AND CC812

SLANTED APRON OF
3/4" DURAPLY

3/4" DURAPLY
BACK SUPPORT AND
MOUNTING STRIPS

TOUCH LATCH

3/4" DURAPLY
BOTTOM

NON-TILED EXTERIOR
PANELS ARE OF 3/4" SEN
PLYWOOD

PLYWOOD
RED WITH
OD TRIM

DOORS MOUNTED WITH 1-1/2"
STANLEY BRUSHED CHROME
CONTINUOUS HINGES

# BATHROOM VANITY

although it is not necessarily the most attractive solution in a room larger than this one.

The bi-folding enclosure doors over the tub and in the passage through the partition were real time-savers. A special, three-dimensional, translucent glass was used for privacy, but without the sacrifice of safety.

Alternate 1-x-1-inch and 4-x-4-inch tiles in the same color as the fawn beige American Standard fixtures were used on all the walls. The marblechip Misa flooring used was the same as that in the Family Bath (page 81), but in a different color scheme. The Conceal-All storage and utility units, the lighting, ventila-

Fig. 12.   This picture illustrates the partitioning of the multi-area bathroom.

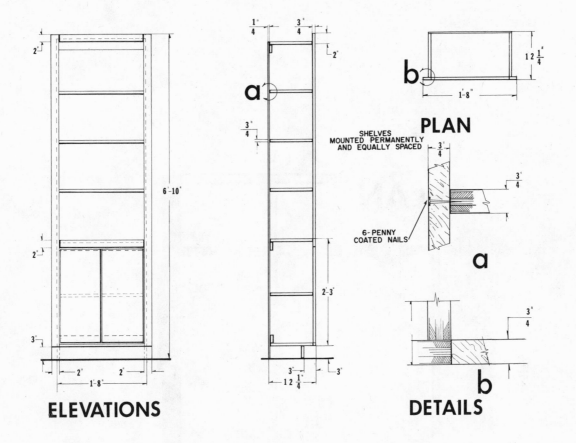

## ELEVATIONS

2"

6'-10"

2"

3"

2"    2"

1'-8"

1/4"    3/4"

2"

3/4"

SHELVES
MOUNTED PERMANENTLY
AND EQUALLY SPACED

2'-3"

3"    3"

1 2 1/4"

## PLAN

1 2 1/4"

1'-8"

3/4"

3/4"

6-PENNY
COATED NAILS

## a

3/4"

## b

## DETAILS

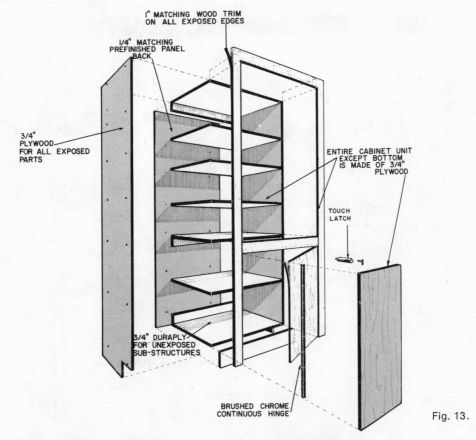

1" MATCHING WOOD TRIM
ON ALL EXPOSED EDGES

1/4" MATCHING
PREFINISHED PANEL
BACK

3/4"
PLYWOOD
FOR ALL EXPOSED
PARTS

ENTIRE CABINET UNIT
EXCEPT BOTTOM
IS MADE OF 3/4"
PLYWOOD

TOUCH
LATCH

3/4" DURAPLY
FOR UNEXPOSED
SUB-STRUCTURES

BRUSHED CHROME
CONTINUOUS HINGE

Fig. 13.

# BUILT-IN BATHROOM TOWEL CABINET

# PLAN

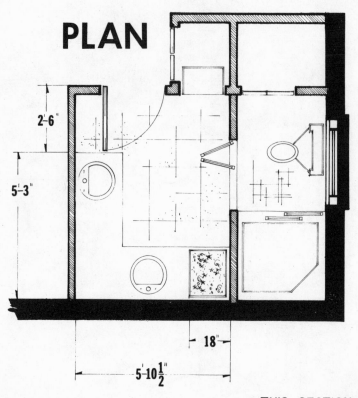

2'-6"

5'-3"

18"

5'-10½"

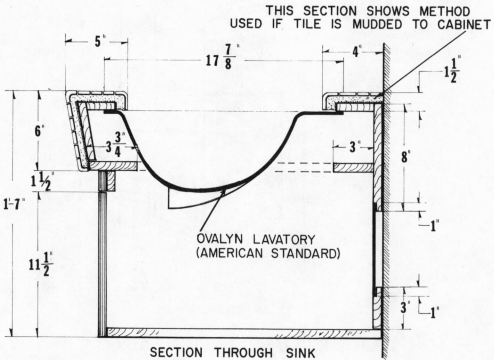

THIS SECTION SHOWS METHOD
USED IF TILE IS MUDDED TO CABINET

5"

17⅞"

4"

1½"

6"

3¾"

3"

8"

1½"

1'-7"

1"

11½"

OVALYN LAVATORY
(AMERICAN STANDARD)

3"

1"

SECTION THROUGH SINK

Fig. 14.

Fig. 15.

VIEW TO BATHROOM ENTRANCE
SHOWING TOWEL SUPPLY CABINET,
ENTRANCE TO TOILET AND
BATH TUB SECTION

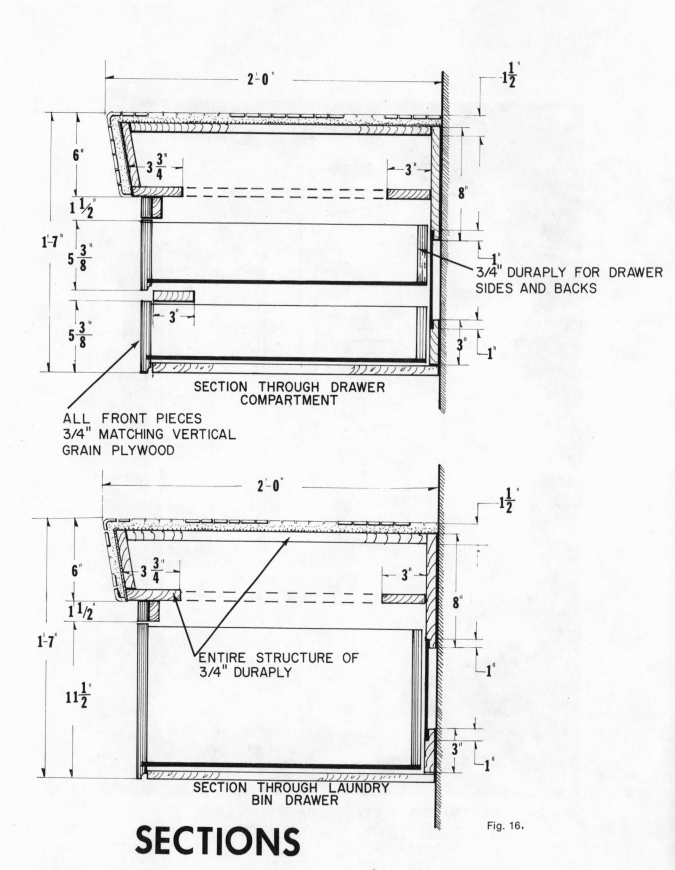

SECTION THROUGH DRAWER
COMPARTMENT

ALL FRONT PIECES
3/4" MATCHING VERTICAL
GRAIN PLYWOOD

3/4" DURAPLY FOR DRAWER
SIDES AND BACKS

ENTIRE STRUCTURE OF
3/4" DURAPLY

SECTION THROUGH LAUNDRY
BIN DRAWER

# SECTIONS

Fig. 16.

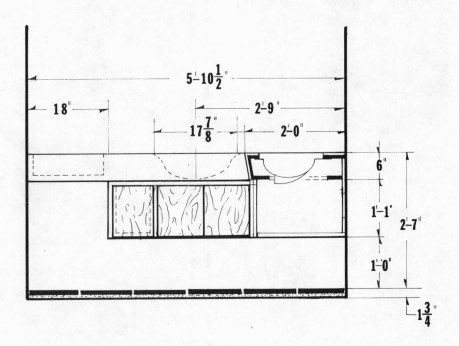

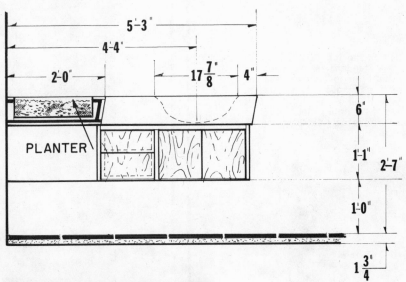

PLANTER

# ELEVATIONS

# BATHROOM DETAILS

Fig. 17.

Fig. 18. Structural and exterior walls are cement coated over wire mesh after all necessary pipes and wires have been installed.

Fig. 19. Restal tub (3 x 3 feet) by American Standard is installed and connected prior to framing. After all structural framing is done and installation of all pipes and wires is completed, a bath after hours is welcome in the only bathroom so far functional.

Fig. 20. Another day adds wire mesh and cement undercoating, thus further developing the area.

Fig. 21. View into a compact two-part area of this functional bathroom.

Fig. 22. Rough cabinetry (corner vanity) advances this bathroom even further.

Fig. 23. Final touches of decor around stainless steel planter brings this face to end.

tion, and heating, and the remote steam bath installation all showed careful planning. There is also a corner double-bowl vanity counter made of ¾-inch Sen plywood finished to withstand exposure (Figure 11). (See more about wood finish on page 271.) All of these account for easily maintained beauty and efficiency.

There is still enough room to install a few decorative and useful items such as a built-in towel storage wall unit (Figure 13 and Figure 15), a counter-top planter with an overhead spotlight for decor (see Figure 23), and a linen closet in the far corner. The combined Conceal-All medicine cabinet units were installed in their proper place (Figure 17). Nothing was left out because of a lack of space. Additional drawer space, as well as a small drawer for soiled clothes, could even be worked into the vanity counter. There was also plenty of storage space for cleaning and maintenance items behind the doors under each wash basin.

The room was done in blending shades of beige, some rose, and light brown. The bathroom fixtures are of fawn beige, blending with the large tiles. The small tiles, as well as the vanity top, are a blending of pale rose for accent. The general decorative attitude is friendly, and, most important of all, the children don't have to fight to use the room.

### The Mediterranean-style master bath

It is rare to find a bathroom with a versatile layout, good accessories, and adequate storage for all necessities. Somehow the decor of most bathrooms—even in very fine homes—disappears in the clutter. Since guests seldom see the master bathroom, the average homeowner feels that basic function is the most important consideration, sometimes even at the expense of the appearance. Such a concept need not and should not hold true.

The room in Figures 24 through 27 is best described as a perimeter-function bathroom of fair size. Its uncluttered appearance is achieved by including little more than is absolutely necessary.

### Sunken tub

Perhaps the main feature of interest in this Mediterranean bathroom is its sunken tub—a luxury many people dream of, but discard as impractical. Building a sunken tub can have its drawbacks. First of all, in an upstairs bath, it involves losing part of the room below, which often rules out the idea completely. Secondly, a sunken tub made of ceramic tile should have a cast concrete box to contain all the tile work. Because this is a costly procedure, many sunken tubs are installed without the concrete box and this causes many problems. When anything goes wrong, it means expensive repairs.

Despite these drawbacks, there are situations in which a sunken tub becomes feasible. In a downstairs bathroom, especially over a basement, builders can find ways to properly support the structure. By combining outstanding custom features with modern prefabricated products, one can go a long way toward achieving a desirable result without costly preparation. Prefabricated products are not only budget-saving, but also provide a low maintenance factor because of their durability. People are therefore able to plan larger and better-equipped master bathrooms with sunken tubs where possible.

In this master bathroom, fitting substitutes were found for expensive and difficult-to-build areas. By using a nearly square tub, approximately 48 x 42 inches (the largest corner tub available), placed 18 inches (or 1 foot minimum) from the left wall and snug against the back wall, an interesting effect was created. The planter strip along the left wall achieved an imaginative and expensive look. And, the sunken tub was installed at minimal cost.

When this feature of the bathroom was planned, a special alteration was ordered from the manufacturer so as to test a new approach in the technique of creating a sunken bathtub. The tub's apron, the one important support and sealing factor, is usually 12 inches high. As the proposed finished exposure for the recessed tub was to be only 4 inches above the finished floor (6 inches above the rough floor sheathing), the apron was cut by the manufacturer to 6 inches prior to enameling the new tub.

To reduce the 6-inch apron exposure to the desired 4 inches, the 2 inches were ab-

Fig. 24.

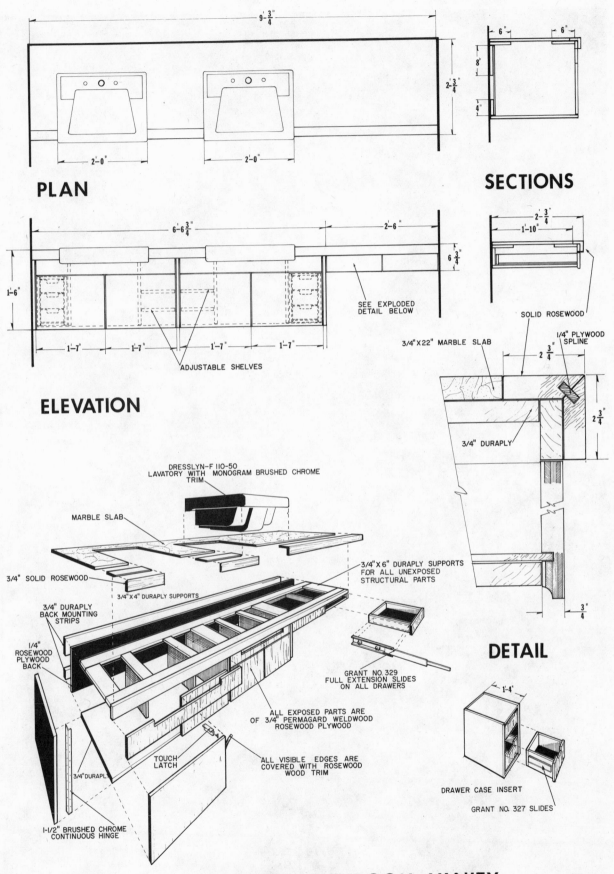

**PLAN**

**SECTIONS**

9'-3¾"

6"    6"

2'-3¾"

8"

4"

**ELEVATION**

6'-6¾"    2'-6"

6¾"

1'-6"

1'-7"    1'-7"    1'-7"    1'-7"

ADJUSTABLE SHELVES

SEE EXPLODED
DETAIL BELOW

2'-3¾"

1'-10"

SOLID ROSEWOOD

3/4"X22" MARBLE SLAB

1/4" PLYWOOD
SPLINE

2 3/4"

3/4" DURAPLY

2 3/4"

3/4"

**DETAIL**

DRESSLYN-F 110-50
LAVATORY WITH MONOGRAM BRUSHED CHROME
TRIM

MARBLE SLAB

3/4" SOLID ROSEWOOD

3/4"X 4" DURAPLY SUPPORTS

3/4" DURAPLY
BACK MOUNTING
STRIPS

1/4"
ROSEWOOD
PLYWOOD
BACK

3/4"DURAPLY

TOUCH
LATCH

1-1/2" BRUSHED CHROME
CONTINUOUS HINGE

3/4"X 6" DURAPLY SUPPORTS
FOR ALL UNEXPOSED
STRUCTURAL PARTS

GRANT NO. 329
FULL EXTENSION SLIDES
ON ALL DRAWERS

ALL EXPOSED PARTS ARE
OF 3/4" PERMAGARD WELDWOOD
ROSEWOOD PLYWOOD

ALL VISIBLE EDGES ARE
COVERED WITH ROSEWOOD
WOOD TRIM

1'-4"

DRAWER CASE INSERT

GRANT NO. 327 SLIDES

# MASTER BATHROOM VANITY

Fig. 25.

Fig. 26.

sorbed by the wire mesh, cement, and marble floor. This final process, however, did not take place until the bathtub itself was firmly anchored in place at the bathroom level as well as secured and supported on the support structure in the basement. (See Figure 27.) If this had been impossible, the floor cutout would have had to be larger toward the front (at the apron location) to accommodate the additional rim width as well as the thickness of the apron. In this case, the resting support would have to compensate for the additional burden, as well as the sealing of that joint after the tub was in place. Therefore, it would have to be closed off and sealed from underneath, and one would have to be able to gain access to the area from beneath the tub.

However the tub is supported temporarily,

Fig. 27.

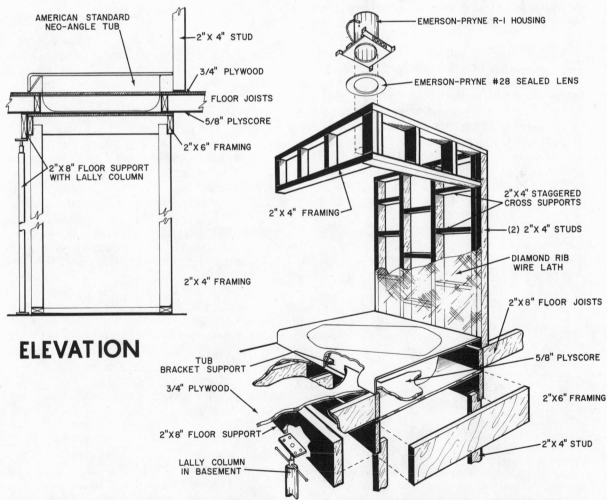

## SUNKEN-TUB SETTING & ENCLOSURE DETAIL

the main support (but definitely not sole support) is provided by a table underneath (see Figure 27). This table is built of 2 x 4 (or preferably 2 x 6) fir verticals with 2 x 6 (or preferably 2 x 8) horizontal cross members and a ¾-inch fir plywood top—or if needed for extra support (recommended in any case), 2 layers of ¾-inch plywood. Once the support table is completed, it is slid under the tub. Shims are used to seat the tub properly, maintaining an appropriate slant for drainage. Plumbing connections are made accessible through cutouts in the table support. The table is then anchored to the concrete floor below with steel angles to prevent possible movement or opening of joints around the tub area by accidental bumping.

To avoid this rather costly and involved tub alteration, which is not absolutely necessary (however desirable), follow the instructions above. Make sure that the tub seat cutout in the plywood floor sheathing is well sealed, using caulking and copper flashing before applying the flooring material.

This sunken tub technique is not limited to the square tub used for this feature, but if you wish to duplicate it (or nearly so), look into the availability of a square or corner tub; these

Fig. 28. A shelf mounted on the sunken tub support in the basement provided a perfect location for the 3 Thermasol steam units servicing the bathrooms.

have been discontinued by at least two well-known manufacturers. The original tub shown is a Neo-Angle unit, 49 x 49 inches—but no longer available. The tub recommended here is by Kohler, and its size varies slightly to 48 x 42 inches. The 6 inches can be compensated for nicely by building a tiled or marble ledge.

By mounting a second ¾-inch plywood shelf beneath the supporting top, it was possible in this case to place the Thermasol steam-producing units for all three baths of the house here (Figure 28).

## Tub area

The tub area (see Figure 26) in the bathroom was closed in with travertine marble, as was the floor. The back wall is covered with sculptured ceramic tile. The left side panel of the tub enclosure (rigidly framed), next to the planter area, is ⅜-inch plate glass; the folding door panels are plexiglass (by Just Plastic Co., New York, who also made the plastic steps in the foyer), inserted in a frame system (gold-anodized by Keystone). The door panels are smooth on the inside and three-dimensional on the outside. This is done by fusing small multicolored plastic particles randomly to the surface (an original plastic creation by Martha Turi).

The Heritage bath adjustable double shower heads with diverter spout and mixer control are efficient as well as elegant, as is true of the delicately designed but sturdy built-in soap grab and 2 staggered safety handle bars by Marchand. The steam of the remote unit is expelled through a small chrome head mounted near one of the shower heads.

A waterproof light fixture in the center of the ceiling with a flood bulb of 150 watts (type R-1030) illuminates the tub area. A Kliegl spotlight highlights the upper leaves of the artificial plants in the planter strip next to the tub.

## Vanity

The Brazilian rosewood counter with small vanity recess was custom-designed and made to appear as a single unit (see Figures 24 and 25). Three-quarter-inch Duraply (waterproof, with laminated paper, actually fabricated for exterior use) was used for the unexposed main

Fig. 29. Six-foot oval pool with 4″ apron for deluxe sunken-type installations.

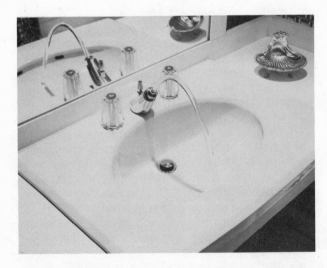

Fig. 30. This Ultra lavatory with Heritage acrylic spout faucets could be used instead of the Dreslyn lavatory described in this feature.

structure. The vanity has two pairs of matched-grain flush doors, which open by pushing the doors against touch latches. Two flush drawers in the recessed vanity section also have no visible hardware; they are opened by coved grips concealed underneath, and roll out practically to their full length on full-extension 329 slides.

The counter unit is 24 inches deep. The marble tops are cut and polished to 22 inches (except where the two basins are fitted). A solid rosewood top-front edge lamination mitered together as shown in the diagram exposes 2¾ inches in front and the same on the top to allow for the 22-inch finished marble (Cremo). This top was in 3 parts, due to its length and to provide the cutout for the American Standard Deluxe Dresslyn basins.

To keep a clean-line appearance around the vanity, scalloped-edge and premounted mirrors (retaining the elegance) were installed above the basins to the marble wall.

Additional medicine and cosmetic storage and a three-sectional toothbrush and glass holder of brushed chrome (Conceal-All) were installed through the paneled side wall in order not to disturb the beautiful marble surface. The ¼-inch unfinished and pregrooved architectural classic Brazilian rosewood paneling matches the vanity counter. Maintenance of this bathroom is simple. Because both the marble and the special wood finish walls can simply be wiped clean, this bathroom will always have a fresh appearance. (See "Wood Finishing," page 271.)

The room is decorated with bold and basic product textures and colors, complemented by a ceiling painted antique gold. The rectangular 4-x-6-foot rug (Portico by Cabin Craft) is an accent in texture, while at the same time a dramatic color blend. The 36-inch-diameter area rug in 3 shades of brown (by Fieldcrest Mills) matches the tricolor border of the main rug. It contributes visual action through color while fulfilling its basic function.

The master bath has 3 lighting circuits—one for the tub only, and a second for the entrance and toilet-bidet area, to which a Chromalox exhaust fan is connected to operate automatically.

The third includes a light over each wash basin (type R-1030 with R30 bulb, 7W) and 2 planter spotlights (one over each) for special effect (Kliegl 2148Q). There is a concealed telephone jack next to the toilet. Next to the light switches (low voltage for safety) is the time switch for the steam bath.

For summer comfort, the overhead hydronic aircooling duct and register (Hart & Cooley) cools the room. Winter comfort is provided by a recessed electric heater and fan combination in addition to the cast-iron hot water heating convectors. The fire alarm button in the ceiling will set off an alarm at 135°.

### A classic powder room

Powder rooms are often planned as rather ostentatious showpieces and as a result money is spent uselessly—while the room, more often than not, is not functional. Simplicity is really the safest way to successful design. This powder room and the Tailored Powder Room on page 103 demonstrate realistic approaches to the problems of designing functional as well as attractive guest baths.

To utilize a leftover bathroom from the original old house (Figure 33), a space barely 3 by 5 feet in the inside shaft of the remodeled House of Ideas where 2½ baths are placed behind each other, a very carefully planned layout was necessary. Because this final area is

Figs. 31 and 32. For a decorative solution to toilet tissue, the Conceal-All unit covers the paper roll and is available in a variety of decorator finishes.

situated in the general vicinity of the entrance foyer and at the same time serves the children to the left corridor and as master bath to the right, it was important to create a compatible plumbing layout while decoratively attaining the proper feeling. The keynotes thus became striking decor, optimal function, and effective use of space.

The lack of available space limited the choice of lavatory and toilet fixtures somewhat. Fortunately, however, a small, handsome, wall-hung lavatory with optional chrome front legs and towel bars (20 x 18 inches) was found. Called Comrade, its sculptured rectangular styling is the prime solution to this challenge.

The decorative emphasis was placed on the surrounding surfaces. The classic beauty of Vinylgard "Early Spring Fox" finish paneling was literally wrapped around 3 of the room's walls. The most important wall—the one which is seen when entering—was covered with sculptured tile, designed on a pattern of vertical stripes in powdered rose and beige. Against the semigloss ivory of the tile, this was just sufficient to control the rhythm of the pattern flow.

Fig. 33. Before: original powder-bathroom of 100-year-old house.

Fig. 34. After: finished powder-bathroom in House of Ideas.

The ceiling was covered with antique gold foil, sponged with orange clouds. The floor was covered with Amtico's classic cut Renaissance, which, in this layout, is easily taken for marble. The color of the fixtures is a popular fawn beige.

In contrast to the Combination Powder Room (page 103), there are no storage gadgets in this one, aside from the Conceal-All toilet paper dispenser (as seen in Master Bath, Figures 31 and 32) and the automatic ceiling fan. While the epitome of simplicity, this room is an extremely useful and beautiful one.

### A tailored combination powder-bathroom

Some people may wonder exactly what a tailored powder room is, and why the description is used for this particular room. In the House of Ideas, paneling was extensively used—even in the bathrooms—because it is quickly installed and extremely economical. Paneling also creates a "tailored" appearance.

The careful integration of water-resistant and prefinished Vinylgard paneling (in many wood finishes), with either sculptured tile or foil wallpaper on alternate walls, is an excellent selection. Because it requires only cleaning, the paneling pays for itself every day, while remaining continuously beautiful. Installation takes only a tenth of the time usually necessary for any other type material. Although unprotected paneling will stand up well in a powder room, the Vinylgard (water-resistant) paneling, which can be obtained for only a slight extra charge, will withstand possible scratching and will remain clean and new-looking with occasional wiping.

This particular combination room (Figure 39) had to accommodate the needs of a growing family by acting as the number two bath in a two-bathroom house. Because it was located at the end of a very versatile family room, it had to be right in every detail so as not to detract from the overall appearance of the larger room to which it was attached.

Accessories include a fine shower enclosure, custom-built vanity, and top grade bath-

room fixtures. The versatile vanity is quickly transformed into a rather elegant make-up table, lined with mirrors and dark blue Carrara (Italian import) glass.

To avoid clutter in this rather small area (3½ x 5½ feet), many small but interesting items were built onto the wall, and were finished to match the paneling—as does the bottom of the

Fig. 35. After removing the old wood lath, pipes and wiring can begin. Next, all walls are resupported and furred out to be straight.

Fig. 36. The vinyl floor is affixed to water-repellent plywood.

Fig. 37. Next, walls are first undercovered with wood where paneling is to be installed, and cement undercoating or gypsum board for tiles. Vinylgard Pasado wall paneling is glued and nailed to sheathing, carefully scribing edges joining ceiling and tile wall.

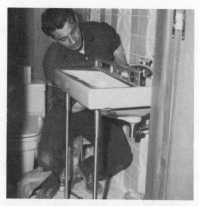

Fig. 38. Final installation of American Standard's smallest and compact washbasin, Comrade (20 x 18 inches), nearly concludes the new powder room.

Fig. 39.

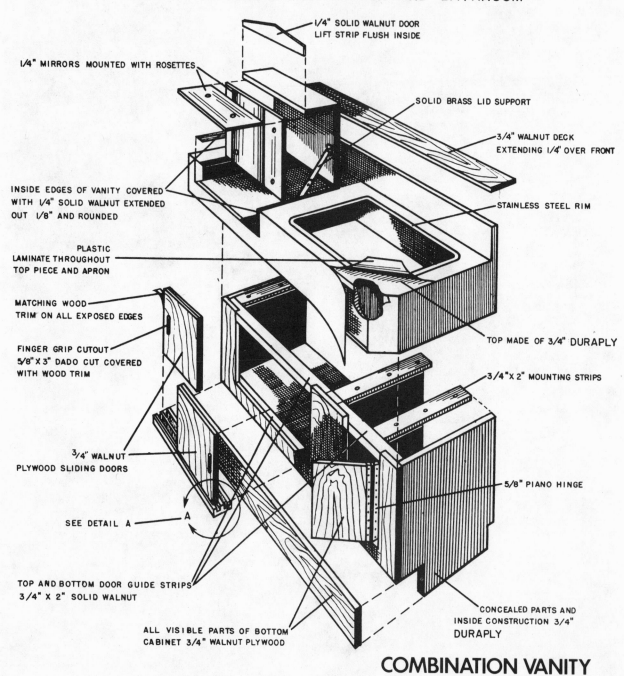

EXPLODED DETAIL OF VANITY FOR A TAILORED
COMBINATION POWDER AND BATHROOM

1/4" SOLID WALNUT DOOR
LIFT STRIP FLUSH INSIDE

1/4" MIRRORS MOUNTED WITH ROSETTES

SOLID BRASS LID SUPPORT

3/4" WALNUT DECK
EXTENDING 1/4" OVER FRONT

INSIDE EDGES OF VANITY COVERED
WITH 1/4" SOLID WALNUT EXTENDED
OUT 1/8" AND ROUNDED

STAINLESS STEEL RIM

PLASTIC
LAMINATE THROUGHOUT
TOP PIECE AND APRON

MATCHING WOOD
TRIM ON ALL EXPOSED EDGES

TOP MADE OF 3/4" DURAPLY

FINGER GRIP CUTOUT
5/8" X 3" DADO CUT COVERED
WITH WOOD TRIM

3/4" X 2" MOUNTING STRIPS

3/4" WALNUT
PLYWOOD SLIDING DOORS

5/8" PIANO HINGE

SEE DETAIL A              A

TOP AND BOTTOM DOOR GUIDE STRIPS
3/4" X 2" SOLID WALNUT

CONCEALED PARTS AND
INSIDE CONSTRUCTION 3/4"
DURAPLY

ALL VISIBLE PARTS OF BOTTOM
CABINET 3/4" WALNUT PLYWOOD

**COMBINATION VANITY**

Fig. 40.

vanity. (See Wood Finishing, page 271.) A small magazine rack, a disappearing ashtray, the built-in Conceal-All utility cabinet and the toilet paper holder (Figures 31 and 32) were some of the space-saving devices used. The small louver door towel-storage cabinet against the wall perhaps does more for appearance than storage, but it is still quite useful. Additional features include a heater-fan vent in the ceiling, a completely tiled shower with a waterproof fixture for lighting, and some smaller details, such as the saddle-step dark tile at the shower door's peripheral edge and the "tap-light" switches and towel bar and towel ring. There is also storage beneath the laminated vanity top, which also provides access to the plumbing through two small doors at the recessed front.

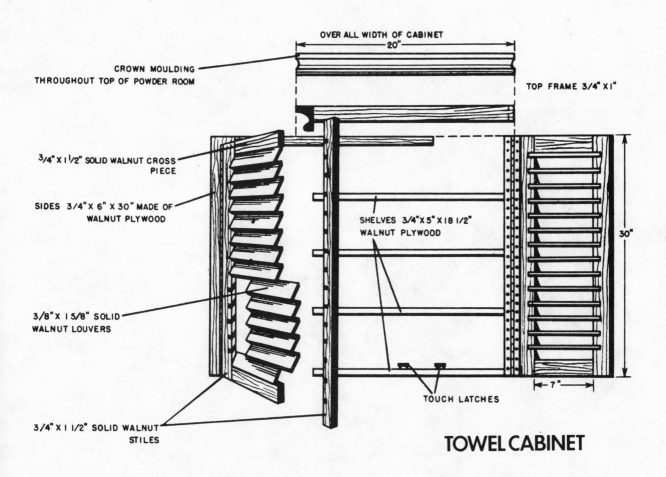

OVER ALL WIDTH OF CABINET
20"

CROWN MOULDING
THROUGHOUT TOP OF POWDER ROOM

TOP FRAME 3/4" X I"

3/4" X I 1/2" SOLID WALNUT CROSS PIECE

SIDES 3/4" X 6" X 30" MADE OF WALNUT PLYWOOD

SHELVES 3/4" X 5" X 18 1/2" WALNUT PLYWOOD

3/8" X I 5/8" SOLID WALNUT LOUVERS

30"

7"

TOUCH LATCHES

3/4" X I 1/2" SOLID WALNUT STILES

**TOWEL CABINET**

Fig. 41.

# 8

# n Living

...sign involves two basic and ...: first, gathering information ... equipment, including its rating ... performance projection; and ... lating a technical layout which ... nnecessary walking and moving ... kitchen by properly placing the

... ry is very important, and while ... signs cannot be recommended as ... olution, they are undoubtedly desir-... important to realize, however, that ... n these matters are subject to the com-... geared planning that governs nearly ... n decisions. With this in mind, a word ... e: the machine—sometimes not too at-... but always necessary—always comes ... en, and only then, comes the cover—... mouflage or decorative part. In order to select equipment, it is best to consider the importance of each item by its cost, not overlooking the repair service connected with the

appliance. Always keep yourself (the operator) in mind as the number one concern and treat the problem accordingly. If you use this procedure, it is impossible to go wrong. Proper organization of the work flow is more difficult, but the details, plans, and pictures shown herein provide solutions to guide you in successfully organizing your own kitchen.

## Remodeling a development house kitchen

Anyone who has ever bought a house has experienced some discontent with the kitchen. Either there was not enough storage, not enough space, or perhaps the kitchen was just not attractive. Of course, everyone has a different need and different solutions, but one condition is that the kitchen be in keeping with the surrounding area, unless it is to be completely isolated.

The remodeled kitchen in Figures 2, 3, and 4 was in a development house. The plan was to open the kitchen into a small dinette area which

Fig. 2. Serve-through counter of remodeled development house kitchen.

Fig. 1. (opposite page) The Living Kitchen in House of Ideas.

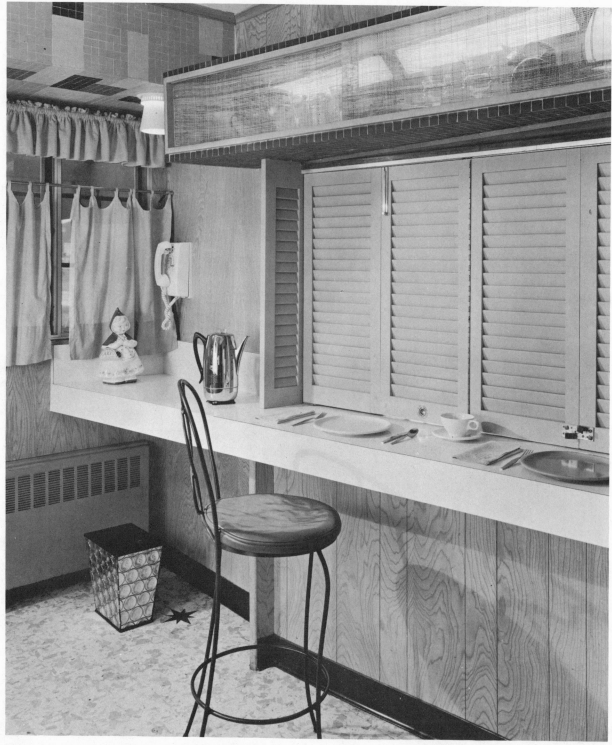

Fig. 3.   Counter area with louver doors closed for privacy.

Fig. 4. Built-in refrigerator surrounded by new plywood structure.

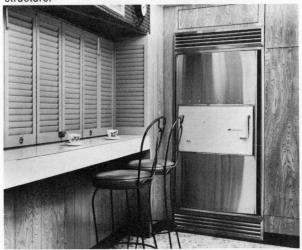

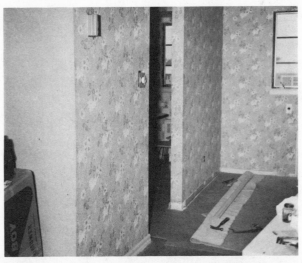

Fig. 5. The door leading from the dinette to the kitchen. (Before removing most of this wall to create the new serve-through.)

Fig. 6. The full extent of the new opening.

was hardly ever used, and thus incorporate the two areas. This structural change would provide more visual depth and create a viable setting for other changes that were envisioned.

The partition wall already had a passage door, ideally situated to become the guiding factor for the structural changes to follow. In order to properly maintain a consistent height throughout, the height of the existing door (6 feet 8½ inches) was used. Since this was not a bearing wall (a very important factor to note when remodeling), the opening from the floor to the ceiling was framed in with 2 x 4 fir supports. Of course, if this had been a bearing wall that supported the ceiling and upper floor, it would have been necessary to support a 4-x-8-inch crossbeam (or two 2-x-8-inch planks placed on edge) on lally columns placed at each end. Another good solution is to cut (shear) part of one side of the wall away on the top to accommodate a 12-inch steel flitch plate, again supported with lally columns on each end. These are structural musts that unfortunately are often neglected by contractors.

The general idea here was to build a service bar with a top unit parallel to it and louver window-doors in between. When the cutting was completed, it was possible to envision a more useful and dramatic solution. The service bar became a snack bar built on a slant. Storage within the snack bar was automatically ruled

Fig. 7. As in nearly all cases, a full-size plan and detail are drawn right on the spot to properly create the conversion.

Fig. 8. The kitchen cabinet (at the refrigerator) soffit is extended forward to create a base for the new and larger refrigerator built-in section. Before planning the wall-mounted cabinets, frames made of 1-x-2-inch fir are mounted snug against the ceiling to provide a base for a decorative soffit.

Fig. 9. After cutting open the floor beneath the built-in oven, the 12-x-12-inch sheet metal chute is installed, connected below, and terminated in the soiled clothing container in the deluxe laundry and storage. This cabinet door was hinged on the bottom and supported on the sides.

Fig. 10. After installation of the Highpoint built-in refrigerator, all available space is utilized with well-planned storage cabinets.

Fig. 11. Decorative facia adds much to the tailored appearance.

Fig. 12. The unit above the built-in oven was well insulated, and provided room for a lazy susan storage system.

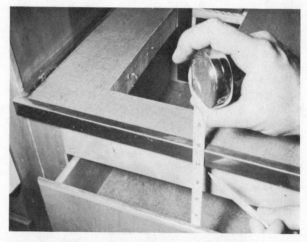

Fig. 13. To expand on the utility aspect of the kitchen, a Nutone mixer-blender food center was installed because it was to be in an area over a drawer. Such operations as narrowing the drawer were necessary.

Fig. 14. Installation of mixer-blender. Cut-out must be snug to keep water from penetrating into the storage area.

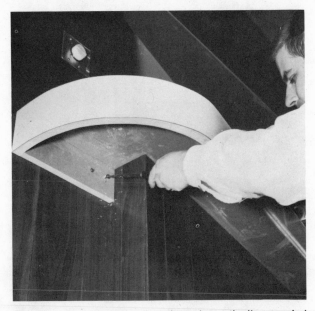

Fig. 15. The slanted serve-through vertically paneled counter front is topped by a ¾-inch Duraply top and apron, covered with white plastic laminate.

out because of the need for proper serving room and knee space on both sides (see Figure 3).

As usual, it was most practical to panel around a newly reconstructed area in order to achieve both a structural cover and a decorative finish at the same time. While still in the construction stage, this led to other not yet planned improvements in the area. To install a built-in refrigerator unit (Figure 4) was very simple and very timely, since material scraps—especially finishing material—came in handy at that time.

When both sides of that wall were finished, building was continued around toward the remaining entrance to the kitchen. It was decided that the bottom section of the former kitchen cabinets should be completely rebuilt; the top portion needed only repair work.

This kitchen illustrates that more and better storage can be achieved without the penalty of poor design. The slideout trays beneath the upper kitchen cabinet units did their share, as did the row of drawers built into the new lower section. The latter is perhaps not too dramatic, but it is certainly worthy of thought when planning a better kitchen.

The counter top was done in a molded plastic laminate called Unitop. Without any sharp corners or edges, this material was the best solution for easier working and cleaning, in that it combined the top edge of the splashboard rounded with the main top and 2-inch front edge, also rounded.

Like many other mass-produced kitchens, this one had a wall-mounted fan over the cooking top area, which of course is not sufficient for exhausting cooking fumes. Today there are more effective means of eliminating odors, even in kitchens where it is impossible to route the exhaust pressure toward the exterior by means of ducts. A ductless hood provides an effective exhaust system without any major installation. In essence, it has a built-in charcoal filter which picks up the cooking odors, filters them out, and returns clean air.

When the soffit was covered with mosaic tiles, it became a permanently clean and decorated area which cut down on the usual repairs and repainting, while adding a very desirable decorative dimension.

Fig. 16. In the remodeled development house, a serving tray storage made the Nutone installation simple. Note slide-out cutting board.

Fig. 17. With the completion of the parallel and level serve-through top and the top cabinet soffit, the louver doors are installed. This versatile serve-through went beyond its expected function in that it enhanced the entire dining area.

Figs. 18, 19. A complete and decorative kitchen in an area of less than 100 square feet, with room for small-family dining.

Fig. 20. Latest American Standard enamel sink with spray faucet, suitable for this kitchen.

## A condensed kitchen

The U-shaped and O-shaped plans for kitchens have proven to be the most successful and functionally advantageous. Each cuts down the unnecessary extra effort that most standard, rectangular, mass-produced kitchens create; a U-shaped counter and cabinet arrangement eliminates the usual elongated plan, consequently condensing the working areas.

Because most kitchen areas have functional limitations, due to existing doors and windows, it is often possible and even advisable to move a window and/or a door, as was done in this case. This key maneuver paved the way for a very successful plan which created an adequately equipped kitchen with a slight recess (Figures 18 and 19) in an area only 10 feet wide and 6 feet deep. Furthermore, there was room for an attractive table and chair set in the newly created eating area.

Not all kitchens are conducive to dining within the area, even if the space is available. Badly designed or dreary surroundings would make dining unpleasant. Proper decor was certainly instrumental to the success of this particular kitchen, which projects the feeling of a country ice cream parlor. The vivid, textured materials that were used are responsible for this feeling. The cabinetry was built of Sen plywood (oriental ash). White-painted brick walls complement the cabinets and the soft pink plastic laminate counter top.

Because a small family used this kitchen, extensive storage space was unnecessary. It was therefore possible to sacrifice some cabinet areas and to design attractive display shelves for the upper cabinet wall (Figure 18). The sliding doors of the center display shelf were made of ¼-inch Acrilan-plastic with a laminated sackcloth within for sliding doors (Figure 19) similar to those of the remodeled development kitchen. The installation of built-in overhead lighting within the unit made it possible to silhouette choice stem glass and fine china pieces, a new and different idea in kitchen design. Even if space is at a premium, using a small portion of the storage units for decor will perhaps make the hours spent in the kitchen

for both cooking and dining much more pleasant.

The sliding auxiliary trays beneath the top units (see page 112, the remodeled kitchen, where the same system was applied) not only provide additional working area, but they also prove to be very decorative even when in use. The functional items include a wall oven (left, Figure 18), a top burner, sink, dishwasher (right), adequate silverware drawers and, most important, very good lighting.

The floor is a solid vinyl slab with beige-brown and slightly pink terrazzo-like textures. It also has a 1-inch-wide dark brown feature strip 1 foot from the cabinets and walls that completely encircles the room. The curtains are Dutch-mounted cafés of white cotton with pink and soft yellow dots.

The kitchen is a small one, less than 100 square feet—but considering that it holds table accommodations for four, it is perfect for the amount of space appropriated.

## The compact "do-all" kitchen

How big must a kitchen be to be efficient; what constitutes the essentials of a good kitchen if there is only limited space? These are pertinent questions which must be answered by any homeowner who intends to either build or rebuild a kitchen.

The small and compact kichen in Figure 21 was actually a second kitchen in a finished basement-playroom. The family did a lot of entertaining and needed an efficient setup close to the entertainment area, which was on a lower level and too far from the existing main kitchen. Nevertheless, after using this new kitchen a few times, the owners felt that it was most efficient, sometimes even preferable to their main kitchen, which actually was better equipped.

Good equipment alone does not make a good kitchen. Properly located appliances and efficient counter work space, as well as properly planned storage, are of vital importance. Although too compact for the well-organized storage that is the ideal, this condensed design would answer the space problem in apartments and small homes. It has all the most important work facilities, and in a more spacious area

Fig. 21.   The compact do-all kitchen.

Fig. 22. Multiple functions give this kitchen versatility in spite of its small area.

with some more counter and storage space it would be more than adequate.

Although less than 6 feet wide, this kitchen has a full-size combination top burner and oven. The top burner unit slides out of the way when not in use. The kitchen is also equipped with a small 18-x-16-inch stainless steel sink with a single lever mixer faucet and a large dishwasher beneath. There is over 12 cubic feet of storage, including silverware drawers behind the doors under the combination cooking unit. (See Figure 22.)

Because there is ventilation built into the oven, an additional wall-mounted exhaust leading through a round duct to the outside is sufficient to take care of odors in the area. A concealed closet beyond the kitchen area provides well-organized food storage.

The area itself is finished in walnut plywood and prefinished walnut paneling. A sand-color laminated top and mosaic ceramic tile covering

the soffit complement the ivory terrazzo vinyl on the floor (by Amtico), making the kitchen unbelievably pleasant and efficient.

## A living kitchen

It is always daring to depart from conventional designs and habits when building or remodeling a house. Most people unfortunately like to see something used by others before they consider taking the risk.

Analysis of the equipment and the space layouts used in many kitchens today proved that several fundamental aspects were entirely inadequate and psychologically wrong. Most women like to spend as little time as possible in the kitchen, especially when family and guests are enjoying themselves in other rooms. The Living Kitchen in the House of Ideas was designed within the family living area to solve this very problem (Figures 23 through 25; see also Figures 29, 55 and 67). Daily chores are taken care of while the entire family sits around the counter talking or watching the portable TV.

Creating such a system without the pitfalls inherent in full exposure of the kitchen meant that everything had to be perfect. Appliances had to be of the finest quality, designed to help keep the kitchen clean, odorless, and extremely functional. In fact, the entire work flow had to be so designed. A full-size plan was therefore made right in place on the floor before any building was done (Figure 54). In this way we could be sure that all necessary kitchen functions could be served no more than a few steps from one another.

The cabinets, all of which are either freestanding or free-hanging, are 8 feet high. This is considerably higher than most ordinary kitchen cabinets due to the elimination of the soffit. Although soffits tend to lower the upper shelves in an ordinary kitchen, making them more accessible, the top shelves are scarcely ever used, and consequently become dust collectors. In spite of the additional height in the Living Kitchen, anyone can reach and use the uppermost shelf by simply bringing the entire inner cabinet unit down (Figure 51). This is accomplished by special Ease Down hardware (Figure 48).

Fig. 23. This view from the inside of the kitchen area exposes the formal dining area. Note the Conceal-All soiled paper and small trash disposal unit with removable plastic bag inside the door. Also note electric barbecue to right. Lighting will separate all exposed areas if desired.

The appliances used were selected on their merits and for proper fit in this type of kitchen living. For example, the Viscount double oven, aside from being efficient and reliable, has an important and necessary built-in device in that it vents with the oven door closed, thereby eliminating cooking odors in the area.

The double sink is a most versatile selection for it has every possible device built in for efficiency and sanitation, including a filter for

(on opposite page)

Fig. 24. This view from the inside of the kitchen area exposes the formal dining area. Note the Conceal-All soiled paper and small trash disposal unit with removable plastic bag inside the door. Also note electric barbecue to right. Lighting will separate all exposed areas if desired.

(on opposite page)

Fig. 25. The 6-x-10-foot working space is an area that can be covered in less than six steps. Within that space one can activate every conceivable appliance, and reach all supply areas.

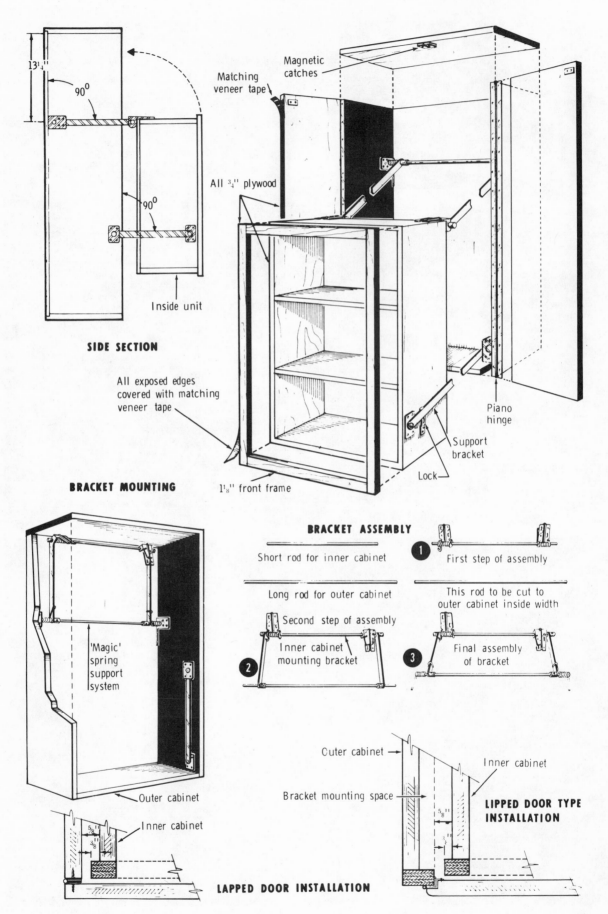

$13\frac{1}{4}''$

$90^0$

$90^0$

Inside unit

**SIDE SECTION**

All exposed edges
covered with matching
veneer tape

**BRACKET MOUNTING**

Matching
veneer tape

All $\frac{3}{4}''$ plywood

Magnetic
catches

Piano
hinge

Support
bracket

Lock

$1\frac{1}{8}''$ front frame

**BRACKET ASSEMBLY**

Short rod for inner cabinet

① First step of assembly

Long rod for outer cabinet

This rod to be cut to
outer cabinet inside width

② Second step of assembly

Inner cabinet
mounting bracket

③ Final assembly
of bracket

'Magic'
spring
support
system

Outer cabinet

Inner cabinet

$\frac{5}{8}''$

$\frac{5}{8}''$

**LAPPED DOOR INSTALLATION**

Outer cabinet

Inner cabinet

Bracket mounting space

$\frac{5}{8}''$

**LIPPED DOOR TYPE
INSTALLATION**

Fig. 26.

Fig. 27. Triple bowl sink, "Fiesta," fitted with Aquarian faucet with spray. For additional convenience, a hardwood board covering one portion will serve as additional work space.

Fig. 28. The Aquamix kitchen single-lever control spout.

the water and a unit which supplies, at once, 195° boiling water for instant coffee, tea, and quicker cooking (Konstant Hot). The stainless steel sink (by American Standard), with attached food waste disposal, single-lever faucet, and spray, is in itself an efficient work area offering counter space and storage beneath. Illumination comes from a nearly invisible source: ⅞-inch-thick miniature fluorescent slimlines which are covered by the additional 1½-inch overlapping of the top cabinet doors. The Kitchen-Aid dishwasher beneath is another work-saving device, as is the Revco built-in refrigerator-freezer combination with built-in icemaker.

The adjacent cabinet-wall section has only small areas to offer because of the slanted free-hanging work counter. This is where the built-in fold-out toaster (for 4 slices) and built-in electric can-opener (matching finish) are installed, side by side. Both eliminate the clutter and necessary clean-up of free-standing appliances. Above and behind 2 small doors is a lazy susan spice rack, efficient enough to hold eight dozen large glass containers. Beneath is a Kitchen Kaddy, also by Swanson, containing 3 roll holders and cutting edges for them in the stainless steel hinged front door. This is used for wrapping, cooking paper, and foil rolls.

The kitchen turns the corner to an interesting wedgelike, slanted, floating counter only 8 inches high, but high enough to hold 4 silverware drawers and a 2-foot-wide solid maple bread or meat cutting board. The board is in a recessed 2½-inch-high borderlike bottom strip and is mounted on Grant heavy-duty full extension slides so it can be pulled out all the way. Even in midair, the board can sustain hard and heavy use, due to the strong slides. Narrowing one of the 4 drawers provided enough space to mount a Nutone built-in food center which is flush, neat, and nearly invisible when not in use. For any type of work, an available attachment fits into the opening of the flush plate which is ready for use by turning a variable speed dial switch.

The top of this suspended counter is covered with Mosaic quarry tile, which will take extreme abuse and heat and be decorative too.

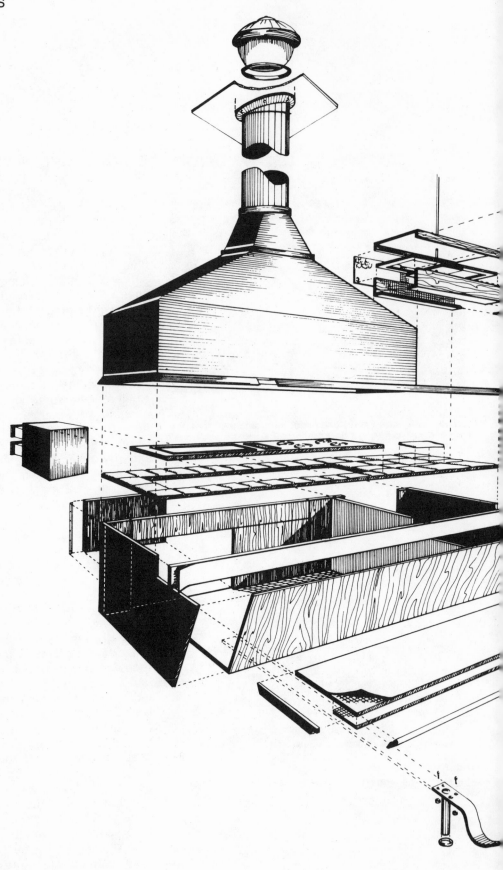

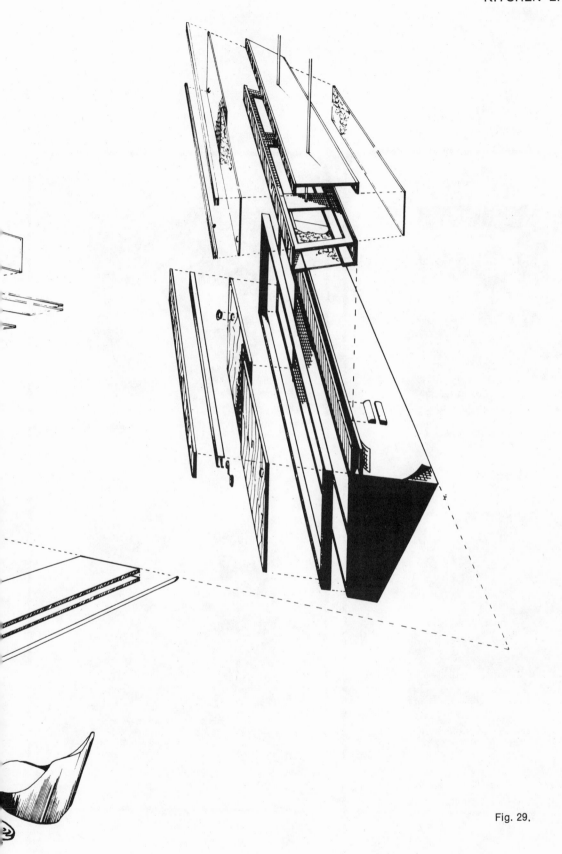

Fig. 29.

Fig. 30. Hollow pipe stainless steel leg with attached ¼-x-8-x-8-inch steel support plate is mounted to bottom of oven cabinet.

Fig. 32. Front counters already built and assembled are sanded on exposed surfaces.

Fig. 31. Floor plug fitting inside of pipe is screwed to floor to lock pipe in place and keep it from slipping.

Fig. 33. Because of narrow wood support, top plates of ⅜-x-3-x-8-inch steel act as additional leg support on the inside of the cabinet bottom.

Fig. 34. Carefully leveled slanted drawer cabinet is mounted to front and back units and against wall.

Fig. 36. After the counter surface is covered with plastic laminate, the upper level is covered with mosaic quarry tile.

Fig. 35. Sliding drawer hardware is installed in drawer compartments.

Fig. 37. To install suspended cabinet, ½-inch stainless steel rods are mounted and checked to make sure they are plumb. Use solid wood block beneath the cedar paneling, well anchored to sustain the weight.

Fig. 38. After installation of upper suspended cabinet, make sure all vertical parts are plumb.

Fig. 39. View of lower part and general structure of suspended cabinet. Note lower support of suspending rod.

Fig. 40. After installation of all lamps, specially textured Belgium glass is laid into grooves.

Fig. 41. Stainless steel shield is mounted and implanted into shingled roof with caulking and mastic. Exhaust motor is connected to exposed pipe above roof.

Fig. 42. Back mounting strips are notched into vertical partitions of upper back cabinet using glue and screws.

Fig. 44. This is the lazy susan disc mounted to the counter stool. Note ¾-x-3-inch stainless steel support welded to disc.

Fig. 43. Upper back unit is put in place.

Fig. 45. Note narrowed drawer opening to make room for the Nutone mixer-blender food center motor.

Fig. 46. Ease-Down hardware completes the pull-down cabinets.

Fig. 48. Hardware is assembled first, then placed in each unit.

Fig. 47. To install the pull-down cabinets, use properly cut spacers to clear the hardware from the main cabinet unit.

Fig. 49. Final bottom brackets of Ease-Down hardware are screwed in place.

Fig. 50. Inside cabinet must clear all sides as well as a full bottom shelf.

Fig. 51. From an 8-foot height, the shelves come down to normal reach.

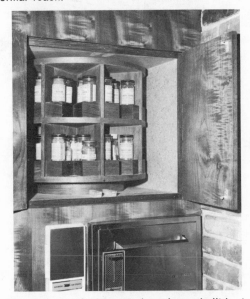

Fig. 52. Not one inch wasted: a large built-in toaster with adjacent electric can opener (all Swanson), with a lazy susan spice rack on top holding 100 bottles of spices, all easy to maintain since they are covered by doors.

Fig. 53. The telephone adjacent to the intercom system provides for better security at hand.

Fig. 54. Because the cast-iron base heating convectors are installed mostly on exterior walls (in this case the garage walk), it was necessary to cantilever all cabinets. This necessitated insulating the bottom of the cabinets and mounting each unit 1 inch above the convector. The bottoms of the cabinets are propped up here to the proper height in order to fit them.

Note the white layout paper on the floor on which the entire kitchen layout was planned and detailed. This was particularly important for this kitchen due to its diverse shape and angles.

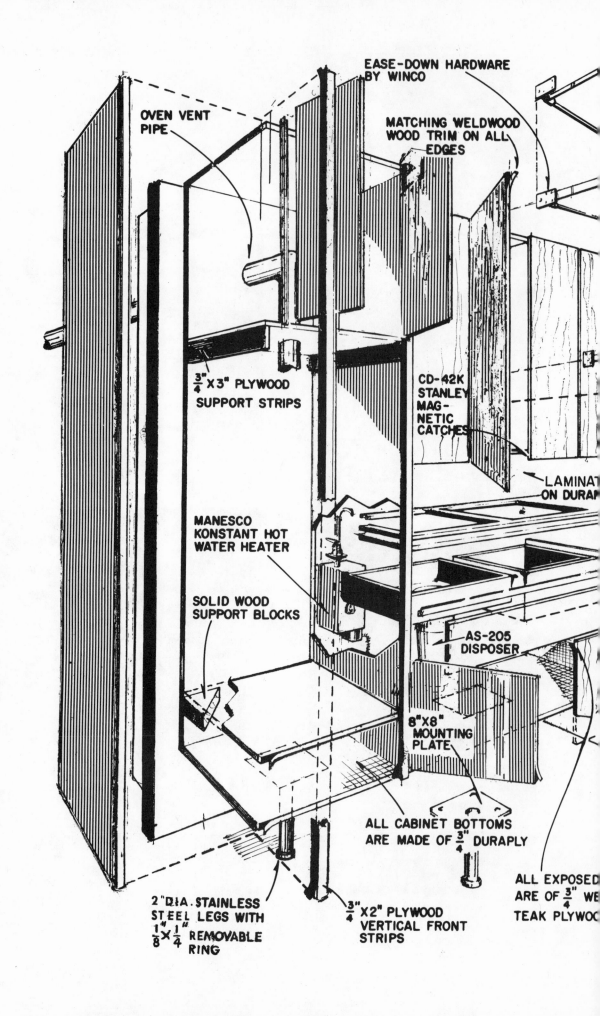

EASE-DOWN HARDWARE BY WINCO

MATCHING WELDWOOD WOOD TRIM ON ALL EDGES

OVEN VENT PIPE

3/4" X 3" PLYWOOD SUPPORT STRIPS

CD-42K STANLEY MAGNETIC CATCHES

LAMINAT ON DURAP

MANESCO KONSTANT HOT WATER HEATER

AS-205 DISPOSER

SOLID WOOD SUPPORT BLOCKS

8"X8" MOUNTING PLATE

ALL CABINET BOTTOMS ARE MADE OF 3/4" DURAPLY

2" DIA. STAINLESS STEEL LEGS WITH 1/8" X 1/4" REMOVABLE RING

3/4" X 2" PLYWOOD VERTICAL FRONT STRIPS

ALL EXPOSED ARE OF 3/4" WE TEAK PLYWOO

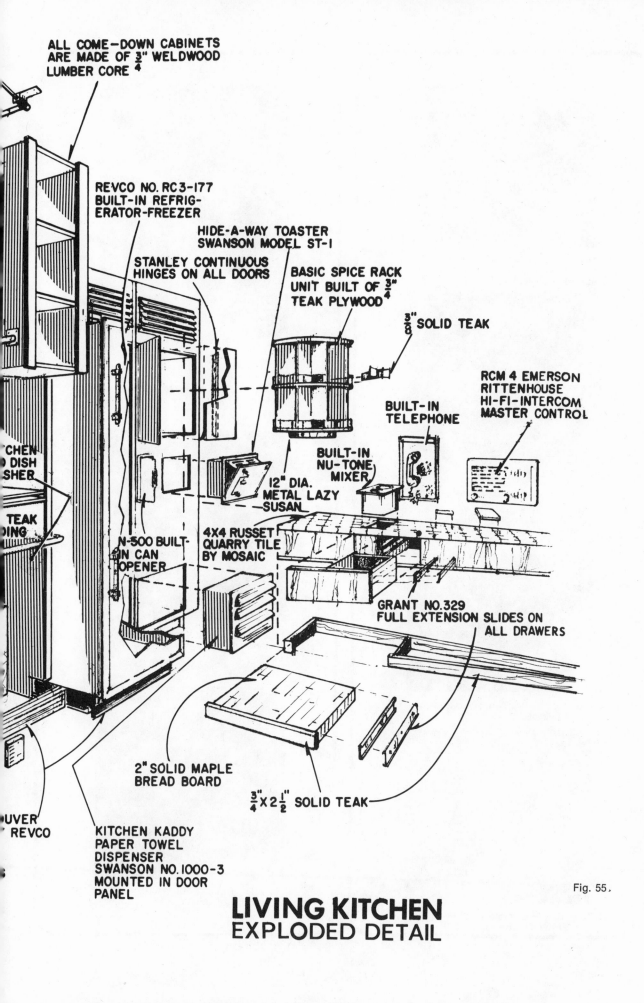

ALL COME-DOWN CABINETS
ARE MADE OF $\frac{3}{4}$" WELDWOOD
LUMBER CORE

REVCO NO. RC3-177
BUILT-IN REFRIG-
ERATOR-FREEZER

HIDE-A-WAY TOASTER
SWANSON MODEL ST-1

STANLEY CONTINUOUS
HINGES ON ALL DOORS

BASIC SPICE RACK
UNIT BUILT OF $\frac{3}{4}$"
TEAK PLYWOOD

$\frac{13}{16}$" SOLID TEAK

RCM 4 EMERSON
RITTENHOUSE
HI-FI-INTERCOM
MASTER CONTROL

BUILT-IN
TELEPHONE

CHEN
DISH
SHER

TEAK
DING

BUILT-IN
NU-TONE
MIXER

12" DIA.
METAL LAZY
SUSAN

N-500 BUILT-
IN CAN
OPENER

4X4 RUSSET
QUARRY TILE
BY MOSAIC

GRANT NO. 329
FULL EXTENSION SLIDES ON
ALL DRAWERS

UVER
REVCO

2" SOLID MAPLE
BREAD BOARD

$\frac{3}{4}$" X 2$\frac{1}{2}$" SOLID TEAK

KITCHEN KADDY
PAPER TOWEL
DISPENSER
SWANSON NO. 1000-3
MOUNTED IN DOOR
PANEL

Fig. 55.

# LIVING KITCHEN
## EXPLODED DETAIL

Fig. 56. Konstant-Hot (instant 195° water heating) by Manesco is installed to cold water pipe.

Fig. 57. This switch, which activates the heavy-duty exhaust fan, is installed at the facia in back of the surface cooking unit.

Fig. 58. Installation of knee switch for magic sliding door.

Fig. 59. Final plate provides spring action switch control.

Fig. 60. This is the sliding magic mechanism. It is covered with a special cornice to avoid soiling and accidental damage.

Fig. 61. With full hands, there is just no other way to open a sliding door.

Fig. 62. Conceal-All waste trap on back door of counter.

Fig. 63. Spout of Konstant-Hot unit can be mounted directly into stainless steel sink's back rim.

The kitchen continues with the cantilevered front counter, one-third of which is used for the combination top burner and broiler unit (by Thermador). The rest of the counter provides work area and room to serve the counter in the front. Built in 2 sections, one is slightly angled into the used-brick wall in order to gain more space for the swivel seats, which are mounted on custom fabricated brackets of ¾-x-3-inch stainless steel for each egress. On the kitchen side, the counter is provided exactly from end to end with good storage. Immediately beneath the work area and adjacent to the top burner is a stainless steel, 2-drawer food warmer (by Toastmaster). This unit, similar to those used on airplanes, keeps food warm and moist and is efficient enough for a large family.

One of the storage doors beneath the top burner has a built-in small waste collector. Made by Conceal-All, this stainless steel lid-frame is cut into the left door and has a plastic bag

Fig. 64. With the protective lid lifted, an electric grill of high power can barbecue a steak in minutes.

buttoned on the inside for little scraps, napkins, etc., and it can be removed easily for cleaning. This unit is extremely important in this open kitchen as all areas are exposed and must be kept neat.

The custom-designed exhaust hood was built by Heifetz Metal Crafts of New Jersey. It had to be very efficient, especially in this case, in order to keep cooking odors out of the living area. A heavy-duty exhaust fan—model GR-235, 1550 rpm, direct drive roof exhauster (by

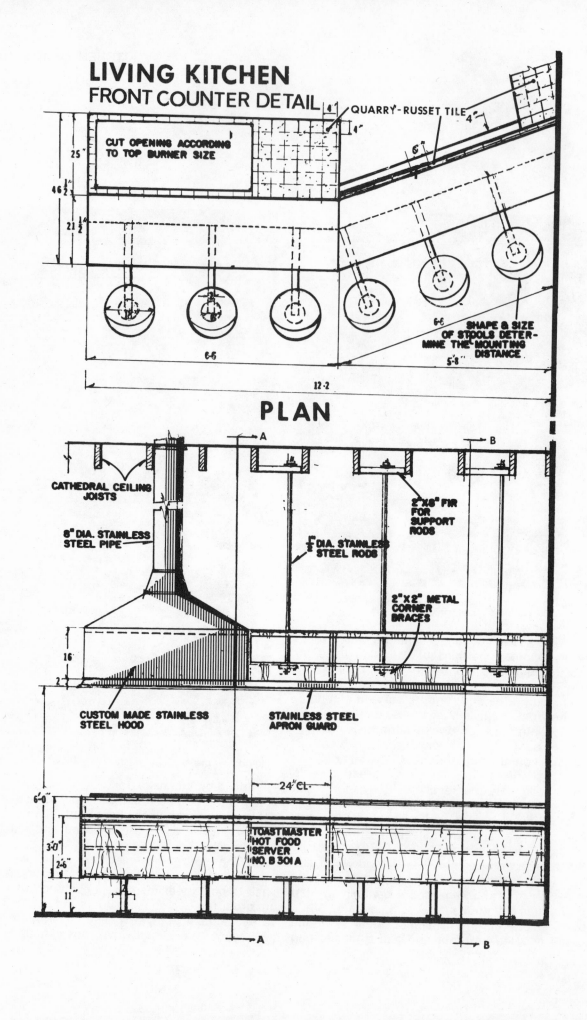

# LIVING KITCHEN
## FRONT COUNTER DETAIL

QUARRY-RUSSET TILE

CUT OPENING ACCORDING
TO TOP BURNER SIZE

25"

46 ½"

21 ¼"

6-6

6"

4"

6-6

5'-8"

SHAPE & SIZE
OF STOOLS DETER-
MINE THE MOUNTING
DISTANCE

12-2

## PLAN

A

B

CATHEDRAL CEILING
JOISTS

8" DIA. STAINLESS
STEEL PIPE

DIA. STAINLESS
STEEL RODS

2"X8" FIR
FOR
SUPPORT
RODS

2"X2" METAL
CORNER
BRACES

16"

2"

CUSTOM MADE STAINLESS
STEEL HOOD

STAINLESS STEEL
APRON GUARD

24" C.L.

6'-0"

3'-0"

2'-6"

11"

TOASTMASTER
HOT FOOD
SERVER
NO. B 301 A

A

B

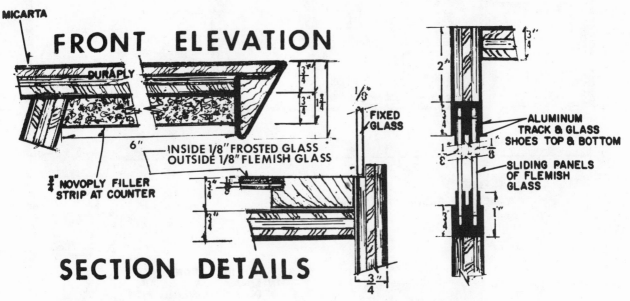

**MICARTA**

# FRONT ELEVATION

DURAPLY

$\frac{3}{4}''$

$\frac{3}{4}''$

$\frac{3}{4}''$

$\frac{1}{8}''$

FIXED GLASS

6"

INSIDE 1/8" FROSTED GLASS
OUTSIDE 1/8" FLEMISH GLASS

$\frac{3}{4}''$ NOVOPLY FILLER STRIP AT COUNTER

$\frac{3}{4}''$

$\frac{3}{4}''$

# SECTION DETAILS

$\frac{3}{4}''$

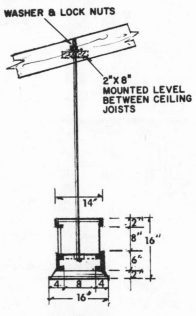

$\frac{3}{4}''$

2"

$\frac{1}{8}''$

$\frac{1}{8}''$

$\frac{3}{4}''$

1"

ALUMINUM TRACK & GLASS SHOES TOP & BOTTOM

SLIDING PANELS OF FLEMISH GLASS

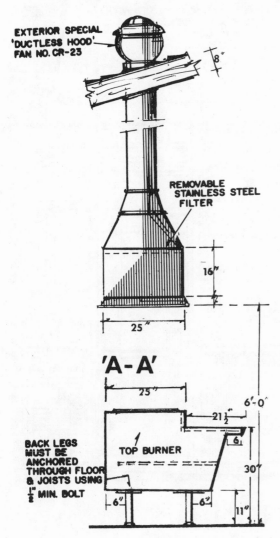

EXTERIOR SPECIAL 'DUCTLESS HOOD' FAN NO. CR-25

8"

REMOVABLE STAINLESS STEEL FILTER

16"

25"

## 'A-A'

25"

6'-0"

$21\frac{1}{2}''$

6"

BACK LEGS MUST BE ANCHORED THROUGH FLOOR & JOISTS USING $\frac{1}{2}''$ MIN. BOLT

TOP BURNER

30"

6"

6"

11"

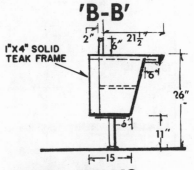

WASHER & LOCK NUTS

2"X 8" MOUNTED LEVEL BETWEEN CEILING JOISTS

14"

$\frac{1}{2}''$

8"  16"

6"

4  8  4

16"

## 'B-B'

2"

6"

$21\frac{1}{2}''$

1"X4" SOLID TEAK FRAME

6"

26"

6"

11"

15"

# SIDE VIEWS & SECTIONS

Fig. 65.

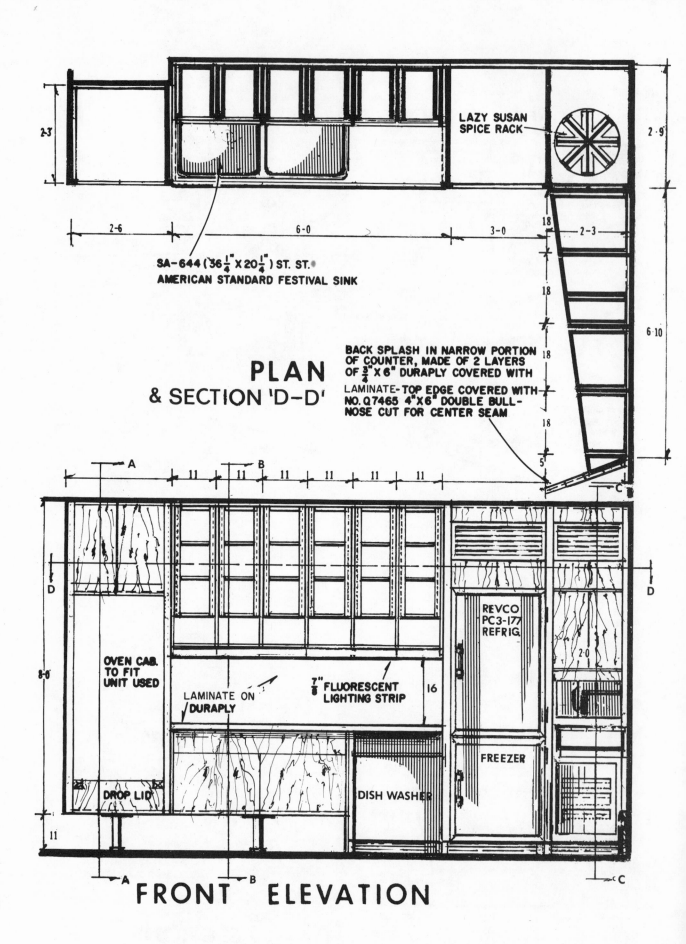

2-3

LAZY SUSAN
SPICE RACK

2·9

2-6

6-0

3-0

18

2-3

18

6·10

18

SA-644 (36¼" X 20¼" ) ST. ST.
AMERICAN STANDARD FESTIVAL SINK

18

**PLAN**
**& SECTION 'D-D'**

BACK SPLASH IN NARROW PORTION
OF COUNTER, MADE OF 2 LAYERS
OF ¾" X 6" DURAPLY COVERED WITH

LAMINATE-TOP EDGE COVERED WITH
NO. Q7465 4"X6" DOUBLE BULL-
NOSE CUT FOR CENTER SEAM

5

A

11

B

11

11

11

11

C

D

D

OVEN CAB.
TO FIT
UNIT USED

REVCO
PC3-177
REFRIG.

2·0

8-0

LAMINATE ON
DURAPLY

⅞" FLUORESCENT
LIGHTING STRIP

16

FREEZER

DROP LID

DISH WASHER

11

A

B

C

**FRONT ELEVATION**

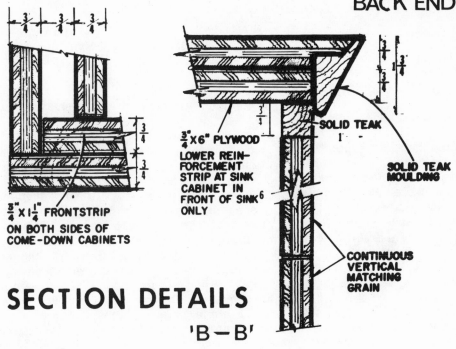

$\frac{3}{4}$ X $1\frac{1}{4}$" FRONTSTRIP
ON BOTH SIDES OF
COME-DOWN CABINETS

$\frac{3}{4}$" X 6" PLYWOOD
LOWER REIN-
FORCEMENT
STRIP AT SINK
CABINET IN
FRONT OF SINK
ONLY

SOLID TEAK
1"

SOLID TEAK
MOULDING

CONTINUOUS
VERTICAL
MATCHING
GRAIN

# SECTION DETAILS
## 'B—B'

Fig. 66

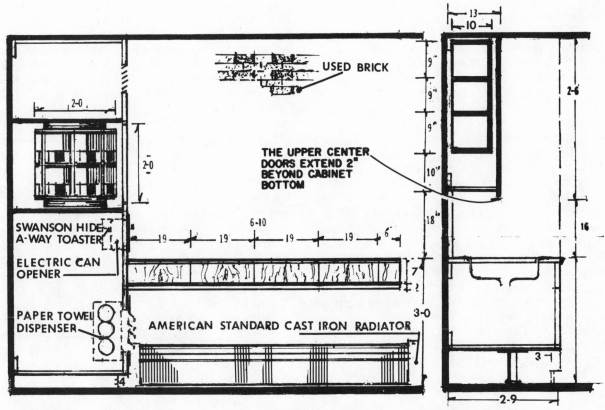

USED BRICK

THE UPPER CENTER
DOORS EXTEND 2"
BEYOND CABINET
BOTTOM

SWANSON HIDE-
A-WAY TOASTER

ELECTRIC CAN
OPENER

PAPER TOWEL
DISPENSER

AMERICAN STANDARD CAST IRON RADIATOR

# SIDE VIEW & SECTION 'C-C' & 'B-B'

Swanson)—was mounted to the roof, to eliminate any excessive noise coming from this powerful unit.

Cabinets constructed in 2 parts (upper and lower) are suspended from the cathedral ceiling (see Figure 37) with three ½-inch stainless steel rods. The cabinets are anchored to the brick wall by the insertion of leg-bolts into lead shields and connected to the exhaust hood with screws from within. The structure is self-bracing because of the angle at which the cabinets are constructed. The height of this unit as well as the exhaust hood can of course be adjusted easily.

The interesting appearance of the suspended cabinet is largely due to the imported Belgian glass which covers most of the area, the direct and indirect lighting creating interesting silhouettes, and the unusual type of construction itself. All this is enhanced by the fluorescent fixture which creates a direct down light, very dramatic during meal time. The entire area is illuminated with a rather soft glow projected by deluxe WW bulbs.

This kitchen plan effectively encourages and provides for an organized work flow. There is sufficient work area near each of the three major action centers, and the storage system is easily accessible. At the same time, the phone, the built-in AM-FM audio intercom and a portable TV with custom-installed video intercom are all within easy reach.

The surface coverings used provide a safe area for hot pots and casseroles as well as for easy maintenance. Laminate covers the top surface and back splash of the sink section and the eating counter; Mosaic quarry tiles top the cooking area and the suspended counter. Both contribute to the warm and modern country life atmosphere of the room, especially in combination with the beautiful Weldwood teak plywood of matching grain (architectural line).

The teak cabinetry is finished to achieve a semi-gloss finish similar to that of Danish furniture. It also must be durable and easy to maintain. (For further suggestions about finishing, see Chapter 14.)

By suspending all the cabinets (except the refrigerator-freezer and the dishwasher), the cast iron heating convectors installed in these areas could function properly. The stainless steel supports of all suspended cabinets also create a transparent look, making it appear as if everything were floating in midair. By using stainless steel legs and supports, the suspension is not at all visually interrupted. The expansive stretch of Barcelona flooring (by Amtico) also contributes to the continuity of the design.

The hardware too was carefully planned to contribute to overall function and appearance. Touch latches and magnetic catches were used to eliminate surface hardware which would tend to clutter clean surfaces. Continuous hinges allowed for constant and reliable door function, avoiding warpage. With Grant 329 full extension slides, the drawers could be pulled all the way out quickly and easily without damage or mishap. Additional advantages were gained by using Noiseless Stanley 2800 sliding door hardware. The stainless steel clock (by Edwards) built right into the used-brick wall made this a truly all-inclusive kitchen.

And finally—as an added luxury in an electric indoor barbecue—a Baker's Pride oven is installed at the edge of the kitchen in the used-brick section of the fireplace structure.

The perfect kitchen, however, is not complete without a attractive color scheme and pleasant surrounding decoration. The room must be appealing, but at the same time easy to maintain. Stainless steel was used extensively in this kitchen for both decorative and maintenance reasons.

When a kitchen is in the midst of a living area, it is preferable to have heavy storage and pot and pan washing, etc., behind closed doors. This was done by building a specially equipped annex laundry-pantry (see Chapter 9) where another sink with waste disposal is installed and there is room for another dishwasher. The door between the two rooms is activated by a knee switch to avoid dropping things when in a rush. When the door slides aside, the lights are turned on electronically by a low-voltage limit-switch. The door can be closed again by a similar knee switch inside the pantry.

Fig. 67.

# Chapter 9
# Laundry and Storage Ideas

Depending on the degree of importance attached to a laundry room, it may range from a dismal basement corner to an attractive, functional combination room.

Since laundries are seldom glamorized by improvement-minded homeowners, efficiency and convenience are the keynotes. Although many builders provide washers and dryers, they leave the design and building of more elaborate and useful laundry areas to the homeowner himself. Using the laundry room as a combination room is often the best solution. Try building a pantry and general storage area or a general household repair and ironing area into the laundry room.

## Deluxe laundry and pantry

In the House of Ideas, the laundry room combined with a pantry and china storage area (Figures 1 and 2) was designed as an extension of the Living Kitchen (page 106). It was separated from the kitchen by a convenient knee-activated sliding door (see Figure 61 on page 132). Because of its proximity to the kitchen this room could hold all of the usual kitchen eyesores such as additional sink space with garbage disposal and the many other items which would tend to clutter up the kitchen.

Literally filled with cabinetry, this relatively small room (6½ x 13 feet) has nearly 150 cubic feet of cabinet storage, and it accommodates a washer, dryer (Speed Queen Atlantic), built-in freezer (by Revco), and a portable metal unit which fits exactly beneath the built-in freezer. This unit provides for an ironing board to slide out and be firmly supported when in use. Behind doors, metal shelves provide for the storage of irons, etc. When rolled into its niche, the unit blends inconspicuously into the cabinetry (Ironing Kaddy by Manesco).

The sink, used for dirty pots, pans, and dishes during a party, is built into a suspended counter which contains a slide-out compartment for soiled clothing (Figure 5). There are also fold-down shelves (Figure 6) for extra dishes and glassware. An additional fold-out container can store large quantities of dog food.

The strong accent on storage worked out nicely because it was rather simple to build these versatile and multipurpose units by apply-

Fig. 2.

ing all structural sections in modulars, screwing them directly onto the already paneled walls.

Tilt-out containers, as shown in Figure 7, add to the storage areas, making them so complete and well organized they seem almost a store within the house. Supplies of canned food and dry staples are provided for on well-divided shelving covered with sliding doors. The storage on the far end of the room holds housecleaning supplies, as well as brooms, mops, and vacuum cleaner attachments. In spite of all this varied storage and equipment, the room is neat, colorful, and well illuminated. Space for an additional dishwasher may be achieved by making merely minor adjustments.

The floor is covered with ⅛-inch Renaissance 12-x-12-inch vinyl (by Amtico). The cabinetry is made of ¾-inch Sen, an oriental

Fig. 1. (opposite page) Deluxe laundry and pantry.

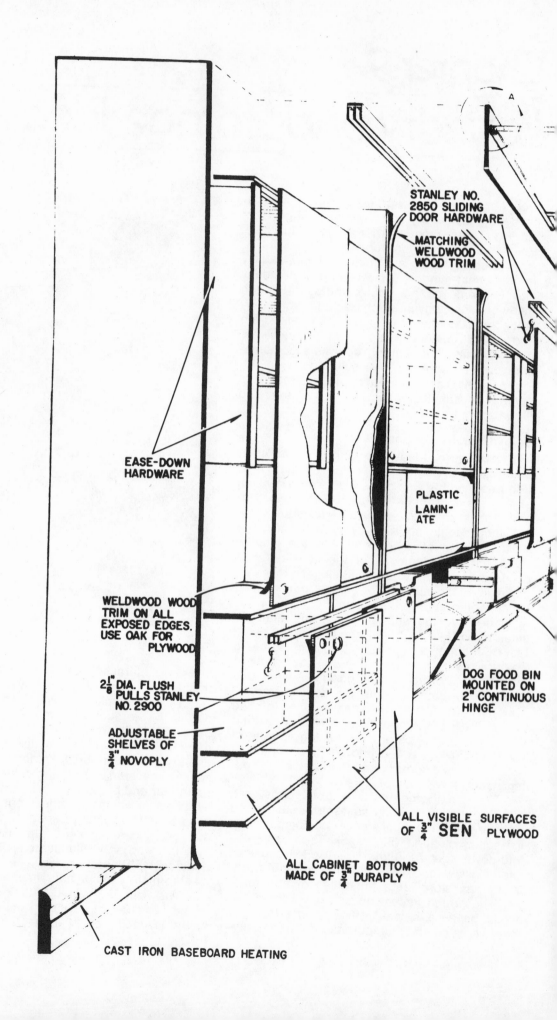

STANLEY NO.
2850 SLIDING
DOOR HARDWARE

MATCHING
WELDWOOD
WOOD TRIM

EASE-DOWN
HARDWARE

PLASTIC
LAMIN-
ATE

WELDWOOD WOOD
TRIM ON ALL
EXPOSED EDGES.
USE OAK FOR
PLYWOOD

DOG FOOD BIN
MOUNTED ON
2" CONTINUOUS
HINGE

$2\frac{1}{8}$" DIA. FLUSH
PULLS STANLEY
NO. 2900

ADJUSTABLE
SHELVES OF
$\frac{3}{4}$" NOVOPLY

ALL VISIBLE SURFACES
OF $\frac{3}{4}$" SEN PLYWOOD

ALL CABINET BOTTOMS
MADE OF $\frac{3}{4}$" DURAPLY

CAST IRON BASEBOARD HEATING

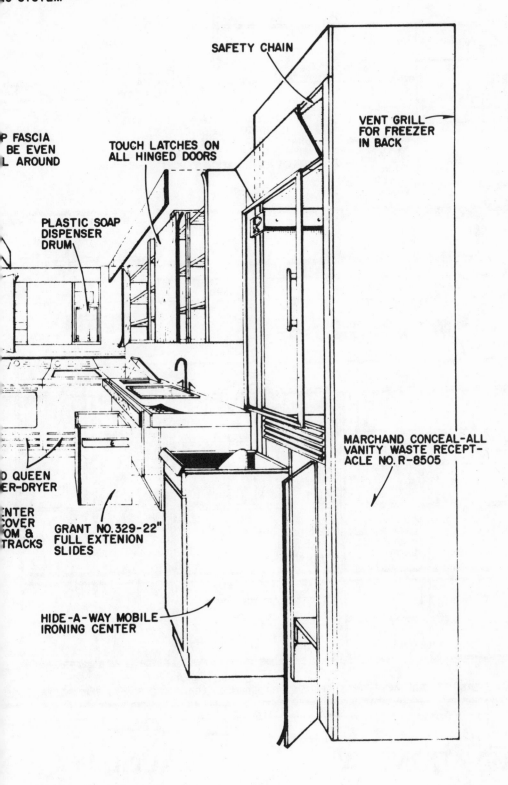

GLAS SUSPENDED
G SYSTEM

SAFETY CHAIN

VENT GRILL
FOR FREEZER
IN BACK

P FASCIA
BE EVEN
L AROUND

TOUCH LATCHES ON
ALL HINGED DOORS

PLASTIC SOAP
DISPENSER
DRUM

MARCHAND CONCEAL-ALL
VANITY WASTE RECEPT-
ACLE NO. R-8505

D QUEEN
ER-DRYER

NTER
COVER
OM &
TRACKS

GRANT NO.329-22"
FULL EXTENION
SLIDES

HIDE-A-WAY MOBILE
IRONING CENTER

Fig. 3.

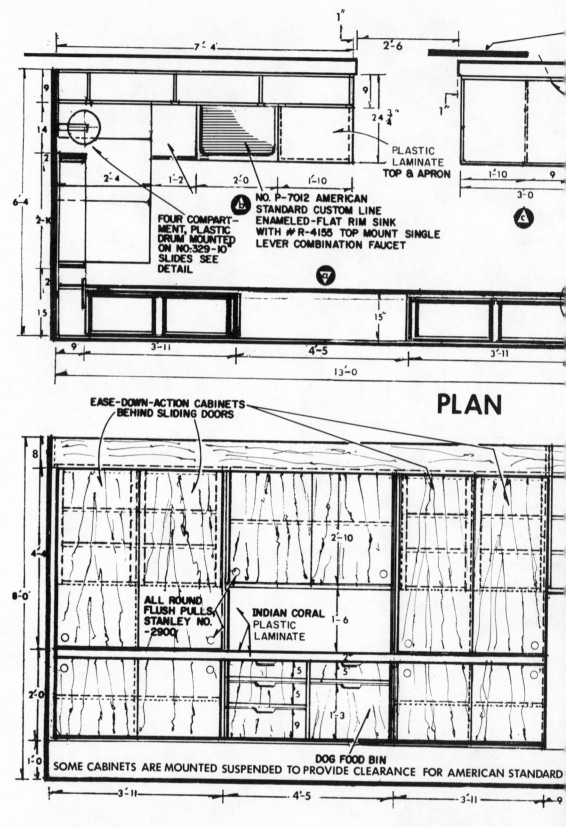

**PLAN**

FOUR COMPART-
MENT, PLASTIC
DRUM MOUNTED
ON NO. 329-10
SLIDES SEE
DETAIL

NO. P-7012 AMERICAN
STANDARD CUSTOM LINE
ENAMELED-FLAT RIM SINK
WITH № R-4155 TOP MOUNT SINGLE
LEVER COMBINATION FAUCET

PLASTIC
LAMINATE
TOP & APRON

EASE-DOWN-ACTION CABINETS
BEHIND SLIDING DOORS

ALL ROUND
FLUSH PULLS
STANLEY NO.
-2900

INDIAN CORAL
PLASTIC
LAMINATE

DOG FOOD BIN

SOME CABINETS ARE MOUNTED SUSPENDED TO PROVIDE CLEARANCE FOR AMERICAN STANDARD

**ELEVATIONS-'A'**

**LAUNDRY & PAN**

PLAN—ELEVATIONS &

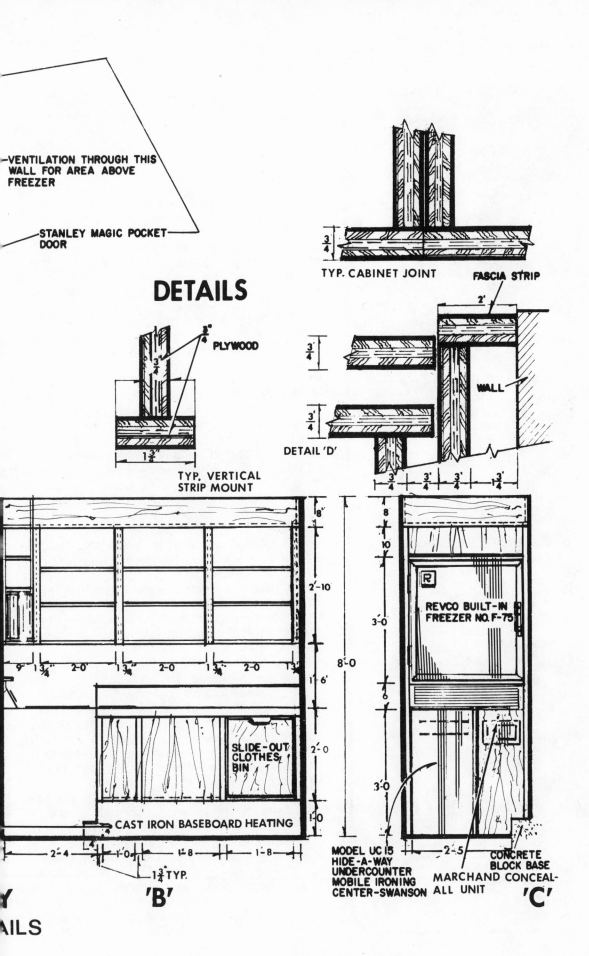

VENTILATION THROUGH THIS WALL FOR AREA ABOVE FREEZER

STANLEY MAGIC POCKET DOOR

TYP. CABINET JOINT

FASCIA STRIP

## DETAILS

PLYWOOD

$\frac{3}{4}$

$\frac{3}{4}$

$1\frac{3}{4}$"

TYP. VERTICAL STRIP MOUNT

DETAIL 'D'

$\frac{3}{4}$  $\frac{3}{4}$  $\frac{3}{4}$  $\frac{3}{4}$

WALL

2'

8'

2'-10

1'-6'

2'-0

1'-0

SLIDE-OUT CLOTHES BIN

CAST IRON BASEBOARD HEATING

8'-0

2'-4    1'-0    1'-8    1'-8

$1\frac{3}{4}$" TYP.

9'  $1\frac{3}{4}$"  2'-0  $1\frac{3}{4}$"  2'-0  $1\frac{3}{4}$"  2'-0  $1\frac{3}{4}$

'B'

8

10

3'-0

6

3'-0

REVCO BUILT-IN FREEZER NO. F-75

2'-5

MODEL UC 15 HIDE-A-WAY UNDERCOUNTER MOBILE IRONING CENTER-SWANSON

MARCHAND CONCEAL-ALL UNIT

CONCRETE BLOCK BASE

'C'

AILS

Fig. 4.

Fig. 5. Looking toward connecting sliding kitchen door. On left side beneath the Revco freezer is the rollout ironing Kaddy. Further front is the slide-out drawer for soiled clothing.

Fig. 6. Opposite the sink wall is continuous storage with pull-down cabinet shelves covered with sliding doors. The center of this unit has shorter doors to provide a utility and decorating niche covered with colored plastic laminate.

Fig. 7. Dog food bin holds 50 pounds of dry dog food. Container is held by a safety chain.

ash of gray-beige. The horizontal surfaces and back splashes are covered with colorful coral plastic laminate. The ceiling panes (Owens-Corning Fiberglas), which are mounted in a metal frame in 2-x-4-foot sections and are removable, serve to evenly soften and disperse the lighting, as well as to absorb some of the machine noise generated by the washer and dryer. Further leakage of noise is prevented by well-insulated walls and a 1¾-inch solid core door, electronically activated (by Stanley).

### Deluxe laundry and storage in the basement

In contrast to the pantry in the House of Ideas, where sufficient room was found on the same level and adjacent to the kitchen to install the laundry, the laundry-storage combination in Figure 8 had to be built in the basement. As an integral part of a basement-remodeling job on a below-ground level, its functions had to correspond to its location. This meant that some activities would be eliminated, while others would be incorporated into the plan.

Obviously, building an elaborate laundry just for the sake of washing and drying clothing would be unreasonable. A related or complementary activity or even several activities must be planned to accompany such a room in order to justify its existence. The secondary use of this laundry in the basement was off-season clothing storage.

The laundry setup in this room even surpassed the one in the House of Ideas, for it had a large soiled-clothing container fed by a laundry chute connected to the upstairs floors (Figures 9, 10 and 11). Intake stations at the kitchen and in a linen closet next to the bedrooms fed this chute. Since the house was a 3½-floor split-level, the chute was certainly a step-saving idea.

Built of Novoply (chipboard) with plastic-covered top surfaces, this laundry turned out to be a simple and relatively inexpensive feature. The room was painted pink and pink appliances were used. Combined with deluxe warm white fluorescent fixtures and bulbs above, the color scheme made even this windowless basement seem as if it were filled with daylight.

The availability of good, space-saving devices makes it very easy to solve almost any

Entrance Gallery and Staircase

# Family and Living Areas

Family and Living Areas

# Fireplaces

# Children's World

Children's World

# Master Bedrooms

# Best Bathrooms

Best Bathrooms

Best Bathrooms

# Kitchen Living

Kitchen Living

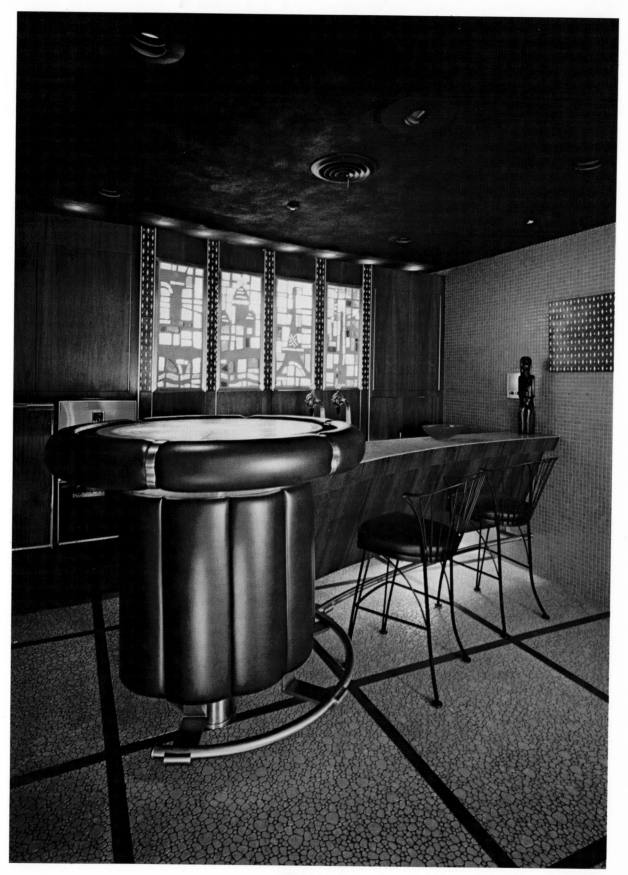

# Bars

Bars

# Outdoor Living

# Family Living and Entertainment

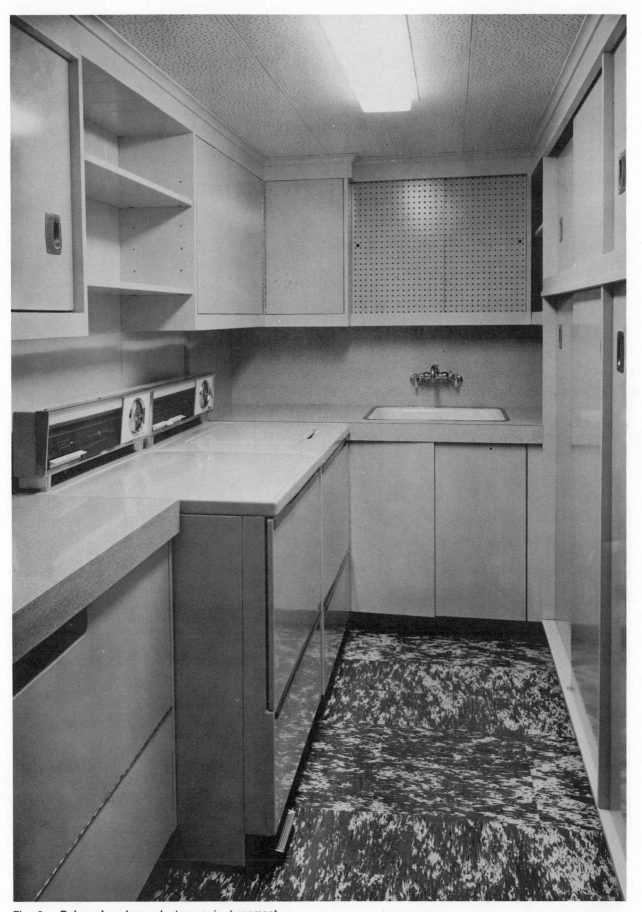

Fig. 8.   Deluxe laundry and storage in basement.

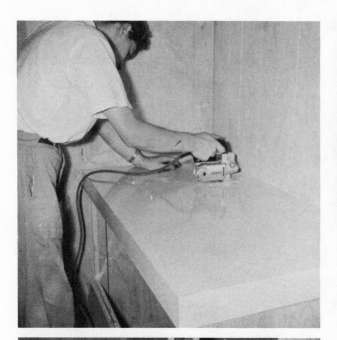

Fig. 9. The top corner of the soiled clothes container is cut open to receive the sheet metal chute.

Fig. 10. Sheet metal chute is now attached to the cabinet.

Fig. 11. To dress up the area in conformity with the rest of the room, matching ¾-inch Sen plywood covers the metal chute.

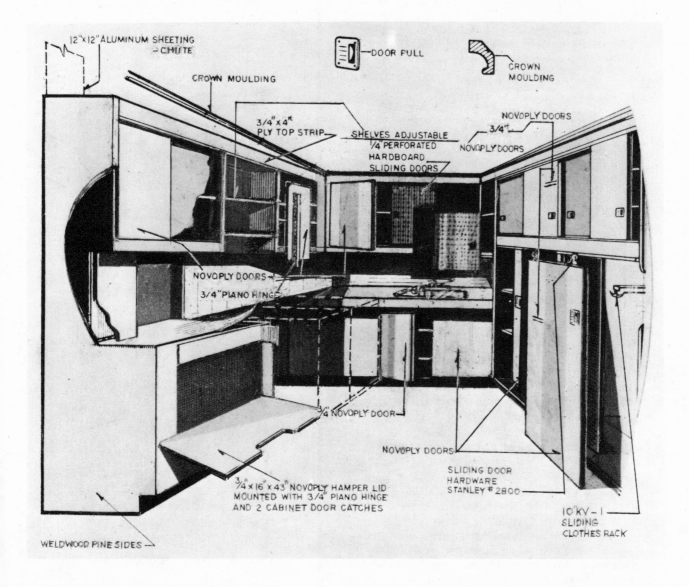

12"×12" ALUMINUM SHEETING – CHUTE

DOOR PULL

CROWN MOULDING

CROWN MOULDING

CROWN MOULDING

3/4"×4" PLY TOP STRIP

SHELVES ADJUSTABLE 1/4" PERFORATED HARDBOARD SLIDING DOORS

NOVOPLY DOORS

3/4" NOVOPLY DOORS

NOVOPLY DOORS

3/4" PIANO HINGE

3/4 NOVOPLY DOOR

NOVOPLY DOORS

3/4"×16"×43" NOVOPLY HAMPER LID MOUNTED WITH 3/4" PIANO HINGE AND 2 CABINET DOOR CATCHES

SLIDING DOOR HARDWARE STANLEY #2800

WELDWOOD PINE SIDES

10'KV–1 SLIDING CLOTHES RACK

Fig. 12.

design problem. In this case, it was possible to build a relatively small area into a larger room without obstructions because of the sliding doors, used even at the entrance. The result is a serviceable and attractive laundry and storage area, with ample space for ironing and folding. While most women do not particularly look forward to clothes washing, a well-organized and pleasant laundry area may well change this outlook.

## Best closet ideas

Today closets are usually built in one of two ways. The first type is built in a double-walled shaft with a 2-sided, or 2-room, opening. These openings are treated differently by different builders. Some like to install a single door (approximately 2 to 3 feet wide), thus creating a walk-in closet with more airtight and dustproof storage than is found in a 2-door installation. On the exterior, a 1-door walk-in closet is very unobtrusive and sets up no obstacles for further room planning or decoration.

The other kind of closet most widely used is the surface closet covered in the front with sliding doors. In order for this type of structure to be attractive and functional, it is necessary to install a good front casing and door system. Whether the door is a folding, accordion, or sliding type, a good door system is usually expensive. Consequently, many homes are ailing with sticking and warped closet doors and a score of other annoyances.

It is fair to say that a good closet is one that has been creatively designed and uses the best available hardware as well as the best doors or panels. Another must is the use of ¾-inch plywood cut to the desired size of the shelf, rather than the less expensive 1 x 12 shop pine more broadly used in development homes, which is very inferior. After these basics are covered, it is merely necessary to remember that a good and versatile closet must always be given high priority in a home furnishing plan.

Homes with basements usually have stairs leading down. This can become a very useful area for storage beneath. Some basements even have the oil tank in them. Enclosing the tank

Fig. 13. A laundry conversion in a basement: before.

Fig. 14. After, with sliding doors open.

Fig. 15. After, with sliding doors closed.

Fig. 16. Typical old staircase to basement with storage beneath.

Fig. 17. Same staircase finished. Note refrigerator enclosure.

Fig. 18. Enclosure of oil tank. Upper wall will become vital storage besides hiding the tank behind fine paneling.

Fig. 19. Additional sliding door cabinets in general area provide more desirable organized storage.

Fig. 20. Even water and gas meters are tucked away. But all essential items are accessible with flush touch latch doors.

Fig. 21. There is no limit to good storage ideas. Here, in an entertainment area, folding tables and chairs slide into a decorative feature wall structure.

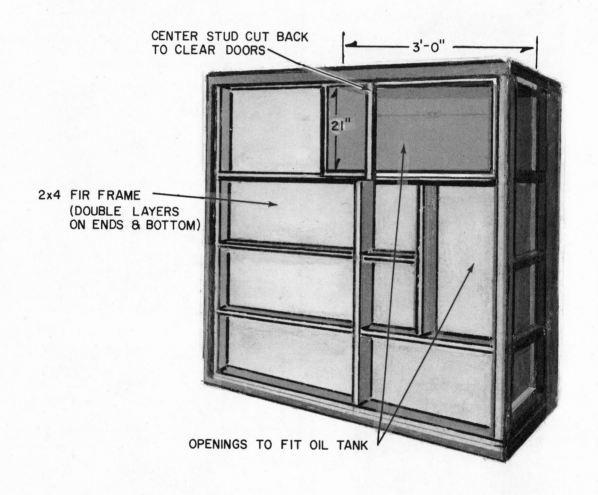

CENTER STUD CUT BACK
TO CLEAR DOORS

3'-0"

21"

2x4 FIR FRAME
(DOUBLE LAYERS
ON ENDS & BOTTOM)

OPENINGS TO FIT OIL TANK

Fig. 22.

not only removes an unsightly thing, especially if the basement is to become a play area, but it can add more storage.

By just utilizing portions of attics, one can create storage for boxed-in goods, such as off-season recreation items.

By shortening any narrow and long room, one can create a fair-sized storage or cedar closet just by building a stud wall and door. At the same time an odd-shaped room can be remodeled into a more desirable one, and, in the process, can provide a variety of useful storage areas.

Often, existing closets are badly planned. With a little rearrangement, the inside function can gain in usefulness. This is possible, as hardware availability is surprisingly broad in selection and is well designed for our ever-

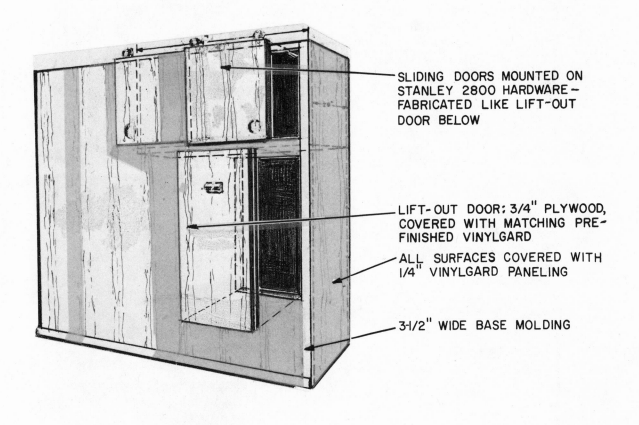

SLIDING DOORS MOUNTED ON
STANLEY 2800 HARDWARE —
FABRICATED LIKE LIFT-OUT
DOOR BELOW

LIFT-OUT DOOR: 3/4" PLYWOOD,
COVERED WITH MATCHING PRE-
FINISHED VINYLGARD

ALL SURFACES COVERED WITH
1/4" VINYLGARD PANELING

3-1/2" WIDE BASE MOLDING

Fig. 23.

increasing need and use of space. When was the last time you visited your neighborhood hardware store?

**A man's closet**

The closets built in the early 1900s are good examples of high-grade workmanship and top-grade materials. They featured regular drawers behind doors, and so-called French and English sliding trays—drawers with cutout sides and slender front strips (usually used for shirt or underwear storage). Even today this type of drawer system is a fine suggestion for a closet. Note the Man's Closet in Figure 28, which is behind the mirrored structural column in the bedroom of the House of Ideas. Figures 29 through 33 contain all the necessary information for building this deluxe convenience closet. Some of its many features include: a slide-out pivoting mirror, "magic pull-down shelves" with clothing carrier, built-in shoe shine equipment, and shoe, belt, slack, and tie racks. Figure 33 illustrates how the clothing rod is installed.

While the same basic solution was used for the woman's closet of the House of Ideas, it only proved that a closet is not just a closet. The best closet perhaps is one that offers every conceivable storage and function once the door is open.

Fig. 24.   As if the walls didn't have enough functions, a small area near the workshop and laundry was used for a built-in telephone.

Fig. 25.   Such built-ins usually have to be worked out with your local telephone company. Once the phone is in, the fold-down door is hinged in place and secured with a chain.

Fig. 26.   A pad is attached. Pencil can be added, too.

Fig. 27.   When closed, the door holds in place with a touch latch and is flush. Even the wood grain is uninterrupted because the door piece was cut out of the same piece of plywood.

Fig. 28.   The man's closet.

# SECTIONS

**K–V NO. 1, 10"
CLOTHING CARRIER**

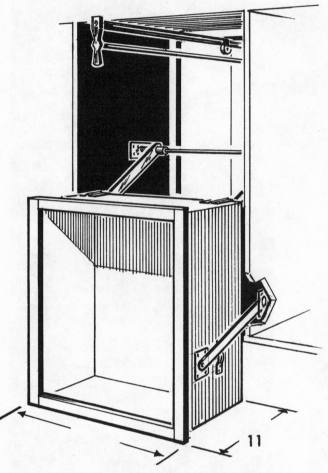

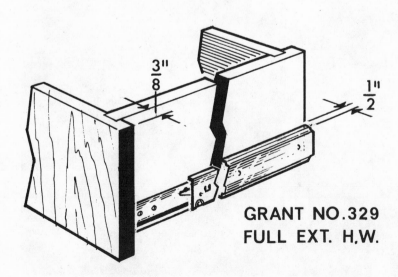

**DETAIL OF "MAGIC SHELF"**

11

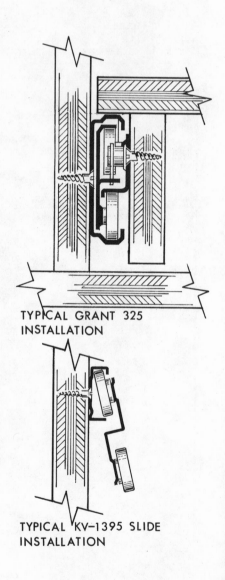

TYPICAL GRANT 325
INSTALLATION

TYPICAL KV–1395 SLIDE
INSTALLATION

$\frac{3}{8}$"

$\frac{1}{2}$"

GRANT NO. 329
FULL EXT. H.W.

**DETAIL OF DRAWER**

Fig. 29 ·

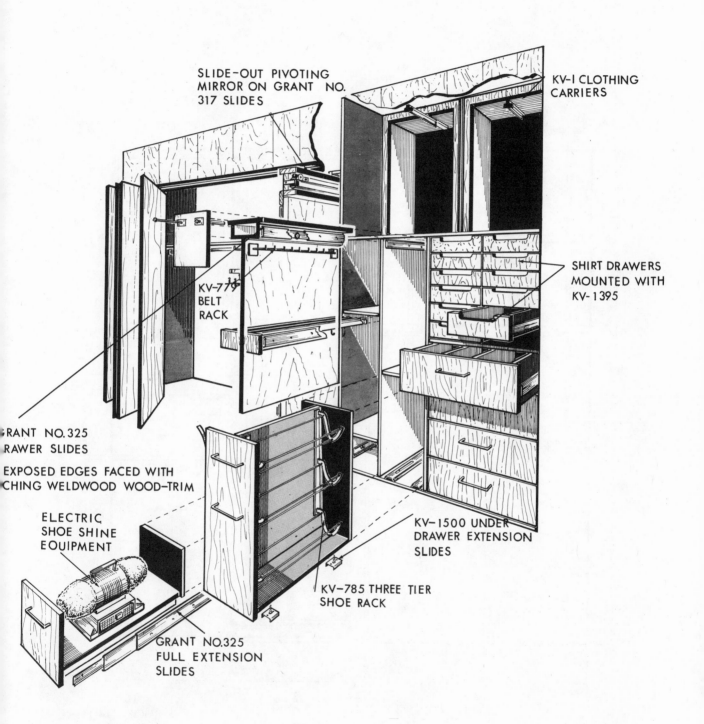

SLIDE-OUT PIVOTING
MIRROR ON GRANT NO.
317 SLIDES

KV-1 CLOTHING
CARRIERS

KV-779
BELT
RACK

SHIRT DRAWERS
MOUNTED WITH
KV-1395

GRANT NO.325
DRAWER SLIDES

EXPOSED EDGES FACED WITH
CHING WELDWOOD WOOD-TRIM

ELECTRIC
SHOE SHINE
EQUIPMENT

KV-1500 UNDER
DRAWER EXTENSION
SLIDES

KV-785 THREE TIER
SHOE RACK

GRANT NO.325
FULL EXTENSION
SLIDES

Fig. 30.

# ELEVATION

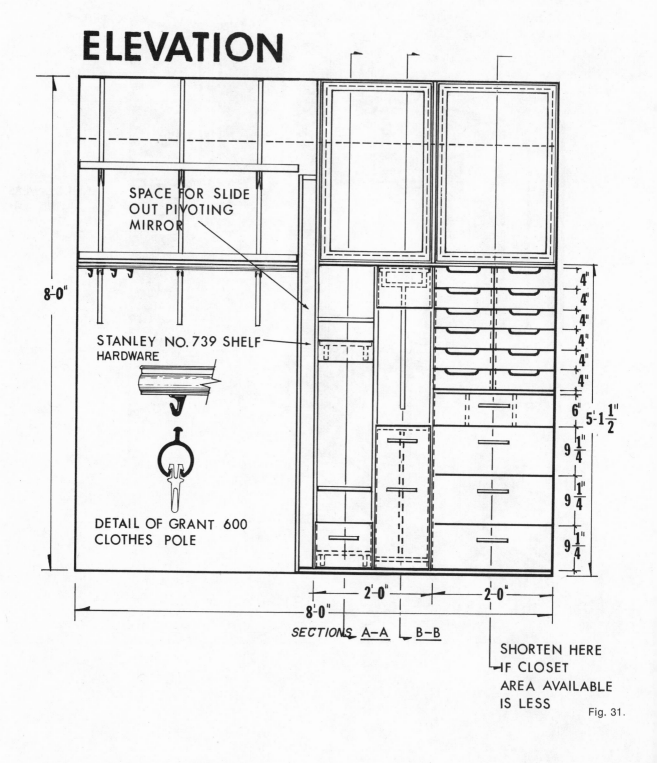

SPACE FOR SLIDE
OUT PIVOTING
MIRROR

STANLEY NO. 739 SHELF
HARDWARE

DETAIL OF GRANT 600
CLOTHES POLE

8'-0"

4"
4"
4"
4"
4"
4"
4"

6"
9¼"
9¼"
9¼"

5'-1 1½"

2'-0"

2'-0"

8'-0"

SECTIONS A-A  B-B

SHORTEN HERE
IF CLOSET
AREA AVAILABLE
IS LESS

Fig. 31.

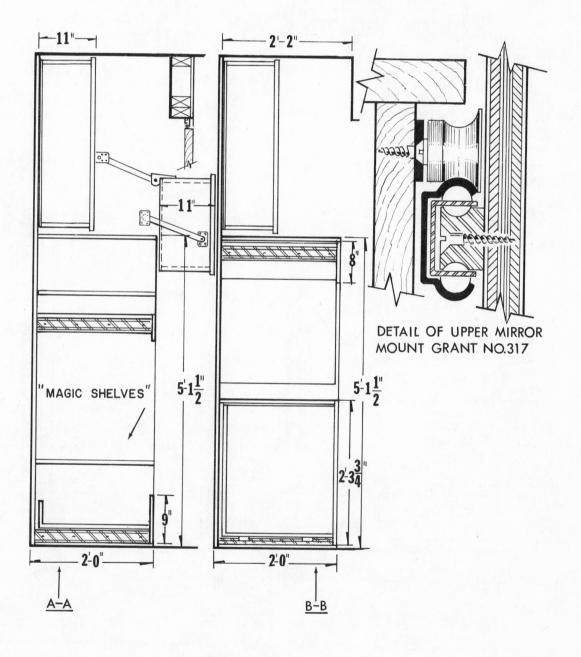

—11"—

—11"—

"MAGIC SHELVES"

$5'\text{-}1\frac{1}{2}''$

9"

2'-0"

A–A

2'-2"

8"

$5'\text{-}1\frac{1}{2}''$

$2'\text{-}3\frac{3}{4}''$

2'-0"

B–B

DETAIL OF UPPER MIRROR
MOUNT GRANT NO. 317

Fig. 32.

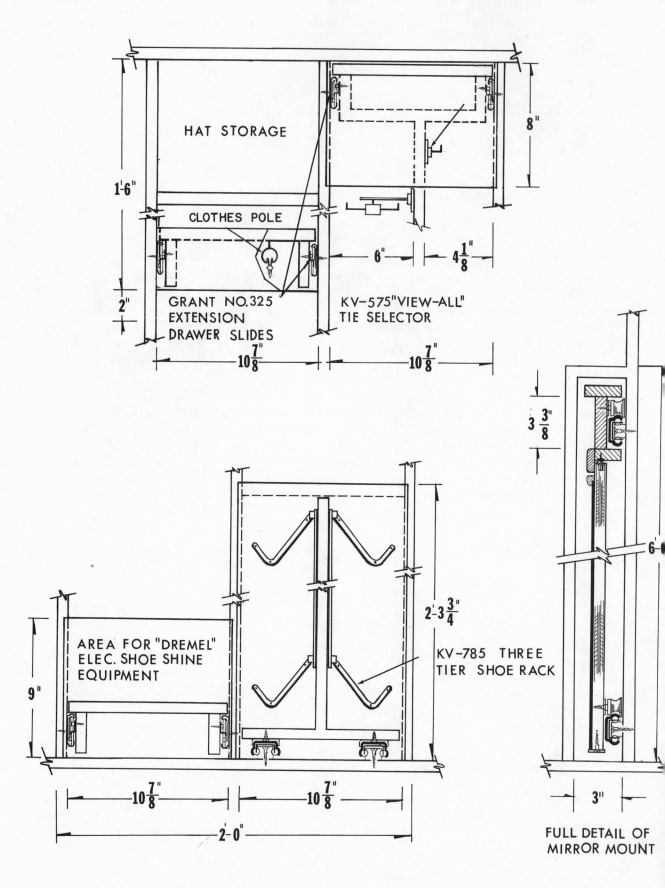

HAT STORAGE

1'-6"

8"

CLOTHES POLE

6"

4 1/8"

2"

GRANT NO. 325
EXTENSION
DRAWER SLIDES

KV-575 "VIEW-ALL"
TIE SELECTOR

10 7/8"

10 7/8"

3 3/8"

6'

AREA FOR "DREMEL"
ELEC. SHOE SHINE
EQUIPMENT

2'-3 3/4"

KV-785 THREE
TIER SHOE RACK

9"

10 7/8"

10 7/8"

2'-0"

3"

FULL DETAIL OF
MIRROR MOUNT

Fig. 33

Fig. 1.   Built-in sewing room.

# Chapter 10
# Sewing Centers and Hobby Workshops

## Sewing centers

Although sewing is an immensely popular and useful pastime, it is often the most disorganized activity in the home. The sewing "center" is usually an ill-defined and untidy area. The sewing machine itself doesn't take up a great deal of space—it is the yards of material, half-finished projects, and other paraphernalia that cause unsightly problems.

To solve the problem, what needs to be set up is a single place where all the supplies needed for sewing and mending can be kept together. Such a center could be permanent or a compact portable setup.

A very convenient arrangement for sewing is a U-shaped area with the sewing machine in the center and surfaces on the right for cutting fabric, and on the left for pressing. Underneath these surfaces, supplies may be stored in drawers. A swivel chair would be best suited for this arrangement.

A built-in sewing center is of course most desirable, since everything would then be out of the way and concealed when not in use.

## Built-in sewing room

Sewing rooms can vary greatly in dimension, depending on the size and number of objects to be included. But to tuck a whole sewing room into a built-in enclosure only 6 feet wide, 2 feet deep, and 6 feet high is indeed an accomplishment.

The complete sewing room in Figure 1 consists of 3 compartments nearly equal in size. In the first is a large Singer sewing machine, a stool, a spool rack holding 10 dozen spools of thread, organized hangers for scissors, shears, etc., 2 racks for sewing manuals and patterns, an adjustable lamp, and a ¾-length mirror.

The slightly wider center section contains three interesting features, each designed to support the other. While using the sewing machine, the seamstress needs an area on which to lay scissors, tape, and other small items. The 20-x-20-inch all-purpose slide-out board below the standard-size ironing board is perfect for this. To iron, simply pull out and fold down the ironing board, holding it in place by pulling down the support legs. To use the 6-foot-x-32-

Fig. 2. Sewing machine folds into housing before it slides in.

Fig. 3. Wood strip latch to support the fold-out table.

Fig. 4. Plastic drawers (optional) get hardboard partitions.

inch cutting table, leave the ironing board down and fold the cutting table out on top of it. Also included in this center area is a 4-cubic-foot container for odd cuttings below the ironing board.

The third compartment includes an insulated box for the electric iron and 10 drawers with dividers for small items (plastic drawers shown in Figure 4 are optional).

To put all of these objects into operational position required not a miracle, but only mathematical calculation. Since they are housed in a wall, they can be folded, pushed, and rolled away, so that the space in the room can be used with maximum efficiency. It is also advantageous to store sewing equipment when it is not in use in order to make cleaning and storing very easy. This work area is virtually messproof since there are no permanent horizontal surfaces to become cluttered.

According to the original plan, most of the items in the room would roll into or out of the wall in a semifolded state. But because the baseboard heating convectors got in the way, the alternative was to use Grant heavy-duty slides (#317) to suspend the sewing machine like a free-hanging drawer and roll it out without the superfluous base structure. In fact, the Singer sewing machine console (base and leg structure removed) was custom-made of Sen plywood to fit the requirements of this feature, and mounted on Grant #317 slides.

A mixture of Sen plywood (oriental ash) and Novoply (chipboard) makes this setup decoratively desirable and fairly inexpensive. Whether built into a wide closet that is already there, or into an enclosure prepared in a suitable area of the family room, it will be one of the most rewarding and simple projects in the house.

A similar but condensed version of the Built-in Sewing Room is shown in Figure 5. Built into a storage closet, it contains many of the important features of the more thoroughly planned room but has less storage space and fewer conveniences, making it an ideal solution in a confined space or an area where the space is needed for other purposes. This unit was built in a developed family-basement area. The multipurpose closet arrangement made this sewing area not only feasible but also desirable. This, in contrast to the all complete Built-in Sewing Room described before, shows the extent of possibilities.

### Hobby workshops

Unfortunately, most hobby workshops are often unnecessarily dull and dreary rooms, built with little imagination or care. In this section, you will find some ideas for well-organized, neat, attractive home workshops, the type a hobbyist will look forward to working in.

The various installations here provide different solutions to different problems. The type of shop you build, of course, depends on your needs and the amount of space at your disposal. The important thing is that the room, or perhaps just a part of an area, be not only efficient but also inviting and decorative.

Other important considerations are safety and adequate lighting and properly placed electrical outlets. It will be well worth while to spend a lot of time planning and preparing for contingencies. Storage must be carefully and amply provided for as well.

It is important to realize and accept the fact that a hobby workshop is entirely different from a professional establishment, even if the latter is a small one. It is hard to believe that the two can be so different from one another, but the features and the storage provisions in a hobby shop can be used effectively only at home. For example, for safety and cleanliness, the radial arm saw in a home shop might be mounted on a pull-out platform, which slides on heavy duty Grant slides so it can be pushed out of the way when not in use (as in Figures 8 and 9). Once in the enclosure, the machine can then be turned inward and the doors closed and even locked for additional safety if there are children around. In a professional shop, this entire procedure would be considered a waste of time and space.

### A built-in hobby work center

The workshop in Figures 8 and 9 is really a model setup, taking into account every one of the hobbyist's possible needs and desires.

Fig. 5. Sewing center built within a closet storage area.

Among these is a device for the storage of small items. To meet this requirement, little partitions in the drawers as well as small glass jars mounted on a turn plate or just beneath the upper cabinet shelves are imperative. The shelves in all upper cabinet units are adjustable in order to provide for changing storage needs. It is a good idea to install the shelves on adjustable supports, and all drawers, large or small, on full extension slides. A rollout scrap box such as the one beneath the machine in Figure 9 is also an absolute must.

The proper placement of the light fixtures is important to a well-planned workshop. If lights are to correctly illuminate the workbench top and adjacent area, the fixtures must be mounted so that the center of the fixture depth (front to back) is plumb and parallel to the edge of the workbench top (front).

A workshop structure such as this built-in

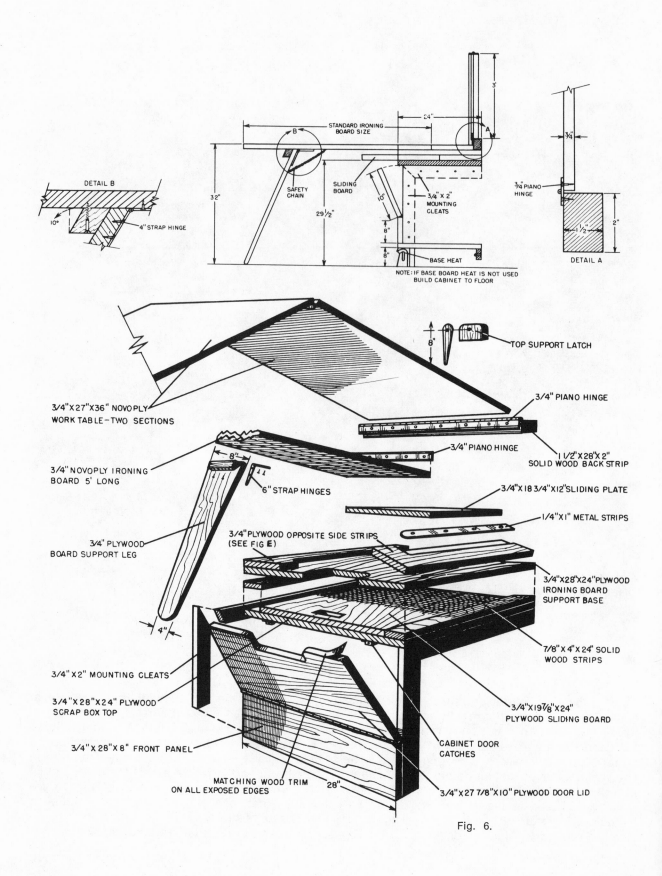

DETAIL B

10°

4" STRAP HINGE

STANDARD IRONING
BOARD SIZE

24"

3'

B

A

32"

SAFETY
CHAIN

SLIDING
BOARD

29½"

10°

3/4" X 2"
MOUNTING
CLEATS

8"

8"

BASE HEAT

NOTE: IF BASE BOARD HEAT IS NOT USED
BUILD CABINET TO FLOOR

3/4"

3/4" PIANO
HINGE

½"

2"

DETAIL A

8"

TOP SUPPORT LATCH

3/4"X27"X36" NOVOPLY
WORK TABLE—TWO SECTIONS

3/4" PIANO HINGE

3/4" PIANO HINGE

1½"X28"X2"
SOLID WOOD BACK STRIP

3/4" NOVOPLY IRONING
BOARD 5' LONG

6" STRAP HINGES

3/4"X18 3/4"X12"SLIDING PLATE

1/4"X1" METAL STRIPS

3/4" PLYWOOD
BOARD SUPPORT LEG

3/4"PLYWOOD OPPOSITE SIDE STRIPS
(SEE FIG E)

3/4"X28"X24"PLYWOOD
IRONING BOARD
SUPPORT BASE

4"

7/8" X 4" X 24' SOLID
WOOD STRIPS

3/4"X2" MOUNTING CLEATS

3/4"X 28"X24" PLYWOOD
SCRAP BOX TOP

3/4"X19⅞"X24"
PLYWOOD SLIDING BOARD

3/4"X 28"X 8" FRONT PANEL

CABINET DOOR
CATCHES

MATCHING WOOD TRIM
ON ALL EXPOSED EDGES

28"

3/4"X27 7/8"X10" PLYWOOD DOOR LID

Fig. 6.

center, in spite of its versatility, cannot be considered the only solution for organized shop space. It is therefore important to have an extra work and assembly area with a straight, nonskid floor and adequate lighting. Additional power tools must be placed in an area that is at least 4 times the square footage of any machine for clearance. Good lighting in a machine area is also imperative. A nonglare fixture placed at the machine feed and directly behind the operator as he stands at the machine is the safest setup. To cast shadows or block the lighting at the cutting area of any machine can be very dangerous.

If power tools are on casters and are movable, assigned areas should be marked on the floor with a painted line for space-saving reasons, for proper location and illumination.

Another way to solve this decoratively would be to inlay a slightly different shade of flooring tile in these planned areas.

Avoid electric cords, especially extension lines. The proper fixtures will be determined on the basis of the ceiling height. In any case, a fire extinguisher must be on the shop premises. A shut-off switch connected only to the electric power supply of the shop near the work area is another must. If small electric portable power tools are to be used extensively, it is also advisable to install a wire mold on the work bench beneath the top overlap in front or above the protective top splash in back. Another piece of equipment that should be acquired immediately is a good shop vacuum cleaner drum (such as the one manufactured by Rockwell-Delta).

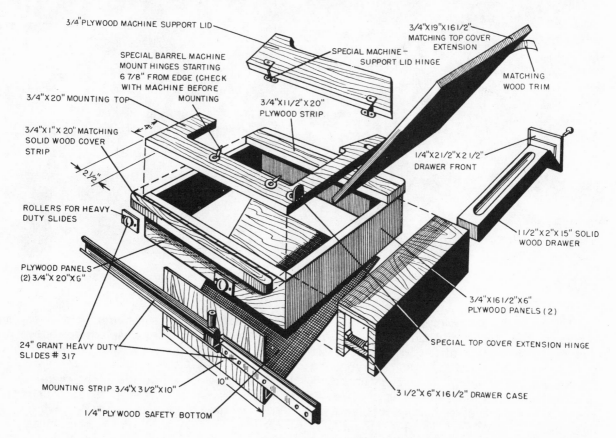

**SLIDING SEWING MACHINE CABINET**

Fig. 7.

Fig. 8. Multi-purpose hobby workshop. Note radial-arm saw (center) which folds away for safety.

The vise should be of a special type for woodwork only and should be mounted about 4 to 6 feet from the left end of the counter if you are right-handed (or from the right end if you are left-handed). The most important thing to remember about mounting a vise is to be sure that there is at least an 8-foot clearance either way between the vise and the nearest point of obstruction. It may be necessary to mount the vise in the center of the bench top in order to meet this requirement. A very outstanding woodworking vise, perhaps above your budget but extremely versatile, is the one shown in Figure 17.

The selection of the right materials for building such a workshop is very important. This model shop was built of ¾-inch Sen plywood (oriental ash), and to economize, Novoply (chipboard) coated with sealer was used for shelves and unexposed parts. Coral-colored

Fig. 9. Roll-away trash box (center) is seen in this view. The tool rack (rear center) is mounted on a 30-inch-wide panel. The inside of the panel is installed on 2 pivots (in center of top and in center of bottom). It has a locking stop inside the cabinet, on one side only, which enables it to revolve in one direction. You push, here are the tools; push again, they are out of the way.

satin plastic laminate was used instead of paint. Sen or any ash, or even a light oak, are sturdy and strong-grained materials which, even if damaged, will not show it, even in ¾-inch plywood. (For suggestions about wood finishing, see page 271.) Plastic laminate is used on the back cabinet because it is nearly indestructible and projects color brilliance far better than paint. Both materials are usually found only in home interiors, but their durability makes

them practical in this heavily used workshop; their decorative qualities make them especially desirable in a basement feature even without surpassing a reasonable budget.

The bench top should be fabricated with ¼-inch tempered hardboard pasted onto ¾-inch fir plywood; if possible, cover the under surface with ⅛-inch hardboard. The edge should be solid ash or oak with slightly rounded edges. All sliding doors are mounted

Fig. 10. Each pegboard leaf has a ¾-x-1-inch solid oak spline, with a ⅜-inch dowel on each end which fits into the top and bottom half disc supports.

Fig. 11. Two recessed 1-x-2-inch oak strips hold both half discs together while at the same time acting as wall mount.

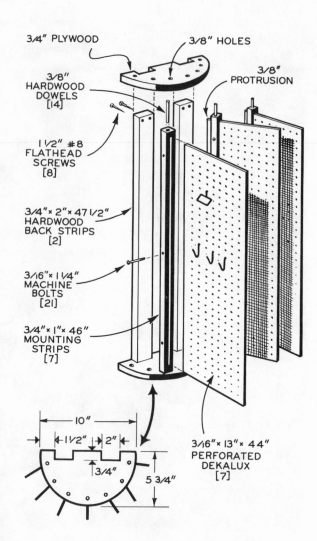

3/4" PLYWOOD

3/8" HOLES

3/8" PROTRUSION

3/8" HARDWOOD DOWELS [14]

1 1/2" #8 FLATHEAD SCREWS [8]

3/4" x 2" x 47 1/2" HARDWOOD BACK STRIPS [2]

3/16" x 1 1/4" MACHINE BOLTS [21]

3/4" x 1" x 46" MOUNTING STRIPS [7]

10"

1 1/2"

2"

3/4"

5 3/4"

3/16" x 13" x 44" PERFORATED DEKALUX [7]

Fig. 12. Folding tool rack.

on Stanley #2800 hardware, which is quickly installed. Flush pulls are important and extending hardware must be avoided. Where hinges are used in a shop, continuous hinges (piano hinges) of solid brass or stainless steel are best. To avoid slivers, all exposed plywood edges should be capped off with either ¼-inch matching hardwood edging or matching Weldwood wood trim (on doors only) following manufacturer's instructions.

### Father-son workbench

To create a good relationship between father and son, this workbench innovation is perhaps better than a bad fishing trip. Grant (vertically mounted) #313 24-inch heavy-duty slides permit the small unit to be raised to the desired height, thus allowing it to grow with the boy. Adjustable legs on both ends, slotted, and two ½-x-2-inch carriage bolts in each slot through bench end panels with washers and wing nuts, will secure the bench at the desired height.

### Built-in shop wall in basement

Using the same building techniques as for the hobby work center and as shown in Figures 17 through 19, this built-in wall is completely self-contained. Clean when not in use, good storage was the aim of this feature. The toolrack is similar to the one used for the Built-in Hobby Work Center. A broader wall area allowed the expansion of the tool storage peg-boards by mounting them to ¾-inch x 2-foot strips (top and bottom) rather than a 10-inch half disk as in the other feature (see Figure 12). This system provided twice the storage of the half disk system.

Good lighting and a soothing color scheme will entice every member of the family to make justifiable use of the area. This area was made even more inviting by the installation of a ceiling speaker connected to an AM-FM radio.

### Foldaway bench in the garage

The "before" picture, page 176, is an all-too-familiar sight to many homeowners. Too often we find our suburban friends parking their cars on the street; after a day's work, who feels like storing away the odds and ends of hobby materials to make room for the car? No wonder.

Fig. 13.   Father-son workbench.

A first look at a mess like this would discourage just about anyone. However, we must consider the fact that the garage, in many homes, provides the only viable storage and shop area.

Solution: A shallow but well-organized wall storage unit with sliding doors on one side only. This will provide enough clearance for the car. At the end of that storage unit, a folding bench suffices for one's hobby and as an instant facility for maintenance and repairs. Next, ⅛-inch tempered perforated hardboard mounted on 1 x 2 furring strips enables one to attach a broad variety of mounting hooks neatly to the walls, even for the mower.

As Figure 1 shows, a small and useless area can become a pleasant and well-organized multifunction addition so important to any home in this time of constantly dwindling space.

*Other helpful features:* A continuous wire mold on the cabinet edge and back workbench wall, good lighting, and an automatic garage door opener are convenient for this small area.

Whether one uses the workbench frequently or just likes lots of storage and the car in the garage where it belongs, this is perhaps the best solution.

Fig. 14.

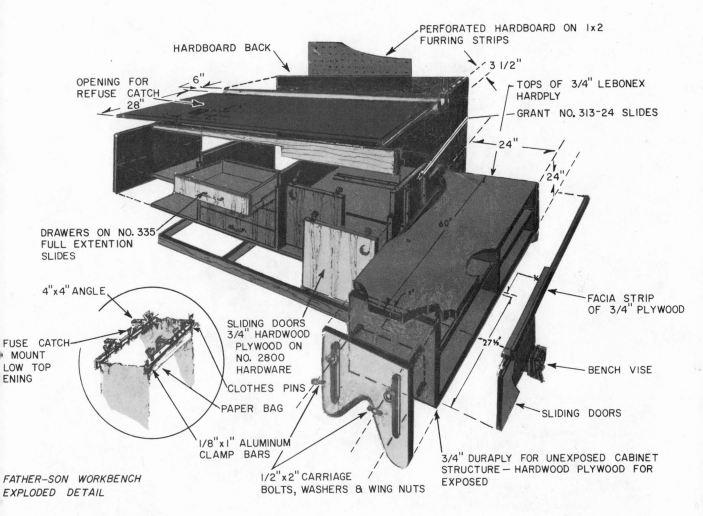

HARDBOARD BACK

PERFORATED HARDBOARD ON 1x2 FURRING STRIPS

OPENING FOR REFUSE CATCH 28"

6"

3 1/2"

TOPS OF 3/4" LEBONEX HARDPLY

GRANT NO. 313-24 SLIDES

24"

24"

60"

DRAWERS ON NO. 335 FULL EXTENSION SLIDES

4"x4" ANGLE

FUSE CATCH MOUNT LOW TOP ENING

SLIDING DOORS 3/4" HARDWOOD PLYWOOD ON NO. 2800 HARDWARE

CLOTHES PINS

PAPER BAG

1/8"x1" ALUMINUM CLAMP BARS

FATHER-SON WORKBENCH EXPLODED DETAIL

1/2"x2" CARRIAGE BOLTS, WASHERS & WING NUTS

FACIA STRIP OF 3/4" PLYWOOD

27½"

BENCH VISE

SLIDING DOORS

3/4" DURAPLY FOR UNEXPOSED CABINET STRUCTURE—HARDWOOD PLYWOOD FOR EXPOSED

Fig. 15.

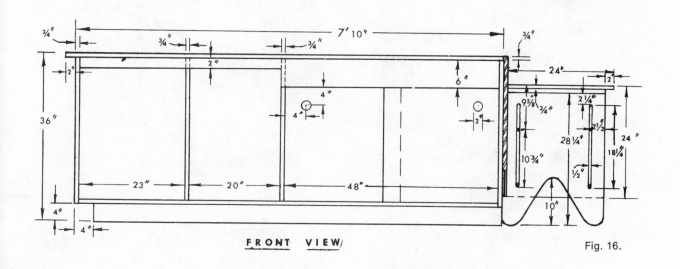

3/4"

7' 10"

3/4"

3/4"

3/4"

2"

6"

24"

2"

36"

4"

4"

9⅝"

3/4"

2¼"

2½"

2"

28¼"

24"

18¼"

10¾"

4"

4"

1/2"

10"

23"

20"

48"

FRONT VIEW

Fig. 16.

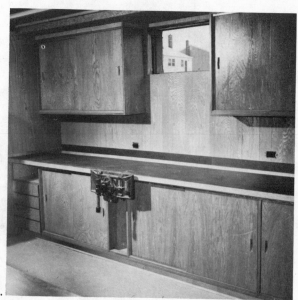

Fig. 17.

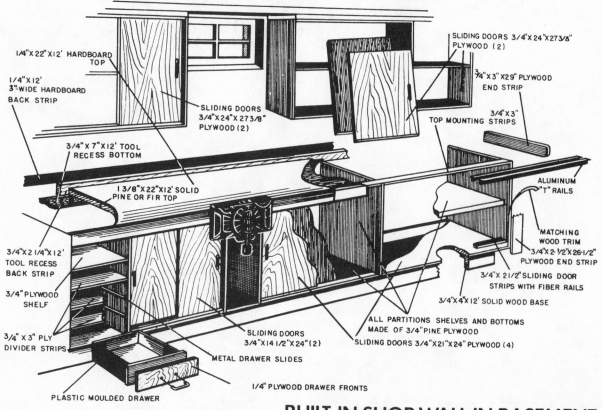

1/4"X 22"X12' HARDBOARD TOP

1/4"X 12' 3"·WIDE HARDBOARD BACK STRIP

SLIDING DOORS 3/4"X24"X 273/8" PLYWOOD (2)

3/4"X 7"X12' TOOL RECESS BOTTOM

1 3/8"X 22"X12' SOLID PINE OR FIR TOP

SLIDING DOORS 3/4"X 24"X 273/8" PLYWOOD (2)

3/4"X3"X29" PLYWOOD END STRIP

3/4"X3" TOP MOUNTING STRIPS

ALUMINUM "T" RAILS

MATCHING WOOD TRIM 3/4"X 2-1/2"X 26-1/2" PLYWOOD END STRIP

3/4"X 2 1/4"X12' TOOL RECESS BACK STRIP

3/4" PLYWOOD SHELF

3/4" X 3" PLY DIVIDER STRIPS

3/4"X 2 1/2" SLIDING DOOR STRIPS WITH FIBER RAILS

3/4"X 4"X 12' SOLID WOOD BASE

ALL PARTITIONS SHELVES AND BOTTOMS MADE OF 3/4" PINE PLYWOOD

SLIDING DOORS 3/4"X21"X 24" PLYWOOD (4)

SLIDING DOORS 3/4"X14 1/2"X 24"(2)

METAL DRAWER SLIDES

1/4" PLYWOOD DRAWER FRONTS

PLASTIC MOULDED DRAWER

Fig. 18.

# BUILT-IN SHOP WALL IN BASEMENT

Fig. 19.  Built-in shop wall, showing multi-leafed tool rack.

Fig. 20. Construction of workbench in basement shop wall.

Fig. 22. Multi-leafed tool rack constructed on 1-x-2-inch top and bottom support strips (used in built-in shop wall in basement).

Fig. 21. Installation of woodworking vise.

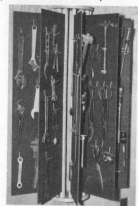

Fig. 23. Multi-leafed tool rack mounted on half-round top and bottom support plates (as used in hobby workshop).

Fig. 24. Before: cluttered garage.

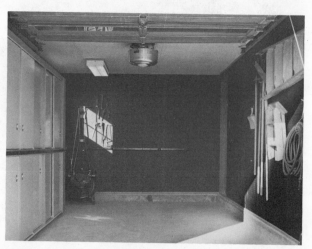

Fig. 25. After: storage units convert garage into useful space.

Fig. 26.  Corner workbench, folded down, and ample storage in renovated garage.

# Chapter 11

# Family Living and Entertainment

The field of home entertainment has progressed so rapidly in recent years that there is presently available an almost bewildering array of televisions, radios, recording devices, movie and slide projectors, and stereo systems. Matching the technological excellence of this equipment with the best possible setting and arrangement in the home is, therefore, an important task. Although the components themselves may be decoratively attractive, they are frequently out of proportion to one another and usually not in harmony with the decor of the room.

It is inconsistent, and certainly inconvenient, to have many pieces of expensive equipment gathering dust in a corner of a children's play room, a family room, or a closet. Much of the wear and tear incurred by just sitting about could be eliminated if all this fine equipment were properly mounted and really used. Because fitting a home entertainment center to an individual setting is such a complex task, any strictly commercial solution is virtually impossible. Unfortunately, an integrated and harmonious home entertainment center is simply not available.

In this chapter, you'll find several suggestions for keeping all your equipment permanently mounted and ready for use, yet out of sight and out of the way when not in use. One of these is a roll-out movie theater in a 12-inch-deep closet with a separate, built-in disappearing music theater wall. There are also combination walls with several compact built-ins which can be completely concealed. Another solution is a multiarea disappearing sound-sight layout. It includes mechanically and electronically moving platforms, doors, and components as well as a separate stereo wall unit with adjustable speakers.

An innovation called the "Living Wall" is also described. It provides an attractive and technically perfect audio-visual entertainment center for use in the privacy of the home.

Although this chapter is concerned primarily with entertainment facilities such as mechanized entertainment walls and their modifications, you will find many other ideas and features as well. Noteworthy is the fact that all of these functions can be either manually controlled and activated, or, as will be described in this chapter, include the most sophisticated electronic control systems known to man; yet these systems or any parts are readily available.

**Built-in home movie theater**

Most people do not take full advantage of their slide and film projectors because of the inconvenience involved in setting up and putting away the equipment. The built-in movie theater shown in Figure 1 was created to change this attitude. It consists of a roll-out cart that holds slide and film projectors mounted on lazy susan disks, a Picture Master screen, and enough space to store at least 80 canned films, many boxes of slides, a movie camera, tripods, and any extras you might have. All of this can be built into a space 6 feet high, 5 feet wide, and 12 inches deep. In this particular case, the cabinet was built all the way to the 8-foot-high ceiling, adding nearly 10 cubic feet of vital storage space.

This unit requires so little area it can be installed in an apartment with limited wall space, while actually improving the decor in that area. Mount ¾-inch-thick by 3-inch-wide back cross pieces to the bottom of the cabinet top and the bottom of the two fixed shelves. The cabinet remains fixed to the wall with 6 screws through the strips into the wall studs, using 2½-inch-long screws.

The 10-inch-deep roll-out cart has 2 vertical support panels mounted to a 2¾-inch recessed center panel made of ¾-inch plywood with 8-inch folding brackets (Stanley 8 x 8 inch). These brackets lock the panels into position (90 degrees) once the doors of the main built-in unit are open (Figure 2). The cart itself rests on 2 casters mounted to the recessed bottom. The back wall and the folding doors keep the cart from tilting over. Therefore, the panel supports must be opened once the main doors are opened. When the panels of the portable cart are open, a ¾-x-3-inch-wide by 18-inch-long hardwood sliding leg slotted in the center and made adjustable by using bolts, washers and wing nuts to lock them in place, puts the cart into a self-supporting position and ready to roll. Three-inch-square blocks (1½ inches thick)

Fig. 1.   (opposite page) Living Wall.

Fig. 2.　Built-in home movie theater.

on the bottom of each leg support the additional 2 casters. The cart is rolled away from the enclosure, where a permanently mounted screen can be pulled down and hooked into position. Depending on the type of projector and the lens, the distance of the cart from the

Fig. 3. Three ¾-inch tops make up the upper portion of the portable projector cart. The first is a plain top to which the metal turn discs are fitted. The second top just clears the turn discs by ¼ inch all around. As the discs are nearly 1 inch thick, they will extend beyond the ¾-inch plywood so as to allow it to turn freely.

Fig. 4. The final top is cut into segments to clear the turning platforms while joining all parts neatly.

screen is determined and the proper picture size and focus are achieved.

Simply position the projectors by turning them on their adjustable disk bases (Figures 3 and 4) in order to conserve space. The ¾-inch plywood bases attached to the 8-inch-diameter metal turn disks were cut straight on 2 parallel sides to conform with the depth of the top.

To put away the equipment, the projectors turn sideways to occupy the least amount of space. The support wings are folded in, and the adjustable caster leg strips are loosened and moved back up and the wing nuts are tightened again. The cart is then pushed back into its original spot. The bi-fold doors to the enclosure which are mounted on Stanley hardware are closed, and everything is out of sight. This operation should take a maximum of two or three minutes to set up or put away. Because of the shallow construction of this unit, it appears as only a paneled section; the use of beautifully matched grain Weldwood walnut makes it a decorative asset as well.

**Built-in combination TV-stereo music theaters**

Because television entertainment has become a way of life in most homes, the TV has been accepted as part of the surroundings and decor of a room. There is no reason why this situation cannot be improved—why not do something with the TV when it is not in use? The answer was to build an enclosure to provide TV storage and to make all stereo, record, and tape equipment readily accessible (Figures 6 and 7). The three main sections containing the TV set, the tuner and amplifier, and the record player are individual compartments each on separate slides (available from Grant Pulley & Hardware Corp., through your dealer) which carry the weight to full extension. The main reason for designing a slide-out unit containing the tuner and amplifier was that it was advisable to allow easy access to the equipment whose chassis were exposed on the top.

While meeting the major goals of TV storage and readily accessible equipment, the system provided for adjustable TV viewing through the use of sliding as well as turning platforms.

Fig. 5.   Built-in combination TV-stereo music theater, with paneled doors closed.

Fig. 6.   TV-stereo unit inside built-out wall.

Fig. 7.   TV-stereo unit pulled out and TV turned around to desired position.

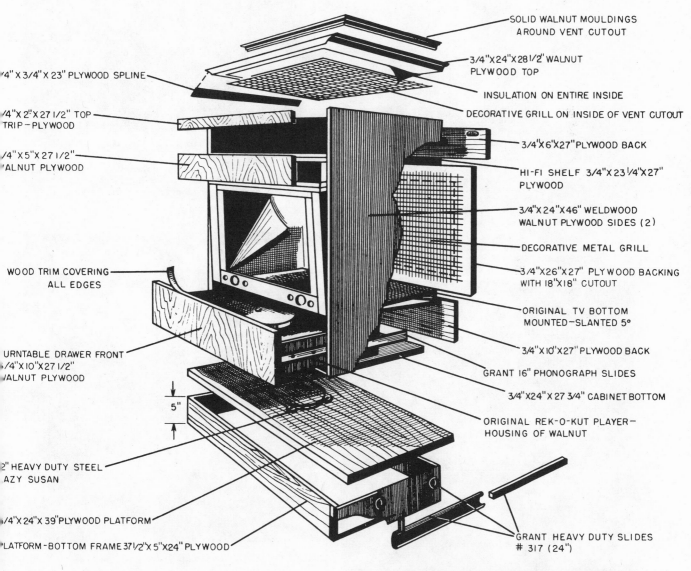

SOLID WALNUT MOULDINGS
AROUND VENT CUTOUT

3/4"X24"X28 1/2" WALNUT
PLYWOOD TOP

INSULATION ON ENTIRE INSIDE

DECORATIVE GRILL ON INSIDE OF VENT CUTOUT

3/4"X6"X27"PLYWOOD BACK

HI-FI SHELF 3/4"X 23 1/4"X27"
PLYWOOD

3/4"X 24"X 46" WELDWOOD
WALNUT PLYWOOD SIDES (2)

DECORATIVE METAL GRILL

3/4"X26"X 27" PLYWOOD BACKING
WITH 18"X18" CUTOUT

ORIGINAL TV BOTTOM
MOUNTED—SLANTED 5°

3/4"X10"X27"PLYWOOD BACK

GRANT 16" PHONOGRAPH SLIDES

3/4"X24"X 27 3/4" CABINET BOTTOM

ORIGINAL REK-O-KUT PLAYER—
HOUSING OF WALNUT

GRANT HEAVY DUTY SLIDES
# 317 (24")

4"X 3/4"X 23" PLYWOOD SPLINE

/4"X 2"X 27 1/2" TOP
TRIP—PLYWOOD

/4"X5"X27 1/2"
ALNUT PLYWOOD

WOOD TRIM COVERING
ALL EDGES

URNTABLE DRAWER FRONT
/4"X10"X27 1/2"
ALNUT PLYWOOD

5"

2" HEAVY DUTY STEEL
AZY SUSAN

/4"X 24"X 39"PLYWOOD PLATFORM

LATFORM-BOTTOM FRAME 37 1/2"X 5"X24" PLYWOOD

## SLIDE-OUT TV-STEREO UNIT

Fig. 8.

Fig. 9. Corner unit contains elaborate speaker system (bottom), a lazy susan record storage (top), with a pull-out tape player in center.

Fig. 11. A wall-like folding door system (made of ¾-inch Novoply covered outside with ¼-inch prefinished paneling) covers a multitude of entertainment equipment and storage. The TV slides out and turns easily through the doors and permits clear viewing from all sides.

Fig. 10. Pull-out tape player in open position.

Fig. 12. One of the stereo speakers was convenient for a forced air outlet on top. (Note vent grille above.) TV is mounted on a steel turn disc and slides out on a platform nearly to full extension. Lazy susan record storage adjacent and tape drawers below take up just about every inch of available space. The tape deck in the drawer is mounted on full extension slides (Grant 300 series).

Upkeep of the equipment and home maintenance were simplified by the elimination of horizontal surfaces. Besides the decorative advantages of such a system, it makes it easy to keep the stereo equipment covered.

The corner music unit in Figures 9 and 10 contains a speaker system, handy revolving record storage and a semicircular drawer which holds a tape recorder.

The built-in basement wall in Figures 11 and 12 illustrates a setup similar in concept, but slightly different in execution. Similar components are included, but they are built in along a flat wall section as opposed to a corner space.

In each of the above built-ins, the use of folding doors to close off the systems is both desirable and practical.

### Remote-controlled multisectional entertainment

A room does not always permit the incorporation of centralized setups such as those just described. Entertainment centers have to be designed so they will function properly no matter what the physical nature of the room. The

Fig. 13. As part of a multiple entertainment system, left and right end cabinets both contain all necessary stereo equipment and controllable speaker housings which, when closed, match the cabinets.

Fig. 14. The platform is mounted on Grant heavy-duty ball-bearing slides in back and the 2-x-7-foot door that covers the housing is opened and closed with an electronically controlled motor. As soon as the door is open and the projector platform starts to move out, the ceiling cover of the movie screen opens and at the same time and with the same speed the projectors turn, the speakers turn, the screen lowers, the drapes close, and the lights dim to 15 percent. Sight and sound begin with the same timing. At the end of the program, the entire procedure reverses itself: everything is hidden and the lights go back to their preset original intensity. This can be overpassed by the manual "hold" switch which enables you to change film and if necessary also to change the synchronized sound track on the tape deck, unless of course you are using a sound film. The interconnected sound system of this feature is illustrated in Figure 13.

important thing to remember is that all means of entertainment, such as movies or even TV, should be installed so that they do not obstruct the main function of the room (Figures 13 and 14).

Because of two large windows with low casements, this entertainment room was partially encircled with low cantilevered cabinet units. Stereo equipment as well as adjustable speakers were built into the 2 units on either side of the fireplace on the north wall. On the south side, the 2 full walls on either side of the terrace doors were built out 20 inches, thus creating 2 large enclosures. The one on the left side was used for portable table and chair storage, and the one on the right was used for a disappearing movie and slide projection platform as well as for film and slide storage (Figure 13). The only other item necessary to complete this overall setup was the movie screen, which was attached to the false ceiling cross-beam farthest from the projection booth.

In order to appreciate this feature fully, it is important to see what happens when the entire system is activated. Movie or slide viewing requires only pushing one of the three buttons which control the movie projector, the slide projector, and the sound system. A fourth switch turns off all systems.

If a sound movie is selected, the 2 speaker enclosures flanking the fireplace turn to the correct position; the amplifier turns on at once; the lid in the ceiling beam opens and the screen lowers itself (weights mounted to the bottom strip ensure a taut, well-stretched screen). Simultaneously, all drapes close and all lights dim out except for 3 wallwasher lights which remain at 20 percent illumination. At the same time and at the same speed, the door of the projector booth opens and a cart that holds the projectors on turning discs slides out. One of the discs (according to the selector) turns the projector to the correct projection aim. Once the projector clicks into position, it will start (unless manual control is desired). In other words, if the projectors are carefully and properly loaded and everything prepared, the push of one or two buttons begins a dramatic series of events.

When the show is over, merely push the

off button and everything will return to its original position and the lights will go on to their original setting.

When the system is shut off, thus cutting electric power feeding this circuit, everything can be operated manually by utilizing the slip clutches that are mounted on all the sprocket pulleys (for safety as well as for manual operation). Slip clutches are attached to motorized chain driving pulleys (as in all such installations) in order to allow the motor to idle should it be obstructed.

The adjustable speaker units on both sides of the fireplace are controlled from 3 different positions: behind the bar, at the projector booth, and at the entrance to the room. The FM channel of the amplifier can also be turned on remotely from any one of these 3 positions. Stereo speaker units function best when the listening point is about 12 feet from the speakers. In this system, the sound projection from

each of the 2 speakers is automatically adjusted to meet in the area where the control was pushed. This produces a more precise sound. When not in use, the speakers turn into their cabinet housing and all that is exposed are matching grain wood panels.

A great deal of action has been added to this area without tarnishing the clean lines of the room. If the same equipment were used in a conventional, nonbuilt-in setup, the room would be cluttered by many different-sized machine units with different finishes.

Although this particular room involved a generous budget, a smaller budget should not rule out such designs. It is true that very fine materials were used here (Macassar ebony, for instance), but the room would function equally well if pine or birch were selected. What really counts are the functional and creative aspects of the room which give it infinite action without any sign of mechanical rigging.

Fig. 15. The Living Wall in closed position.

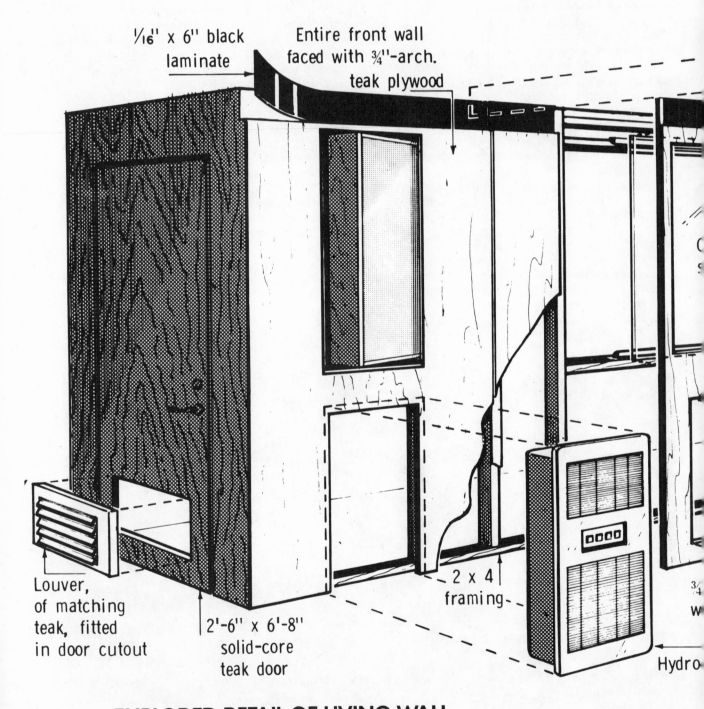

1/16" x 6" black laminate

Entire front wall faced with 3/4"-arch. teak plywood

Louver, of matching teak, fitted in door cutout

2'-6" x 6'-8" solid-core teak door

2 x 4 framing

Hydro

## Fig. 16. **EXPLODED DETAIL OF LIVING WALL**

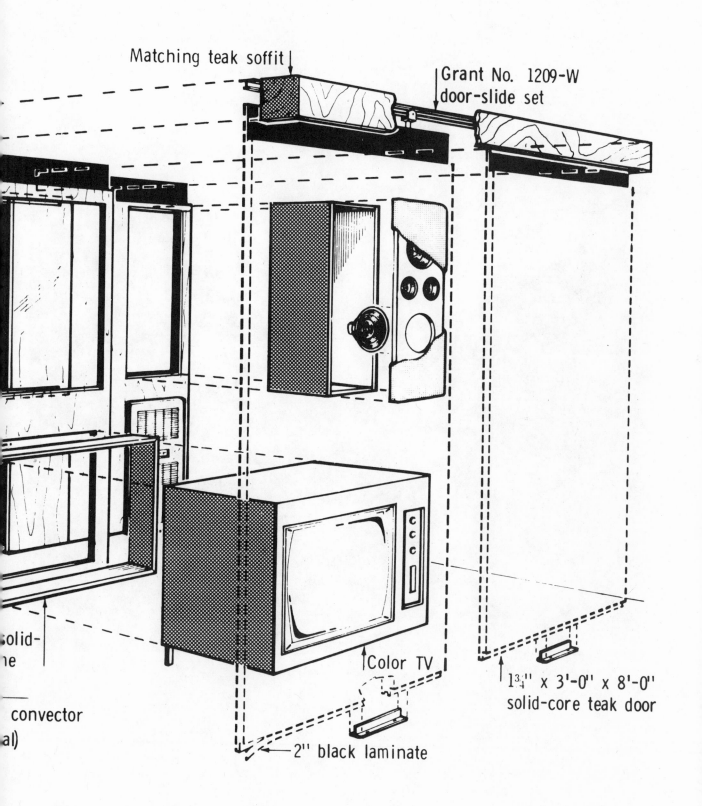

Matching teak soffit

Grant No. 1209-W
door-slide set

Color TV

$1\frac{3}{4}$'' x 3'-0'' x 8'-0''
solid-core teak door

2'' black laminate

Solid-
ne

convector
al)

Fig. 17. The Living Wall in open position.

## The Living Wall

More than any of the areas discussed so far, the Living Wall shown in Figures 15, 16, and 17 represents the ultimate in home entertainment. Its main component is the rear projection wall, a device first used successfully within the business community. If the business world found this solution so readily acceptable and adaptable to its needs, might not the enterprising homeowner also be ready for such a change? This question led to the idea for a home Living Wall. It is located in the House of Ideas in the far corner of the family living room (see Figure 1).

The Living Wall performs every possible function related to audio-video entertainment. It covers a maximum area of 5½ feet in depth and up to 14 feet in width and extends from floor to ceiling. It has directional stereo speakers which move out of sight when not in use and a minimum 4-x-4-foot movie screen which also disappears. There is even a laboratory for editing films and slides. The design for this intriguing project is offered here as a guide for any who are venturesome enough to try the unusual.

## Projection room

*Size:* A projection room is the key to this entire setup (see Figure 18). It must be no less than 50 inches deep from front to back; 10 feet wide left to right; and 7 feet high. While these minimum dimensions are adequate, more involved activities such as splicing and editing would require increased dimensions, such as 66 inches deep, 14 feet wide, and 7½ feet high, roomy enough to service 8 projectors and allow space for more specialized activities.

The projection room must face a room no less than 16 feet deep (from the screen surface). For example, installing such a setup at the end of a playroom would optimally require an overall room length of no less than 20 feet.

*Entrance:* Constructing a projection room means first building a 2-x-4-inch stud-type partition (16 inches on center), leaving the opening for an entrance door of no less than 2 feet x 6 feet 8 inches. The width of the entrance door, however, must be added to the 10-foot width, which could result in an overall dimension of 12½ feet. A room 12 feet wide and 18 to 20 feet long would certainly be the very minimum. Of course, if the room were somewhat larger, especially wider, it would then be possible to install the entrance door to the projection quarters on the end, as was done in the model. In such cases, the door could be wider by at least 6 inches.

*Screen:* Another item to consider when building the partition is the screen. In order to aid in soundproofing and damping out projector noises, it should be fashioned of ¼-inch polarized glass. The size of the screen, considering the minimum room size available, should be no less than 4 x 4 feet. If the room were much larger, perhaps half again the size quoted, then the glass screen could be 5 feet wide. It would remain 4 feet high because the projection proportion usually works on a ratio of 3 x 2, or, as in this case, 4 x 3 (approx.).

Professional experiences reveal that for best rear projection results, it is advisable to use 1:1.5 lenses. These lenses will give a performance of 1½ times the distance of the screen width. As an example: If you have a 4-foot-wide screen, as in this case, and are using a 1:1.5 lens, you would have to keep the projector 6 feet away from the screen. This would be dividing it up between the distance from the projector lens back to the mirror and to the screen, as shown in Figure 18. There are, however, 1:1.0 lenses available for most projectors, especially slide projectors like the Carousels (all by Kodak) used for this project. These lenses facilitate a performance of a 1:1 ratio, meaning that for a 4-foot-wide screen, the projector has to be a total of 4 feet away from the rear of the screen. This distance, considering that it will be divided between the projector and mirror, comes in very handy where space problems are apparent. However, optical experts feel that a 1:1.0 lens has very little flexibility as far as the characteristic of the projector is concerned, so that if at all possible, a 1:1.5 lens is recommended.

The picture ratio on slide-projected pictures is 4 feet wide and 3 feet high on horizontal, and the opposite on vertical slides. On film projectors the ratio is again 4 feet wide

# PLAN OF REAR PROJECTION SYSTEM

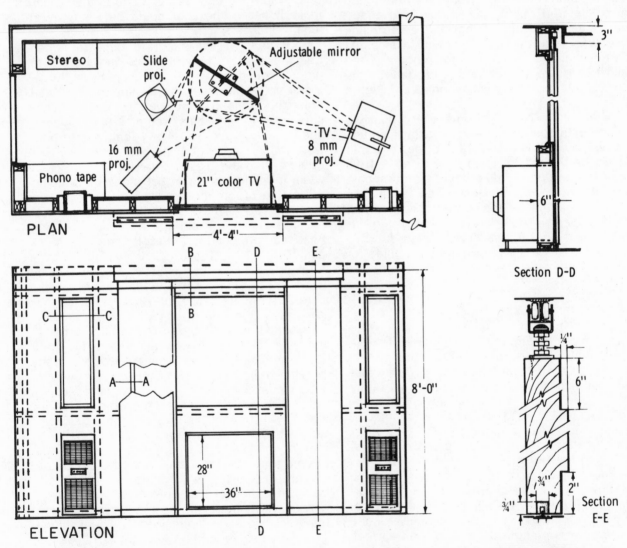

Stereo

Slide proj.

Adjustable mirror

16 mm proj.

Phono tape

TV 8 mm proj.

21" color TV

4'-4"

PLAN

ELEVATION

8'-0"

28"

36"

3"

6"

Section D-D

¼"

6"

¾"

2"

¾"

Section E-E

## FRONT OF LIVING WALL

# REAR PROJECTION DETAIL

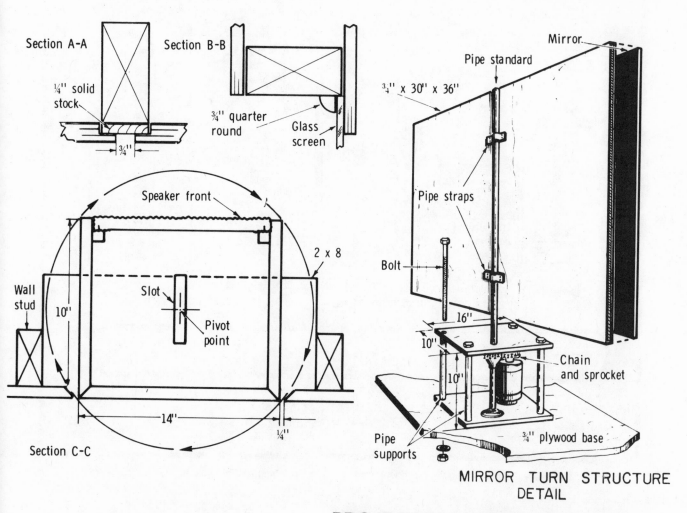

Section A-A

¼" solid stock

¾"

Section B-B

¾" quarter round

Glass screen

Speaker front

2 x 8

Wall stud

10"

Slot

Pivot point

14"

¼"

Section C-C

¾" x 30" x 36"

Mirror

Pipe standard

Pipe straps

Bolt

16"

10"

10"

Chain and sprocket

Pipe supports

¾" plywood base

## MIRROR TURN STRUCTURE DETAIL

# PROJECTION MIRROR SYSTEM

Fig. 18.

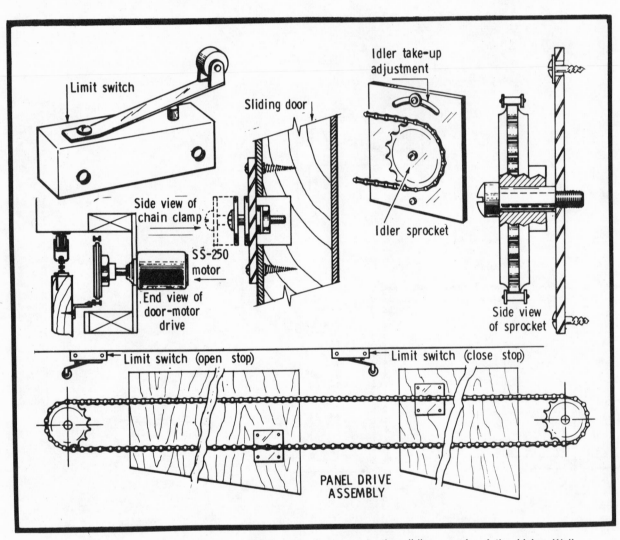

Fig. 19.  This detail refers to all the pertinent parts that operate the sliding panels of the Living Wall.

and 3 feet high. There are slight variations, running into decimals on some projections, but by slightly overshooting the projection screen, one can make it up without any noticeable effect. See plan of Figure 18 for a more complete explanation.

*Speakers:* The speakers on each side of the projection screen must be considered next because an adequate frame support for them must be built into the stud wall. In the model installation, the speakers had to be shorter due to the two heater radiators in the space below them (see Figures 16 and 18). If such heating units are not being considered, then the preferable alternative would be to build the speaker housings floor to ceiling (less the thickness of the top and bottom 2 x 4 plates onto which ¾-inch plywood is mounted on top and bottom, flush in front). These thicknesses would have to be subtracted from the floor-to-ceiling clearance for each speaker, as well as the necessary clearances for the pivots and plates, whether or not they are being motorized. And when the speakers are laid out, there should be an 8-foot minimum center distance (from the center of one to the center of the other) between the two speakers.

While it is desirable to use a factory assemblage of components, as was done originally for the Living Wall, custom assembly was the best solution for other areas and for the overall balance of the sound system. And there still are those who prefer to do what this author did: with proper guidance, create a sound system using a selection of components that they favor most.

*Television casing:* In addition to provision for the speakers and screen, the Living Wall has an opening below the screen (Figure 17) for a large remote-controlled color television set. Although a projection television is included (see page 199) on the inside, it produces only black and white pictures.

*Covering the partition framework:* When the framing is completed, insulation (Owens-Corning Fiberglas friction-fit type pads) is put between the studs. The outside paneling of the partition is ¾-inch plywood, but other wall coverings such as ½-inch plaster wall board or ¼-inch prefinished paneling are also acceptable. The wall enclosure here is covered with ¾-inch architectural continuous grain Weldwood teak paneling on the outside and with ½-inch special sound-deadening boards on the inside walls, painted flat black.

The ceiling, also painted black, is modular fiberglass and aluminum, a suspension system that is fire- and soundproof (by Owens-Corning). Except for the center row of the fiberglass inserts, which are translucent, all inserts of this ceiling structure are of ½-inch fiberglass. The floor is covered with black vinyl-asbestos tiles. A dark color scheme was chosen to keep reflection glare to a minimum.

*Covering the screen:* The floor-to-ceiling covering for the screen section consists of two 3-x-7-foot teak veneer doors. They are mounted on Grant No. 1209-W hardware and fastened to a horizontally installed chain with sprockets and slip clutches which is driven by a Superior SS-250 Slo-Syn reversible motor (Figure 19). This makes it possible to open and close the doors electrically. They could also be manually controlled. Simply mount the doors to heavy-duty Grant hardware and slide them apart manually. The sprocket and chain system, as well as all necessary brackets, are concealed by a matching wood cornice, clearing the doors in depth, flush with the upper edge of the doors and mounted snug against the ceiling.

Instead of doors, a pair of ceiling-mounted heavy drapes could also be installed to function either manually or electrically. They could even be remotely controlled (as these doors are) using a drapery motor.

*Room temperature:* A safe temperature is maintained in the projection room by installing a 22-inch Emerson (Chromalox) exhaust fan with outside self-adjusting louvers on the exterior house wall. This was connected to a self-starting wall-mounted thermostatic switch which would start the fan should the room build up too much heat.

# DETAIL SPEAKER CABINET AND INSTALLATION
## ALSO REAR PROJECTION STANDS & CABINETS

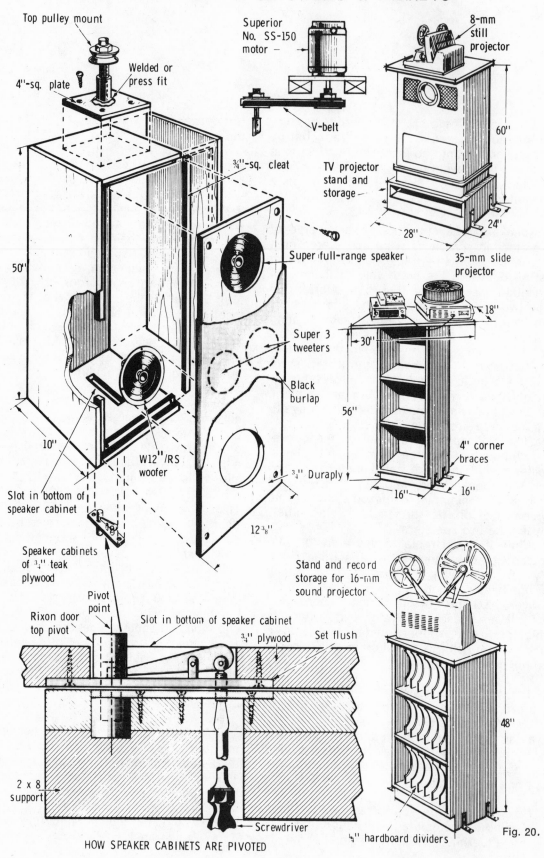

Top pulley mount

4"-sq. plate

Welded or press fit

Superior No. SS-150 motor —

V-belt

8-mm still projector

60"

¾"-sq. cleat

TV projector stand and storage

28"

24"

35-mm slide projector

50'

Super full-range speaker

18"

30"

Super 3 tweeters

Black burlap

56"

W12"/RS woofer

4" corner braces

10'

Slot in bottom of speaker cabinet

16"

16"

¾" Duraply

12 ³⁄₈"

Speaker cabinets of ¾" teak plywood

Pivot point

Rixon door top pivot

Slot in bottom of speaker cabinet

¾" plywood

Set flush

Stand and record storage for 16-mm sound projector

48"

2 x 8 support

Screwdriver

¼" hardboard dividers

Fig. 20.

HOW SPEAKER CABINETS ARE PIVOTED

## Sound system

*Speakers:* The selection of the loudspeaker system was given very careful thought. It had to be capable of both extended and distortion-free reproduction and yet stay within the limitations of reasonable budget and space requirements. The speaker units are interconnected, as shown in Figure 20, and contained within specially designed enclosures. The 12-inch speakers handle mid-range tones, while the treble range is further supported by the tweeters. Further tone expansion is achieved by the 12-inch woofers supporting the low range. A variable control permits adjustment of the level of sound output from the tweeter to suit the acoustics of the room. (High frequency sounds are rapidly absorbed by drapes, carpets, upholstered furniture, etc.) Note that the tweeters are also contained within a special housing inside the cabinet. This is to keep the powerful 12-inch speakers from impressing their bass tones on the lighter and more delicate diaphragm of the tweeters.

*Speaker installation:* When installing the speakers (Figure 21) on the ¾-inch baffle board made of Novoply (chipboard), distribute them so that the center of speaker activity is aimed at the center ear-height of the average person when seated on a dining room chair.

*Technical sound design:* The bass operates as an acoustic transformer in the bass range, converting low magnitudes of energy to levels many times greater and, additionally, purer than was previously achieved. Utilizing a specially designed 8-inch woofer, bass notes as low as 30 Hz can be solidly reproduced with a tight, clean sound, denoting excellent transient response and freedom from audible harmonic distortion.

To provide a proper match for the exceptional efficiency of the bass section, a "mid-range" pyramidal horn/compression driver unit is used, to eliminate the need of the usual crossover network to interrupt the critical, ear-sensitive mid-range spectrum which would produce distortion. The operating range of this unit is 1500 to 15,000 Hz. The wide-angle dispersion pattern is uniform in all directions. Also, a new inert material used in the horn totally eliminates metallic coloration of sound.

Although the "mid-range" horn reproduces frequences well beyond 15,000 Hz, where most modest-sized speaker systems end, it is desirable to extend response to at least 20,000 Hz or beyond, in order to preserve original sonic balance and hence musical timbre of instruments in the lower frequency ranges.

The sensitivity of this new sound system is so high that amplifiers or receivers legitimately rated at as low as 15 watts RMS per channel will produce sound levels that are more than adequate for normal home listening. This speaker system also requires much less amplifier power.

On the other hand, Bic Venturi speakers can handle amplifiers and receivers rated as high as 75 watts RMS per channel with ease and reliability, providing sound pressure levels rivaling the loudest concert hall passages and the noisiest discotheques.

If a custom speaker setup (as shown in this feature) is going to be selected, the speaker enclosures are built as indicated below. However, in order to achieve maximum quality in sound reproduction, the inside surfaces of each enclosure should be lined with insulation, so that no extraneous sound can vibrate or distort the pure sound desired.

First of all, the enclosure cabinet should be built of ¾-inch plywood using tongue and groove construction and a good grade glue for minimum cabinet vibration and a perfect airtight seal (Figure 22). The baffle board should be of ¾-inch-thick chipboard (Novoply) and the speakers should be mounted with bolts rather than screws, countersunk in front.

Because the sound is produced within an area behind the speaker cove itself, the enclosure must be sound-absorbent on the inside, especially if the enclosure is completely sealed in back. This will allow the different frequency sound levels to develop and egress through the front without distortion. A product called Tufflex, which is about ½ inch thick, semifirm, and, most important, three-dimensional, is sound-

Fig. 21. Both identical speaker panels reveal the tweeter, the 12-inch midrange, and a 12-inch woofer and capacitor. There are also 1-x-4-inch slots cut horizontally between both 12-inch speakers to release extensive treble.

Fig. 22. Speaker housing with speaker panel removed (see Tufflex lining on all surfaces).

Fig. 23. Any preferred tuner amplifier (all transistor).

Fig. 24. Garrard record player. Note tone-arm balancer.

Fig. 25. Saba tape recorder-player and Garrard record player.

Fig. 26. Film editing area with editor and Kodak cutter-splicer.

absorbent and very useful for speaker housings. Other products such as fiberglass pads have been used successfully, but the Tufflex technique has proven far more satisfactory, especially when used to line all inner surfaces of the speaker enclosures, as was done here.

The speaker cabinets are built on a pivot (Figure 20) so they can be turned to a perfect preset angle to project sound toward the most desirable area. Or, as in this installation, through remote control and relay connections, these speakers will face the area or spot from which they are "called," thus eliminating the need to sit in one spot to get a perfect stereo reception. Whether you build in a factory-enclosed speaker system or a custom unit, utilize available floor-to-ceiling space by building tall, narrow units which match the outside when closed.

*Speaker cloths:* A few years ago people knew little about speaker cloths. In the mid-sixties, various manufacturers started to supply more decorative, better textured fabrics. A speaker cloth should be webbed of hard fibers, rather than ordinary wool or cotton which could obstruct clear sound projection. Today's cloths are also attractive enough to match the finest decor. Charcoal knobby sack cloth was used for the speaker cabinet fronts in this feature.

Grille material in the newest speakers has changed over, for the most part, to "reticulated" foam, which is far more transparent to sound than any other type of material. It is available in various colors, as well as in black.

When closed, the speaker cabinets match the front surface of the Living Wall enclosure in continuous wood grain, and are therefore concealed.

A TV and FM antenna system is, of course, imperative in an up-to-date installation. Such a system was installed in the House of Ideas along with an amplified booster system to improve the reception. With connecting receptacles in every room for independent FM radio and TV use, this system (engineered and fabricated by the Jerrold Corporation) not only affords consistent spread of the antenna per-

formance for use in various localities, but it also strengthens reception.

Almost all the sound units (6 in this particular installation including sound film production) are connected to the stereo speaker system. Tuning and amplification are, of course, very important, as are the speaker qualities. While the price structure of stereo tuning equipment will vary, the reasonably priced units are good enough to produce very fine sound, providing the speaker system is well balanced and carefully installed.

**The projection television**

This is perhaps the only unusual item in this room, not known to many, but important because it is competitively priced and geared for home consumption. (It must be serviced by a TV repairman, however.) Its unique performance certainly justifies its inclusion in this projection setup. The Saba Telerama used for this Living Wall projects a picture on a movie screen up to 52½ inches wide by 38½ inches high, at a distance of approximately 7½ feet (see plan). The only disadvantage is that it operates on tubes, and these, as well as other parts, come from West Germany and are stocked mostly in German TV and hi-fi sales and service stores. There are also other TV projection units (some made in the U.S.A.) available. General Electric is about to market a color and black and white TV projector.

While the performance, size, and weight, as well as the optical gun (single lens) one-time adjustment, etc., of this G.E. PG 5000 are incredible, its price is in the low to medium five-figure range. However, as nearly all products in the House of Ideas originate from commercially-oriented manufacturers, there is good reason to foresee a projection TV made and serviced by G.E., just like any of the other appliances in our homes. Since this unit was just introduced, perhaps the better knowledge of and demand for a projection TV for our homes may initiate further adjustments, coupled with large production to bring such a unit within the price range of more people.

In the model theater feature, this unit operates via rear projection, as do all the other projectors, movies or slides, generally used. This is only possible with a projection TV system (see Figure 18) similar to those now manufactured by the electronic giants which are in use (as front projectors) in movie houses for closed circuit TV productions of sporting events. Any TV projector can be used for either front or rear projection. The projection lens of the SabaTelerama (Schmidt lens), one of the original devices for this type of projection, is a multi-mirror 8-inch round aperture.

### About rear projection

The picture is projected onto a 30-x-30-inch front surface plated mirror (front surface in order to avoid double ghost-like images). The image is then reflected onto the rear screen, thus correctly exposing the picture. The mirror is mounted with a 1½-inch steel rod to a metal structure (see Figure 18) which houses the SS-250 Slo-Syn motor, the gear, and the limit switches. The mirror automatically turns to the side and to the selected projector which is so aimed as to allow the mirror to complete the proper turn (see plan). It is stopped with a limit switch first, in order to complete the electronic cycle, but it can also be stopped against a magnetic catch. Accuracy is extremely important because if the mirror overrides its stop even by as slight a margin as $\frac{1}{16}$ inch at a time, after several uses it could easily be out of line enough to project the picture partially off the screen. Since the projector stands had to be positioned in certain specific areas, there was very little space available for any movement. In fact, the 2-inch wide-angle lenses used on the Carousel 850 (Kodak), which are stacked (on shelves) on top of each other, clear the mirror by only $\frac{5}{16}$ inch (when it turns), which proves how precise these projector placements must be.

Thanks to this successful arrangement, 8 different projectors produce perfect and undistorted pictures, by projecting them onto a mirror which in turn reflects them to the back of the screen, nearly filling it in its proper proportion. The remarkable fact is that, with the exception of the TV projector and the Kodak 16mm and Super 8 Sound Projectors, the equipment is not specialized or expensive. The only additional expense for any of these projectors is the cost of wide-angle lenses needed to qualify the projectors for a production of a large exposure at a short distance. As found in this installation, to meet the requirements of a regular lens, the projector in this case would have to be placed 8 feet or more from the mirror, and even more from the screen (see plan).

The most outstanding advantage of rear projection is the enormous footage gained by criss-cross projection and special lenses. Ordinarily, this could be achieved only in a much larger area. It is also appealing because the equipment is out of the way during and after presentation. This eliminates projector noises and is better for the equipment itself.

The key to success in planning and organizing an all-complete projection room is to take full advantage of its essential privacy and the proximity of all related equipment.

### Turntable

The Garrard SL95 automatic transcription turntable was chosen for playing records (Figures 24 and 25). A turntable must be capable of many years of trouble-free use with minimum wear to the records, and the low mass tone arm on the SL95 is balanced and calibrated to function satisfactorily at exceptionally low stylus pressure. (See tone arm balancer, Figure 24.)

### Tape recorder

The tape recorder used in the model theater is a popularly priced Saba. In selecting a tape recorder, there are two important factors to consider: the proper speed and the sound projection. Very popular and proven best is 7½ IPS (inches per second). However, there is also a fairly new 15-IPS unit which is not yet perfected enough to be commercially successful. The other factor is system quadraphonic (four-channel reproduction), a double stereo sound projection surrounding the listener. As far as attachments are concerned, a good microphone is an absolute necessity. The Saba

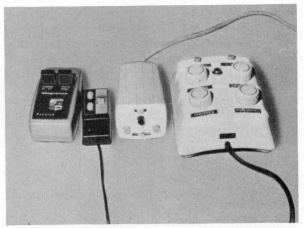

Figs. 27, 28. The permanent remote control panel for the Living Wall. The button above is the activator used before selecting any program. To the right of it is the twist lock slide projector remote control. (This is needed only if a single slide projector is used.) Otherwise, for a complete sound-narrated multi-projector program, push center button (in row of 5), and the programmer takes over.

Left to right: First is off button. Second is movie. (The controls in the projection room must be preset to organize the program since there are several movie projectors and several slide projectors.) Third is slide programmer. Fourth is projection TV. Fifth is hi-fi or stereo. The larger square button below is for 8mm silent film, and is to be preset in the projection booth controls. The smaller multiprong plug (to right) is for full remote controlled Saba stereo. The larger multiprong plug (to left) is for the TV projector. The small flip switch to the left of the larger multireceptacle is the off and on switch which opens and closes all drapes automatically. Above the control board are three banks of illuminated low-voltage switches (only part of one is shown). The entire general living area is controlled by these switches. Two more banks of the same switches, repeating the same functions, are placed in such strategic areas as the entrance, covered by a slim planter, and the Living Kitchen. This rather complete

and fussy control system is mostly covered by drapes and a planter in that corner.

You cannot overrule the lighting from any other station while the master button has activated the electronic brain, unless you push the off button, thus stopping all projection at once. The same is true for the multiswitch drapery controls.

Above, left to right: Magnavox color TV control, slide projector control, Saba stereo control, Saba projection TV control. Further down on the panel (not shown) are three buttons. The first activates the closed circuit camera over the entrance, allowing the occupant to see on the TV screen who is at the front door before using the Emerson Intercom System. To bring the normal TV program back again, the button is released. The second button is a panic button setting off an enormous noise with three bell systems on the outside. The third is to cut off the current entirely from this system, thus enabling one to manually turn the speakers or open the slide wall panels covering the screen as well as the four panels covering the Continental Bar Room.

All the controls shown here will enable one to just sit and play magic. There are more coaxial cables (mostly 8 and 16 pair Belden) for possible future use in the wall. By removing the control panel with a screwdriver, the reserve cables can be coiled and fastened against the stud, ready to be used for new actions. For best performance, thinner cables use less room in and around the electronic brain; for safety, the current which goes through the cables to the switches and instruments is converted from 110 volts to 12 volts by relays.

recorder used here has a split-up microphone which, when needed, becomes a two-microphone stereo recording system. However, the trend is toward cassette-type machines, now that such units have reached the quality of reel-to-reel.

### Remote control

Although simultaneous use of remote and manual control is likely to involve more work than the usual projection, the results are worth it. If the entire operation is done electronically, as in the Living Wall, everything will move smoothly into place at the proper time with just the push of a button.

All the remote controls for this system are installed in a wall panel behind a planter at the end of the room opposite the theater. As shown in Figure 27, the controls are operated by means of buttons on the control panel or plug-in receptacles for removable controls, which are furnished by the manufacturers of this particular equipment. For instance, the Kodak 850 self-focusing slide Carousel unit has a small control to drive forward or backward as desired. By connecting an extension inside the projection room and off the control point in the wall, this control can be operated remotely. The same system is used for the Kodak RA-950 random access Carousel projector. However, in this instance, it carries a much larger remote control device. These controls are removable.

### Slide projection

The slide projectors in the Living Wall serve in a far broader capacity than is commonly expected. In order to avoid the lack of enthusiasm that results when slides are shown in the usual manner, an exciting program using both the 850 and the 950 Kodak slide projectors can be arranged. The use of cinema equipment, especially in concert with any other projector—even slides—can produce stimulating results.

The No. 950 is a random selector projector, while the No. 850 only moves forward and backward. The random selector will show any of 80 slides; just select the number of the slide (usually taken from a guide list) and the Carou-

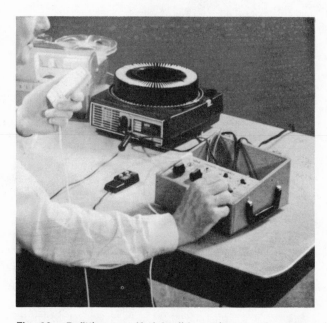

Fig. 29. Befitting any Kodak slide projector, this operation enables one to narrate each slide also using special background music (from a record or tape player) and to synchronize each slide to move on as the programmer (Kodak) provides an electronic trip signal (unnoticeable) that brings about all this motion when projected by itself. The tape recorder remains connected to the programmer and synchronized with the slide—or even a silent film. Once the button is pushed, a narrated musical slide program starts and all 80 slides move when electronically told—without your touching anything. As the library of slides in their organized carousels and background tapes as well as superimposed electronic signals on the same tapes increases, showing your travel or other experiences to your guests will no longer be an imposition.

sel slide tray will turn to the number and release the slide, dropping it into the projector slot and projecting it onto the screen. In slide projection there are newer and better ways of arranging interesting combinations of projecting, more so than are possible even with film projection. Careful planning can produce a stimulating slide program requiring no electronic installation other than just interconnecting the units.

Eighty carefully chosen slides can be projected onto the screen, accompanied by a narrative text. The timing of the text must be very exact so as not to defeat the effect of a constantly moving program. As shown in Figure 29, the narrative is recorded on a tape with the aid of a Kodak Carousel programmer, which is connected to the slide projector and tape recorder. The volume is carefully adjusted and the narrative describing the interesting highlights of the slides is spoken into the microphone. At the same time background music can be recorded from the record player. Simply pushing a button on the programmer activates a "trip" signal into the projected program, which in the final playback will automatically change the slides at the correct moment.

Entertainment becomes a simple matter of setting up the two pieces of equipment, which continue the entire program by themselves, moving the slides and, with the use of the new Kodak 850 Carousel, automatically adjusting the lenses. The host is free to enjoy the program with his guests.

A further technological refinement involves wiring 2 interconnected No. 850 projectors to a Kodak dissolve control unit. This eliminates the abrupt change from one picture to another by slowly dissolving the picture of one projector, jumping to the other projector, and slowly bringing the next picture into focus. By interconnecting the Kodak programmer with the dissolve unit and the tape recorder, these two units could move along by themselves with sound accompaniment. This network, already wired to the stereo amplifier, which in turn was connected to both stereo speakers, could now produce not only stereo sound and narration with an additional 80 slides (a total of 160 in the program), but could also, due to the "trip" signal now on the tape, move both Carousel trays alternately, exposing and dissolving each picture into the next. A program thus arranged can last for nearly a half hour or more, giving a smooth and interrelated performance and creating a memorable impression on the viewer.

Extra "fill-in" slides can be mounted on the 950 random selector Carousel, which is connected to a Kodak portable remote-control selector unit. Leave these extra slides in the random selector on standby duty to fill in a program for those viewers interested in greater details or a more personal touch. The use of the 950 projector also allows you to select whatever fill-in slide you want. These extra slides, however, must be narrated by the operator as well as manually controlled through the remote attachment.

### Film projection

Sound films are, of course, the most desirable. In the model setup the Kodak M-100 projects either Super 8 silent film or sound film. It also has the very useful built-in facility to record sound onto existing Super 8 silent films. It is possible to show a length of interesting silent film (taken with a simple Instamatic movie camera) with background music and narration (added to a tape). Thus you can create your very own custom-built sound film production.

The simplest projector in this Living Wall installation is the Kodak Instamatic 85, which at little cost does a most professional job for both 8 and Super 8 silent film, once the original lens is replaced by a wide-angle lens adjusted to the distance at hand. For instance, the total throw distance in this projection system amounts to 8 feet, requiring the use of a 7.5mm lens (available through the Fairchild Corp.). Using the new wide-angle lens at the short distance of only 8 feet, which is broken up into two 4-foot sectors behind the screen, the projection exposure fills the screen in width and falls just slightly short on top and bottom.

Although an electronic control system produces impressive effects, it is not necessarily an initial objective. The components are all ready to be placed and all structural preparations are geared for the mechanization which actually precedes the electronic controls. The more complicated installations and connections can be done whenever convenient.

### Wiring

The main wiring (such as stringing concealed cables like the 32 pair Belden Cables and a 16 pair shielded cable for the TV projector, as well as the Kodak remote control unit extension cords) must be in the wall while the initial wiring job is being done. It would be advisable to do this during construction.

Further projects along this line will entail ordering the low-voltage relay box for the remote-controlled, multiaction unit which requires the pushing of only one button, activating some 6 to 8 related consecutive actions. A helpful idea for this installation would be to bring various spare lines into the control areas to be used for future expansion.

The Living Wall was designed to set the mood for successful and functional entertainment within a given environment. By pushing a certain button, all drapes in the room close, the room's lights dim to a glow, and the speakers turn outward, while the pleasant sound of music becomes clearer as the door panels part to expose the screen, and the projector flashes on just as the doors are partially open. All this takes perhaps 20 seconds or so, during which time the nontransistorized amplifier (like an old 16mm sound projector) and the Saba Telerama are warming up so that they are ready for immediate action.

While you sit comfortably, you might select for your entertainment slides, film, projection TV, etc. Then things begin to happen: lights dim, drapes close, walls open, speakers slowly turn, and music starts as if coming closer from afar as a sharp and beautiful picture fills the screen. All this, accompanied by unmatchable sound aimed directly at you, will chill your spine every time you push that button.

Fig. 30.   View from door into closed rear projection area. Note screen (at right).

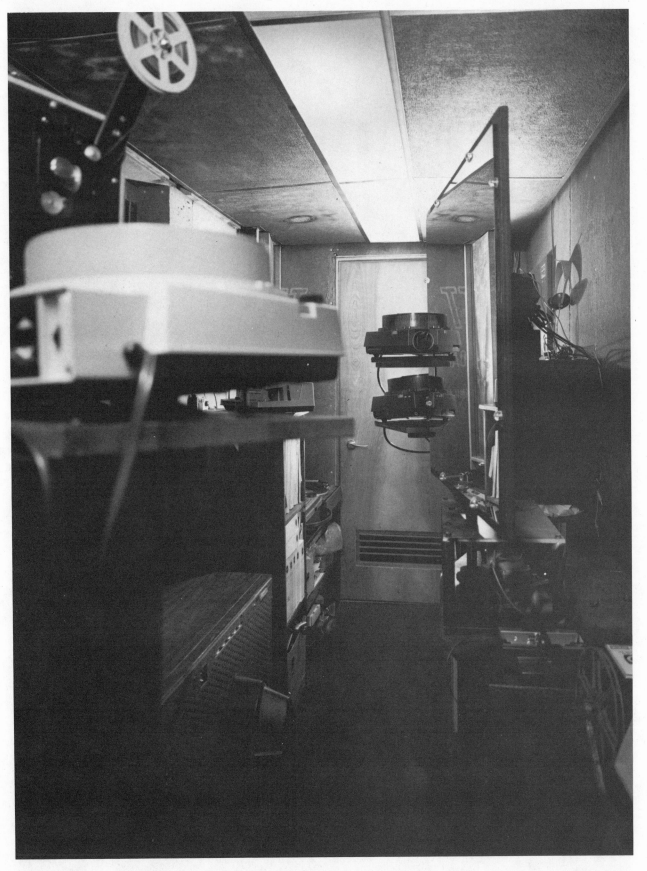

Fig. 31. View from inside rear projection room, toward door. In this case, the mirror facing the back of the projection screen is tilted to project the slides in the foreground.

Fig. 32.  Wide-angle view from door into rear projection room, showing all projectors as well as tuners, amplifiers and recorders.

Fig. 33. The Electronic Brain: a 12-volt transformed miracle built from a script designed by the author to perform infinite functions for both the Living Wall and the Continental Bar.

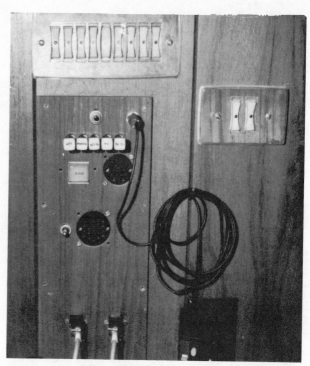

Fig. 35. Terminal of electronic brain is the control pan 1.

Fig. 34. A rare electronic relay system that did more than one had the right to expect. The ingenious and tireless talents of electronic master Stan Goldstein did what it took to put thousands of wires in the right terminals.

Fig. 36. The panel wiring on the reverse side. Due to increased demands for more and better functions, additional smaller boxes (not shown) had to be added.

# Chapter 12
# Bars

Except for its presence in the homes of a wealthy few, the private bar was almost non-existent before the advent of development houses. The usually sizable basements in these houses permitted the construction of bars in every size and shape—hence, the private bar came into its own on a popular level.

Bars have grown increasingly popular with homeowners and apartment-dwellers alike because of their versatile nature. No matter what design you have in mind, a bar can be a decorative and functional addition to any area.

## Budget

Strangely enough, when building a bar, the budget is not the first consideration. It is, of course, important, but because the same budget could apply to an 8-foot as well as a 4-foot bar, expenses are more flexible than they would be in other parts of the house. The reason for this lies mostly in the fact that a simple bar structure up to 8 feet in length (standard plywood of any thickness comes in 4-x-8-foot sheets) requires nearly the same labor and decoration as does a smaller bar. And, if going the big way, one can install back bar equipment for a 4-foot bar on the same budget as for an 8-foot bar. This is not to say that rooms of the same size cannot have entirely different-sized bars. Size is determined by how frequently the bar will be used and how many people will probably be using it.

In a discussion of bars, one should certainly not overlook the smaller-size bars, many of which are portable. A portable bar can serve the needs of its owner as well as a luxury bar can. However, a portable bar is most appropriate in smaller homes and especially in apartments. This does not necessarily mean that a portable bar is an economy. In fact, it can be more expensive to custom-build some portable bars than it is to build a standing bar. The usual reason for owning a portable bar is not economy as much as it is space considerations. Only in isolated cases is a portable bar chosen, for reasons such as space consideration, relative cost factor, decor, or conservatism.

## Proportion and design

Unfortunately, many designers and builders do not carefully consider proportion before building a bar, and as a result, the bar is often overpowering, both proportionally and financially. Too much emphasis is put on the bar structure itself and it is not built in relation to the surrounding area. Frequently this distortion becomes apparent only after the entire job is complete.

Although there is no "safe" size, proportion, or shape, and no reliable formulas to figure them out, there are fundamental considerations that should be taken into account in every case:

1. If a rather large bar is to be built in a small room, the structure must have a free-line shape and the room should become a part of the bar in motif and function. If built against one end of the room, the bar should end in a smooth, closed curve. Or if the room is long and narrow, a bar built at the end of the room and of unusual shape could turn out to be very successful. To visually shorten a long bar without losing seating or standing room, build it in a circular end section.
2. If the bar is to be a small part of a rather large area, it is advisable to create a built-in arrangement surrounding the bar, or build up the wall that leads to the bar, thus making it into a feature wall. This can be done by beginning at one end with a walled-in structure and combining it with other functions such as music centers, closets, etc. This kind of built-in, especially if done parallel to the long wall of a rectangular room, can produce a very interesting design. When the wall containing the built-in is done on a slant, the outer line should flare, stretching toward the other end of the room and reshaping that particular wall. Then there always is the back bar to balance, thus helping the overall appearance by bringing about a desirable proportion.
3. Never have a small bar free-standing in a large room. It is a better design, but still not advisable, to do it the other way around. This at least establishes a bar room, if you have room for it in the house.

After considering these guidelines, you may decide that the area in which the bar is to be built is unacceptable without physical alteration. For instance, there are certainly ways to lower high ceilings in the bar area, and slightly altering a room to accept a certain bar struc-

Fig. 1. (opposite page) The Continental Bar.

ture is entirely possible and often desirable.

### Drop-ceiling

Creating a drop-ceiling structure with an interesting three-dimensional cornice and a textured soffit, of about 12 to 18 inches in height (depending on the height of the room), following the shape of and keeping parallel with the bar rail, can be the solution for those who seek a dramatic appearance where the bar is the main feature of the area. A soffit is the bottom surface or underside of a subordinate part of a member of a building structure, such as an archway, a cornice, etc. An interesting cornice facing a drop-ceiling in a bar area can lend itself to numerous inventive solutions. For instance, the texture and color could become very interesting. Furthermore, a row of pin lights directed toward the bar top, thus creating a multiple spot pattern, is in itself extremely dramatic. A couple of wallwasher fixtures, mounted within the drop-ceiling and aimed toward the back bar, too, will create a mood that only designed lighting can achieve. In conclusion, perhaps the safest way to solve the many different problems involving the shapes and applications of the bar as successfully as possible, and carefully considering the location, is to design first and then to make a full-size projection on the floor and wall of the selected area.

### Other factors

Although a bar must be proportional to the room in size and shape, there are other factors that contribute to a successful setup. In fact, the basic dimensions of a bar are frequently determined by selected and mostly standardized available accessories such as bar stools, and other items used behind the bar like stainless steel splash and drain, built-in containers for crushed ice and ice cream, inserted glass washers, blender, mixers, and sinks—many of which can be found in used restaurant equipment stores. Some custom bars designed by the author where the floor behind the front bar was made 12 inches lower than the floor of the rest of the area were very successful. This enabled the standing host-bartender to communicate with the guests (sitting on standard low bar

stools) at eye level. Because most bars, commercial or otherwise, are 42 inches high, most available bar stools are made to suit that height. The next popular bar height is 36 inches, but stools comparable to those available for the 42-inch-high bar are quite difficult to find for the lower bar unless you choose, as is done rarely in home installation, bar stools which are standard floor-mounted and concrete-anchored (with special base supports), and the 3-inch round steel tube pedestals with self-returning seats. While this is a typical commercial installation requiring a concrete floor, it can easily turn out to be the most successful solution for a higher-budget bar. Besides, perhaps covering the bar top with bronze instead of the usual plastic laminate and covering a rather noncommercial upholstered seat with very decorative material, one can end up with a feature that is not often seen and is successful in the important bar requirements. The fullest overall achievement depends of course on the refinements of the design, especially those of the back bar, the overhead treatment, the color selection, and, very importantly, the lighting. One can choose from a variety of back bar equipment that is attractive and useful. Carefully plan and select only those items that are absolutely necessary. It is advisable, before precise planning of the working areas, to research the availability of equipment. A search for rebuilt, second-hand units may prove rewarding to the budget-minded. Once the equipment has been decided upon, one can establish the placement of the particular unit, and consequently, with all the dimensions at hand, it is possible to lay out the surrounding woodwork. The back bar's working equipment, of which there is a variety —mostly commercial, plus the stainless steel equipment—even if limited, would surprise most people who contemplate a deluxe bar. This is one of those features that if properly handled from the start—designing, planning, selecting, cost analyzing, and carefully watching and never losing control of the spending—will show much more for the investment than most others, even if proportionally analyzed.

Comfort is an important factor in any living space. A bar must insure comfort by supplying adequate support, whether for sitting or standing. Design is therefore of primary importance. Unfortunately, in most bar designs, knocking one's knees against the front is almost inevitable. Stand-up bars are seldom designed with the user in mind. One must be able to rest one foot on a foot railing which would extend far enough and high enough off the floor to be comfortable. Provision for an arm support or railing is also necessary.

Lighting that is both dramatic and functional is another consideration to keep in mind.

## Back bar

While most home bar functions and designs are similar to those of commercial bars, they are condensed and miniaturized. Therefore, behind-the-bar designs will vary considerably. In general, it can be said that a commercial back bar will be more expensive than a home back bar. On the other hand, the home bar in most cases will be relatively more costly in the exterior finish and appearance. Essentially, each bar must efficiently serve its own particular purpose.

When buying a commercially manufactured bar, you can achieve a custom appearance by adding decorative touches and by building a special back bar for it. Here again, a careful combination of shape and size is the fundamental requirement. A well-designed front unit cannot succeed if the back bar is out of proportion.

If possible, the back bar should be no less than 1 foot deep, floor to ceiling, and at least ⅔ the length of the bar. Although there are no rules as to how much working space must be allowed between the front and back bars at home, a minimum clearance of 2 feet will suffice in most cases; 3 feet or a little more is of course ideal if the space is available. If the back bar dimension must be decreased, it should be done at the end of the working space, thus giving more space where needed. The end of the bar is a good place to put a small wash sink. In big bars, designers often place the sink somewhere under the front bar top just as they do in commercial setups. This, of course, is not always practical or possible for a home unit.

Each of the bars in this chapter has its special advantages and is worthy of consideration by those who may be planning to build or acquire a bar. The Continental Bar is definitely a luxury item, but the thinking behind it applies to any type of bar. Especially noteworthy is the Hideaway Bar, which is a practical installation for small areas. Because it is seen only when in use, it is an important answer to problems caused by bars built in areas at above-basement level.

Not all bars are necessarily liquor dispensers. For example, the Continental Bar in the House of Ideas enabled a couple of teenagers and their friends to mix ice cream sodas. This is perhaps a good hint for parents—why not a refreshment bar with real soda-water-dispensing spigots? Used refurbished soda fountain units with all the containers for ice cream, syrup, etc., can be inexpensively purchased. A built-in generator, which will keep the right temperature while supplying cold water and soda water, is also available at used restaurant supply outlets.

## The Continental Bar

The motive for designing the bar in Figure 1 was the desire to create a proper mood for bar entertainment and at the same time to prove an important point: that a bar is not just a piece of furniture or a structure. It is rather an environment which must be inviting and complete.

*Full-size layout:* When this model bar was built, a full-size outline of the bar room was drawn onto heavy paper on the floor. The entire feature was then built from the original sketch and the full-size layout. It is amazing how helpful and instructive such a layout can be, for it provides a correct listing of materials and helps to establish the proper work procedure. This approach will often reveal newer and better solutions as well. In fact, the round standing section of this front bar came into focus when the full-size layout was being worked out.

Moving from the original rough sketch to a full-size layout obviously bypasses the usual scale drawings and blueprints. While the latter are commercially imperative, they are not al-

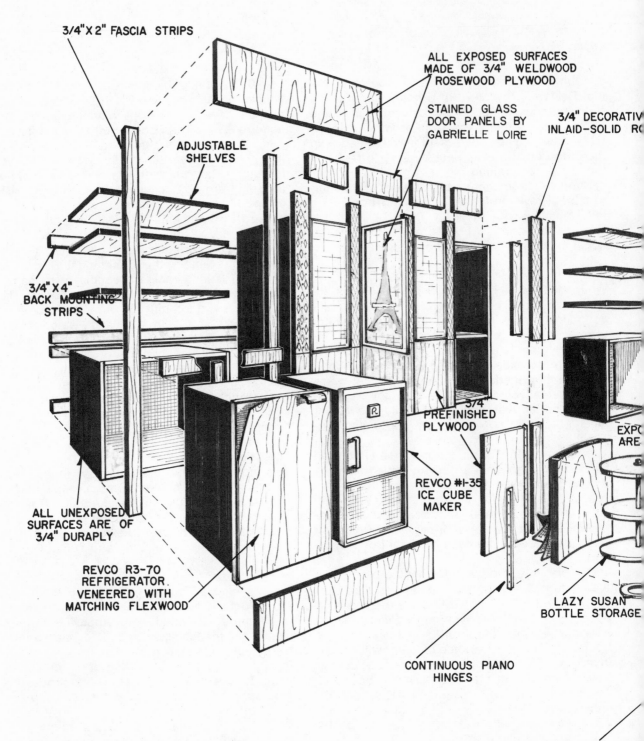

3/4" X 2" FASCIA STRIPS

ALL EXPOSED SURFACES
MADE OF 3/4" WELDWOOD
ROSEWOOD PLYWOOD

STAINED GLASS
DOOR PANELS BY
GABRIELLE LOIRE

3/4" DECORATIV
INLAID-SOLID RO

ADJUSTABLE
SHELVES

3/4" X 4"
BACK MOUNTING
STRIPS

ALL UNEXPOSED
SURFACES ARE OF
3/4" DURAPLY

REVCO R3-70
REFRIGERATOR
VENEERED WITH
MATCHING FLEXWOOD

3/4
PREFINISHED
PLYWOOD

REVCO #I-35
ICE CUBE
MAKER

EXP
ARE

LAZY SUSAN
BOTTLE STORAGE

CONTINUOUS PIANO
HINGES

SCALLOPS UPHOLSTERED IN NAUG.
WITH 3/4" FOAM RUBBER BACK

# BAR CONSTRUCTION

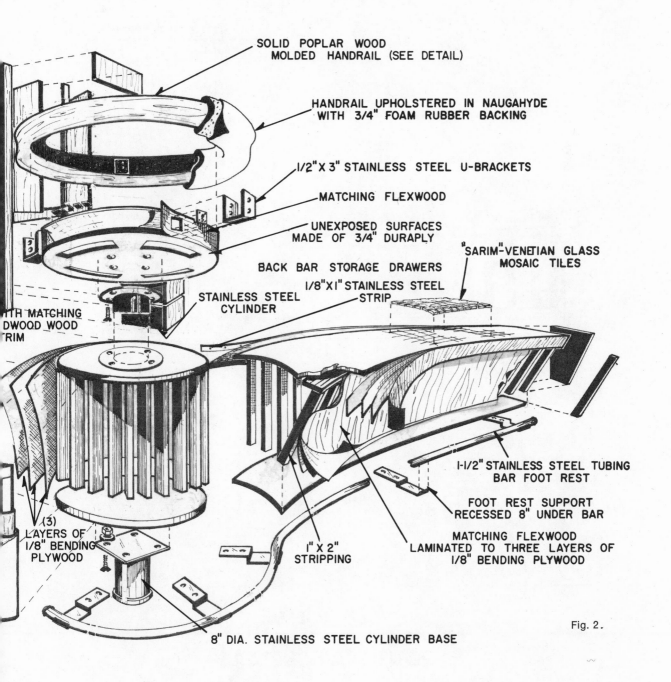

SOLID POPLAR WOOD
MOLDED HANDRAIL (SEE DETAIL)

HANDRAIL UPHOLSTERED IN NAUGAHYDE
WITH 3/4" FOAM RUBBER BACKING

1/2" X 3" STAINLESS STEEL U-BRACKETS

MATCHING FLEXWOOD

UNEXPOSED SURFACES
MADE OF 3/4" DURAPLY

"SARIM"-VENETIAN GLASS
MOSAIC TILES

BACK BAR STORAGE DRAWERS

1/8"X1"STAINLESS STEEL
STRIP

STAINLESS STEEL
CYLINDER

ITH MATCHING
DWOOD WOOD
RIM

1-1/2" STAINLESS STEEL TUBING
BAR FOOT REST

FOOT REST SUPPORT
RECESSED 8" UNDER BAR

MATCHING FLEXWOOD
LAMINATED TO THREE LAYERS OF
1/8" BENDING PLYWOOD

(3)
LAYERS OF
1/8" BENDING
PLYWOOD

1" X 2"
STRIPPING

8" DIA. STAINLESS STEEL CYLINDER BASE

Fig. 2.

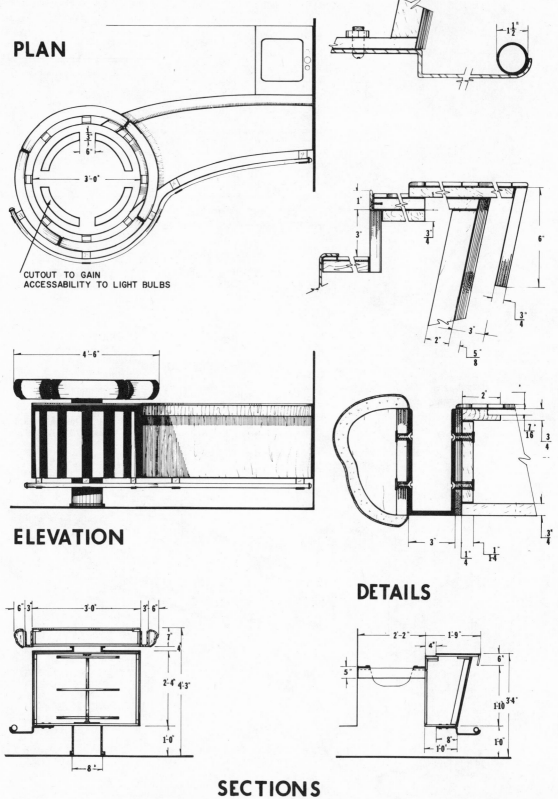

PLAN

CUTOUT TO GAIN
ACCESSABILITY TO LIGHT BULBS

ELEVATION

DETAILS

SECTIONS

FRONT BAR DETAILS

Fig. 3.

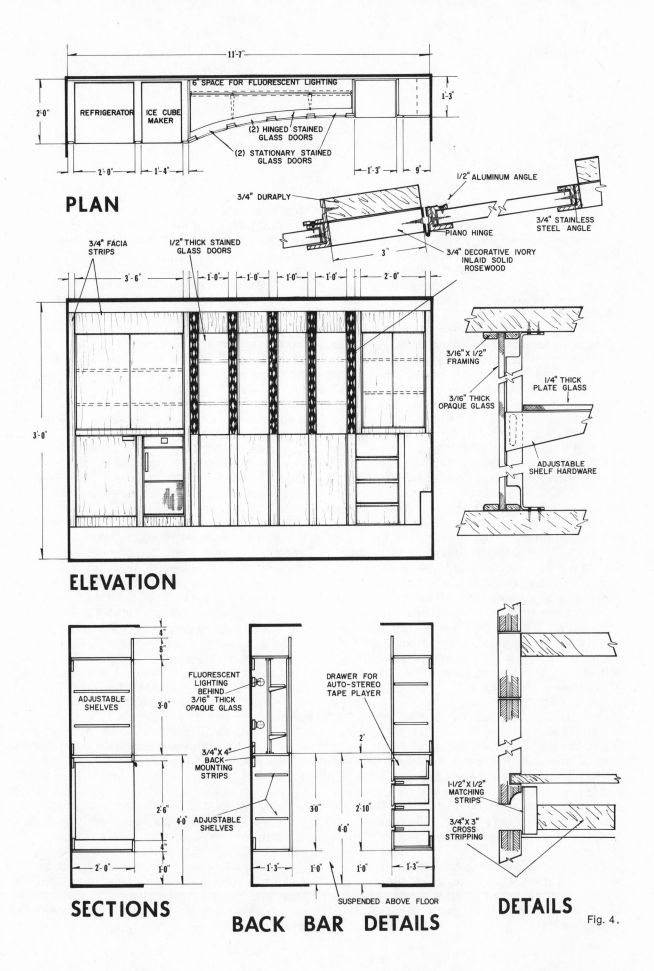

**PLAN**

11'-7"

6" SPACE FOR FLUORESCENT LIGHTING

2'-0"

REFRIGERATOR  ICE CUBE MAKER

(2) HINGED STAINED GLASS DOORS

(2) STATIONARY STAINED GLASS DOORS

2'-0"  1'-4"  1'-3"  1'-3"  9"

1/2" ALUMINUM ANGLE

3/4" DURAPLY

PIANO HINGE

3/4" STAINLESS STEEL ANGLE

3/4" DECORATIVE IVORY INLAID SOLID ROSEWOOD

3"

**ELEVATION**

3/4" FACIA STRIPS

1/2" THICK STAINED GLASS DOORS

3'-6"  1'-0"  1'-0"  1'-0"  1'-0"  2'-0"

3'-0"

3/16" X 1/2" FRAMING

1/4" THICK PLATE GLASS

3/16" THICK OPAQUE GLASS

ADJUSTABLE SHELF HARDWARE

**SECTIONS**

4"

8"

ADJUSTABLE SHELVES

3'-0"

2'-6"

4"

1'-0"

2'-0"

ADJUSTABLE SHELVES

4'-0"

**BACK BAR DETAILS**

FLUORESCENT LIGHTING BEHIND 3/16" THICK OPAQUE GLASS

3/4" X 4" BACK MOUNTING STRIPS

DRAWER FOR AUTO-STEREO TAPE PLAYER

2"

3'-0"

2'-10"

4'-0"

1'-3"  1'-0"  1'-0"  1'-3"

SUSPENDED ABOVE FLOOR

**DETAILS**

1-1/2" X 1/2" MATCHING STRIPS

3/4" X 3" CROSS STRIPPING

Fig. 4.

ways necessary or even useful. For example, a curved line, a slant, or a circle, and especially a compound curve, can never be properly felt and judged in scale, which is at best 10 percent of full size. And a full-size layout is always the best way to discover technical solutions and work them out properly, especially for unusual structures.

Figures 1 and 5 are exact copies of the full-size layout used. To build this bar, the plan and the most important parts of the drawings will have to be made full size again. When doing so, you can alter the dimensions to suit the particular area in which you are working.

*Basic requirements:* Since comfort was one of the main criteria for this bar, ample knee space at the sitting section and a padded finish on the standup portion of the bar were provided.

SLANTED SEATING SECTION: As shown in Figure 5, the recess for knee clearance was achieved primarily by building the seating part of the bar (which was finished in hard surface only for decorative reasons) in the shape of a compound curve, which slanted out more than 10 inches in 2 feet of height. This, of course, was improved by the 6-inch-high apron (overlapping by 4 inches) on the top, without which the incline would have been less than the necessary 10 inches at knee height for sitting at that area. At the same time, the apron established an indirect lighting trough.

Although the usual procedure in many curved bars is to build the top to follow the curve, retaining its width evenly, the bar top in this seating section ranged from 26 inches at the widest part (adjacent to the round section) to 16 inches at the narrowest (against the wall), and had a 4-inch glass trough in the back. Varying the width not only created a better-looking and more dramatically shaped bar, but it also provided much-needed space for behind-the-bar activity.

ROUND STAND-UP SECTION: Included in this area is a foot rest (12 inches above the floor), a smooth padded finish along the bar top, and fluted Koylon foam rubber panels covered with Naugahyde around the sides. The cushioned

arm rest, which extends 8 inches beyond the fluted panels, provides proper support and creates the necessary knee clearance when standing up and even when putting a foot on the bottom rail.

*Bar construction:* With these basic requirements established and fixed on the full-size layout, it was expedient to trace the full-size bar top and bottom on ¾-inch Duraply (exterior plywood), a strong waterproof material used for all the unexposed structural parts. When both pieces were cut out, they became the bases for further structural planning. The two different parts of the front bar—the round section and slanted curved seating section—were built and assembled separately.

SLANTED CURVED SEATING SECTION: The exact angle of the slanted compound curve was taken from the elevation and detail section of the front bar (Figure 3). The proper angle was transposed to the top and bottom end edges of the ¾-x-2-inch vertical pine support strips used for the entire bar front structure, about 3 inches apart. This determined the proper slant of the compound front when uniting the ¾-x-2-inch strips with the top and bottom precisely, after following these preparations: First of all, before assembly and in final preparation, the curved top edge (outside only) had to be cut or planed to the same slant used for this entire area, from the top down. Next, the bottom, after it had been checked against the full-size layout and the top, was cut or planed on the front edge the same way as the top. The top was turned upside down, and a ¾-x-3-inch strip of Duraply was glued, retaining the curve parallel at 4 inches in from the front edge and retaining the same slant. Next, the vertical strips were cut on a slant on each end and were glued and nailed to the bottom flush with the front edge. The strips were next nailed to the 3-inch strip of the top, flush with that slanted edge. After completing the front bar skeleton and before covering any part, additional blocks and cross-pieces were glued to the top and bottom between the strips. Temporary nail braces were used to support the structure in back. You may have to make minor adjustments. It is advisable to block, reinforce, and even fill in pieces (where necessary) which will sustain a strong and properly built body, and it may also support the stress areas. After the glue had dried for 24 hours and after checking all areas well, the entire front was sanded flush with a portable electric sander. The right end panels were then mounted to the structure, using glue and nails into the top and bottom edges as in the diagram. The left end was without end panel because it was fitted and coved to be snug against the round section. To cover the front skeleton of the bar structure and to create a good and solid surface for the Flexwood covering, 3 layers of ⅛-inch special bending plywood (vertical grain) were glued and nailed to the entire front using glue and ¾-inch headnails generously between layers, applying pressure from the center out by fastening each layer in the center first. This insured that the plywood was guided in the right direction and the access glue was pressed out more evenly when the second layer was applied in order to avoid pockets or bumps. However, in order to retain an even application of the plywood, it was necessary to mark center points on top and bottom of the structure and on each layer. Three layers of ⅛-inch bending plywood were sufficient because each cross-grain plywood is a three-layer lamination itself. The reason for the heavy glue application between each layer of plywood is that the plywood veneer used for this type of bending lamination is of poplar wood, a very spongy material that absorbs most of the liquid of the glue. This liquid is necessary to properly spread the substance. Its lack prevents a normal drying process, thus considerably weakening the adhesive strength. It is absolutely unwise to laminate all three layers in succession, for each process needs curing time (24 hours to dry) to first expand and then, as it dries, contract. And because this process tends to change the original form and surface slightly, occasionally necessitating some adjustments, there is always the other layer to rectify the change. The closer you come to the final layer the more even the surface becomes. After the last layer of bending plywood has been applied and glue is dry, you may find areas which did not adhere properly and see some edges separating, and, more seriously, bubbles in the gen-

eral mid-area.

HOW TO REPAIR BAD GLUE JOINTS: These defects, while not uncommon, must be repaired before proceeding. To fix separations on edges, slightly force a screwdriver into the loose area, separating the faulty adhesion. After 24 hours it should not open up much further unless there is something wrong with the glue chemistry.

For any feature, but especially this one where stress is exerted by the compound curve in a relatively small area, it is best to use a slow-drying and somewhat elastic glue rather than other types that dry quicker and crystal hard. The glue used for this project and nearly all others is Weldwood white glue, which has proven its excellence over many years of successful use. To repair the loose edges of this particular tension area, loosen up the part that is partially open and keep blunt instruments such as one or two screwdrivers or other narrow and thin metal tools inserted as deep as possible, jiggling them back and forth while squeezing white glue into the opening. Release the metal pieces, then slightly press down on the center toward the surrounding areas. If there is enough glue in the area it will tend to come out at the least touch. If there is not, add some more and let the glue set for at least 5 to 10 minutes (depending on the temperature; if damp and cold, wait longer) before applying pressure by putting a heavy layer of newspaper and a wood block with rounded edges on top. Tighten the area with a large wood block underneath to disperse the pressure of 1 to 2 good clamps. This Weldwood white glue needs only moderate pressure for best results. Too much pressure tends to squeeze out the vital amount of glue. The more difficult area to repair is a bubble somewhere inside of the area. A hollow empty sound when tapping will indicate that there is no adhesion. To make sure that all areas are tight and ready for further applications, keep tapping with your finger to find a problem area. Then puncture holes with an icepick all around that area until you open the right spot. Even if the bubble is not too large at the time, it may become larger later on.

To avoid this, cut a slot into the hollow area; try to insert a knife and push in some glue in all directions, wait a while, and clamp. If a single clamp cannot reach the area, put a ⅜-inch-thick pack of newspaper on the patch; place a wood block on it. Put a 2 x 6 on top of the block, in the direction shortest to the ends, and apply a clamp on each end with a block underneath each side and slowly tighten both clamps simultaneously. You might need help to do this. If the area cannot be reached with any kind of support or clamp, repeat the entire procedure but nail the block in place strongly enough to exert the necessary pressure, bending the nails over so as to be able to remove the block after 24 hours.

These instructions are important and a good preparation for the application of the Flexwood. If a bubble occurs after applying the Flexwood, cut a slot in line with the grain using a sharp-bladed matting knife, insert adhesive, let it set for a while, and then rub it down with a blunt instrument. Always test with the tips of your fingers before concluding this phase and before setting that portion of the bar aside in order to let it adhere well. After 20 to 30 hours it may, by drying and tightening, shrink enough to eliminate the small bubbles. This is why the finished surface must be dampened before setting it aside. After the last layer of plywood has been applied and is hardened and dry, sand the plywood surface smooth using an electric sander, always checking that the surface is perfectly smooth and without any blemishes. Use wood putty to cover any holes or depressions.

APPLICATION OF FLEXWOOD: Using a special saw-tooth scraper or a short cross-cut saw, scratch the plywood surface to create a coarse texture. Clean the surface with a damp cloth and let dry. If the Flexwood is not wide enough or a better vertical grain pattern is desired, cut the Flexwood with a very sharp matting knife and join the sections on a flat surface, taping them temporary together, first over the joint and also across the joint, every 4 to 5 inches on the good surface. Cut the Flexwood large enough so that there is enough material to overlap the top and bottom and each side by 3 inches to recover the loss taken by the compound shape. Have enough Flexwood on top (at least 10 inches) to cut off for the apron, thus creating a continuous wood grain pattern. Make a double mark on the cut edges of the now-separated pieces in order to match them again. When applying the full sheet, get someone to help. Before applying the adhesive, place the full sheet in position and mark in center to the top and bottom of the Flexwood and the plywood guidelines. Align with corresponding marks on the bar top, as well as on the bottom (where it is best visible). Next, following manufacturer's instructions, apply the special adhesive for the Flexwood to both surfaces. Let it get tacky. When installing the Flexwood, hold both ends up, lining it up first in the center with the guidelines. Slowly lower one end at a time pushing the Flexwood out inch by inch, actually forcing it down from the helper. Leave a safe margin overall, rubbing the surface with a wood block formed to a semisharp edge. Always beware of creases. It is best to rub sideways against the grain until the Flexwood is down on the surface. It may be necessary to use a spatula, carefully pulling the Flexwood until it is down. With a wet cloth, keep the surface of the Flexwood damp, and keep rubbing it until it feels like a solid plywood surface. Put the bar in a 65° to 70° area to dry. Sand and finish after 2 to 3 days.

ROUND STAND-UP SECTION: The construction of the bar's round section is somewhat different from that of the main body of the other structure. In addition, it has two 2-inch-thick by 4½-inch-high hardwood rings, the first of which is the outer ring for the upholstered arm rest. Each of the 3 layers of the curved 2-inch-wide section (1½ inch thick) is assembled in a staggered bricklaying fashion. Each joint is covered by the piece above. This assembly is best done on a ¾-inch piece of plywood marked according to the planned perimeter circle. Each edge is glued to the next (small pieces of paper under the glue joints will prevent adherence to the plywood base) until the ring follows the outline, with the first layer temporarily tacked through the outside edges. To keep all subsequent layers in line, use a small square. The same method is to be followed on the other round top assembly.

The next part is the inner ring which forms

Fig. 5. Note the dramatic down light from the bar bottom. This is created by a series of small bulbs (as behind the bar apron and on top, behind the back bar cornice), mounted behind front and back cover strips.

Fig. 6. With the stained glass doors open, it is apparent that the storage area inside is also dramatic.

Fig. 7. Looking toward the soda water spigots (antique silver), note the bar sink crossover unit. Note also the Emerson intercom built into the antique copper Faientex mosaic-covered wall.

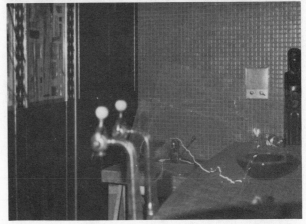

the round top. It is made of laminated hardwood in the same manner as the outer ring, except that it has two rabbets notched into the horizontal edges. The bottom rabbet is to hold the slotted top-base-disk made of ¾-inch plywood, and the top rabbet is to hold the ½-inch glass base (to retain the translucent quality) for the Venetian glass ceramic tile covering all top surfaces. (See Figure 2.)

The third major section is the round body which is covered with 3 layers of ⅛-inch bending poplar plywood. This assembly is much like that of the slanted front section except that here the two round Duraply disks are made into a drum, vertically straight, using the same 1-x-2-inch pine strips about 3 inches apart. A small storage door is also cut from this section to serve as additional storage in back of the bar, but only after the application of all 3 layers of bending plywood.

The two bar sections (the round and the curved) are fitted—the curved open end of the long bar section is now supported with 1-x-2s close together and covered with 2 layers of ⅛-inch bending plywood—and permanently assembled by applying glue and by fastening them in both directions with screws and bolts, starting with nails. The top surface of this two-piece assembly is planed and sanded flush, checking it with a long straightedge. Repeat on the bottom.

SCALLOPED COVERING: Now that the two sections are assembled, the round section can be divided into equal parts to ascertain the width of the scallops or flutes (see Figure 2). Although those in the model bar are 8 inches wide, you could fit in one more scallop to achieve a more fluted effect if you reduce each scallop by approximately 1⅜ inches.

The scallops are made of curved frames covered with 2 layers of bending plywood. These, in turn, are covered with 1-inch latex foam rubber upholstered with Naugahyde.

Except for the 2 scallops fitted into the curved front and apron of the slanted section, all scallops are equal in height.

The apron of the curved bar section (6 inches high) is made of ¾-inch plywood. Due to the stress put upon the plywood by the consid-

Fig. 8. As only the two center panels are motorized, it was possible to push the end panel toward the center without the use of power.

Fig. 10. Closeup of Grant heavy-duty nylon ball-bearing rollers in 2-wheel carrier (center hung) fastened with bolt-on adjustable carrier bolt.

Fig. 9. Push the button, and after a slight delay the center door panels open. When they reach a position where they are even with the solid end panels, a built-in bracket on top picks up the end panels and moves them evenly along until the entire bar room is open.

Fig. 11. The alignment of all sliding door panels is made possible by adjusting and locking an adjustable carrier bolt (stud)—up to ½ inch.

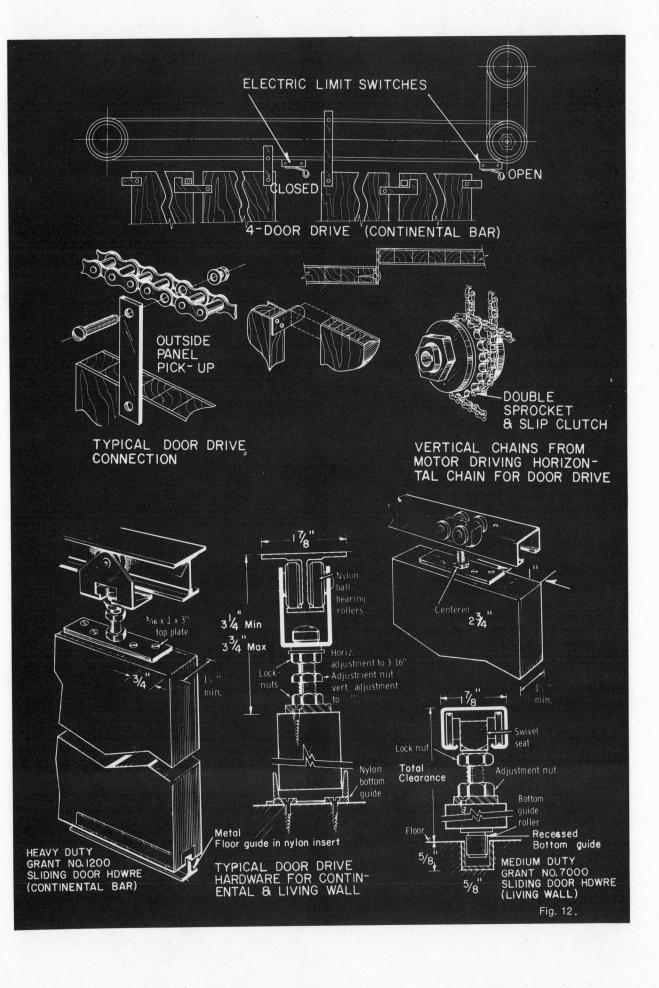

ELECTRIC LIMIT SWITCHES

CLOSED OPEN

4-DOOR DRIVE (CONTINENTAL BAR)

OUTSIDE PANEL PICK-UP

TYPICAL DOOR DRIVE CONNECTION

DOUBLE SPROCKET & SLIP CLUTCH

VERTICAL CHAINS FROM MOTOR DRIVING HORIZONTAL CHAIN FOR DOOR DRIVE

$3/16 \times 1 \times 3''$ top plate

$3/4$

$1\frac{1}{2}''$ min.

HEAVY DUTY GRANT NO. 1200 SLIDING DOOR HDWRE (CONTINENTAL BAR)

$\frac{7}{8}''$

Nylon ball bearing rollers

$3\frac{1}{4}''$ Min
$3\frac{3}{4}''$ Max

Lock nuts

Horiz. adjustment to $3\cdot16''$
Adjustment nut vert. adjustment to ''

Nylon bottom guide

Metal Floor guide in nylon insert

TYPICAL DOOR DRIVE HARDWARE FOR CONTINENTAL & LIVING WALL

Centered $2\frac{3}{4}$

$1''$ min.

$\frac{7}{8}''$

Lock nut

Swivel seat

Total Clearance

Adjustment nut

Bottom guide roller

Floor

Recessed Bottom guide

$5/8''$

$5/8''$

MEDIUM DUTY GRANT NO. 7000 SLIDING DOOR HDWRE (LIVING WALL)

Fig. 12.

erable curve, the plywood had to be water-soaked and clamped in its place overnight. Finally it was permanently mounted with glue and nails.

Because of the compound curve, the plywood for this apron had to be cut wider to accommodate the loss in width in the twist in order to end up with the necessary 6 inches. After the glue set, the top edge was made flush with the bar top first. Next, the 6 inches for the apron was scribed parallel with the top cut and planed at the bottom edge also parallel with the top. The bottom edge of this apron was banded with maching veneer. Next, the apron of the curved bar section was covered with vertical Flexwood matching the wood grain pattern (as marked) of the main bar section. This was the same procedure as on the large Flexwood lamination. To mount the upholstered scallops to the outside of the round bar unit, #8 roundhead screws of diversified length were used. These were long enough to reach from the inside of the vertical support strips of the round section into the vertical and horizontal cross members of the scallops without using glue. This held the scallops temporarily (they are removable for repair or recovering).

BAR SUPPORTS: Once the front bar sections were firmly and permanently united, and after another layer of ¾-inch plywood was glued to the right end panel (cut to the same size), the entire bar was supported at two points: on one end in the center and bottom of the round section with an 8-inch stainless steel cylinder base; and at the narrow end with four $\frac{5}{16}$-inch Lag bolts attached to lead shields in the wall. (See diagram.)

In order to sustain the free-standing bar rigidly, two ¾-inch plywood disks, cut slightly smaller than the inside of the 8-inch diameter stainless steel top and bottom support disks. As shown in Figure 2, this center-top support is act spot where the base was to rest. The bar was temporarily set in place and the proper location carefully marked. This caused the entire bar, which was thus far directly and firmly supported only at one point (the wall), to remain rigid, as the powerful support of the 8-inch stainless steel cylinder base was now locked in place.

The round bar top was also supported with a 3-inch-high 8-inch-diameter stainless steel cylinder, including two ¼-x-16-inch-diameter stainless steel top and bottom support disks. As shown in Figure 2, this center-top support is anchored to the round bar case with stainless steel flathead bolts and is mounted to the round bar top in the same way. However, before attaching the round top to the center support, the top surface of the round case was covered with glass ceramic tile, starting flush with the outside of the plywood cover, continuing in parallel circles, and fitted around the steel disk.

After the round bar top (without its upholstered rim) was mounted on the stainless steel center cylinder, it was covered with the same Sarim Venetian glass ceramic tile too. Then, butted to the round tile surface, the remaining top surface and 4-inch glass trough were covered with the same tile. A water-clear epoxy resin cement was used for adhesive as well as grout. Any excess cement was cleared off and the tiles washed with the proper liquid or thinner (provided by the manufacturer).

When the epoxy was dry (usually within 24 hours), the tiled surface was rubbed down by hand with abrasive waterstones to smooth any sharp outer edges and high spots. Don't try to make the tile perfectly even, because it would lose its desired characteristics.

UPHOLSTERED ARM SUPPORT: The round wood rim is first rounded on top and bottom of the outside. (See diagram.) The arm rest is supported on the suspended round bar top with 6 equally spaced U-shaped stainless steel brackets (¼ inch thick by 2 inches wide by 2½ inches deep by 4½ inches high). (See diagram.) The two top edges of all the brackets are rounded approximately at ¼-inch radius toward the inside. All bolts to support the brackets have Allen holes in the center rather than the usual slots, in order to be able to fasten them with an Allen key, which is easier to use in these narrow areas.

In addition, there are 12 mounting steel plates, ¼ inch thick by 2 inches wide by 4½ inches high. These plates are to support the 6 "U" brackets. All support plates are drilled and countersunk on each corner to receive 8-x-1¼-inch flathead screws to hold them in place. The 6 plates which are to be mounted on the apron of the suspended round bar top will have 2 equally spaced ⅜-inch tapped holes drilled in the center. The other 6 plates have only one ⅜-inch tapped hole in the exact center. These are the plates that are mounted to the inside of the upholstered arm rest before it is upholstered. Most important is the fact that all holes of the mounting plates must line up with those of the "U" brackets. Furthermore, all brackets must be perfectly aligned with their counterpart. This is best done by first recessing each of the equally spaced brackets into the apron of the round suspended bar top, perfectly flush (preferably), before covering the apron with Flexwood. Next, before fastening them permanently, mark the 2 tapped ⅜-inch holes to the wood, remove the plates and bore ⅜-inch holes about 1 inch deep for clearance for the bolts. Bore pilot holes for the 4 fastening screws. Mount the plates permanently and attach a "U" bracket temporarily to each plate using the 2 bolts on each. Slip the armrest support temporarily in place, testing with a straight edge across the round top to make sure that the support ring is perfectly flush. The wood joints must not be at the location of the brackets. Now mark the center hole (⅜ inch) to the 6 locations of the brackets. Draw the outline of the "U" bracket to the wood surface of the arm support. Remove the support ring, and place a corresponding flat support plate on each marked location. Complete the marking of all holes. Scribe the outline of each plate and bore a ⅜-inch hole 1 inch deep and the 4 pilot holes in the corners. Now plow out the wood and mount each plate flush with the wood surface. In order to avoid imperfect alignments, mark each location and the corresponding bracket sets. Replace the arm support and fasten each bracket temporarily with a ⅜-inch bolt. Then remove the arm support and cover the inside edge with vertical grain Flexwood like the other apron if this has not yet been done. The point is to cover the apron's and armrest's plates after they are installed with Flexwood to expose the "U" brackets only. This is the time to send out the arm

rest to be upholstered. If the ⅛-x-1-inch feature strips (stainless steel dividers) are used over the upholstered arm, preparations must be made before upholstery so that a 1-inch groove is further plowed out of the wood ⅛ inch deep behind the top and bottom in the center of each mounting bracket to cover the 1-inch return of the top and bottom of each bracket which is held in place with one 1¼-inch #8 flathead screw on each end and is covered additionally by each plate flush with the wood. (See diagram.)

FOOT REST: The foot rest consists of 1½-inch-diameter stainless steel tubing formed to the outline of the bar in conformity with its location. It is 7 inches o.c. from the bottom front bar surface; it starts 2 inches from the right wall and ends just about one scallop before the curved door in the round bar section, thus visually covering all areas looking straight on. The brackets supporting the foot rest are equally spaced on both the curved and the round bar sections. They are welded neatly to the pipe foot support and finished off smoothly. The supports (shown in the diagram) have 2 countersunk holes. These holes match the holes in the ½-x-3-x-6-inch prebored steel plates on the inside of the ¾-inch Duraply bar bottom, which is concealed after all parts are aligned. The holes are marked and are bored through the bottom. The foot rest support brackets are bolted to the steel plates with ½-inch flathead bolts, washers, and nuts on the inside of the bottom. This assembly, as well as the permanent mounting of the arm support rim, can best be done after completing the entire room, or at least the bar.

THE SINK TOP: This is built and mounted to the bar with a 3-inch apron support strip anchored to the wall and front and back bar. The sink, which should be as small as possible, is optional. The model bar is outfitted with an American Standard stainless steel bar sink, drain, and single lever mixer faucet. A ¾-inch fitted plywood cabinet section, 12 inches deep, is mounted beneath the sink. Concealed, it accommodates a hot water unit (Konstant Hot) and a combination blender, mixer, and ice crusher (Nutone). It also provides additional work space. This is done with ¾-inch plywood topped with matching plastic laminate covering the sink. There are also 6-x-6-inch metal corner brackets supporting the sink top (extending all the way into the front bar area) bent to fit the slanted inside of the curved bar section. These brackets are mounted 12 inches down from the inside of the bar top. It would be desirable, but not absolutely necessary, to cover the inside exposed structure with 1 layer of ⅛-inch bending plywood before installing shelves. This, however, can best be done in sections. This shelf should be covered with textured black plastic for easy maintenance. The edges of the shelf and the trough of the main bar top are covered with ⅛-x-1-inch stainless steel, rounded on the top edges. All inside surfaces are covered with satin black acrylic paint. This sink and built-in equipment combination cabinet section backed against the wall form the only and perhaps best suitable connection of the front and back bar.

THE BACK BAR: For consistency and design purposes, the curve of the front bar structure is repeated in the three-part back bar. The slightly curved center section, which features stained glass panels (Figure 6), is flanked by left and right outer units. Although the curve is noticeable, it is not so round as to prevent the installation of the 4 flat 14-inch-wide stained glass panels. Three-inch divider strips of imported Indian rosewood with hand-inlaid diamond-shaped ivory pieces are extended from top to bottom (slightly planing the edges slanted toward the outside in keeping with curved top and bottom). These are covered on each side with ⅛-x-1-inch stainless steel strips which follow the curve, so that at first glance there is the illusion of having curved doors where there are none. All surfaces are flat but ever so subtly tilted to follow the direction of the desired curve.

The entire structure is mounted 12 inches off the floor in order to clear a baseboard heating unit and to conform to the front bar. It was installed with long screws through horizontal back-mounting cross strips and into the 2-x-6-inch wall studs (see Figure 4). The support is important because of the weight of the installation.

LEFT-SIDE UNIT: The bottom section of this unit, which is 24¾ inches deep, contains a refrigerator and ice maker. The rosewood plywood doors in the top half cover an elaborate storage section with adjustable ¾-inch plywood shelves, big enough to hold large trays, and all the special dishes and other items for special occasions.

CENTER UNIT: This section is dominated by 4 magnificent stained glass panels, the outer 2 of which are stationary. The other 2 are hinged doors and are mounted with continuous hinges to the stationary panels. Behind the panels are three ¼-x-8-inch-deep plate glass shelves with rounded edges. They span the entire enclosed cabinet, providing enough room to store more than four dozen mixed glasses (Figure 6). These shelves can be installed in various ways.

For this bar, the 3 shelves were cut 2 inches shorter than the enclosure to allow a 1-inch margin on each end. Each shelf is supported by 2 thick drinking glasses (preferably no less than 3 inches in diameter and 6 inches high) turned upside down. The support glasses are placed in pairs (one behind the other) and are positioned about 10 inches in from the shelf ends on each side and in the center. They are centered over one another. This system is sufficient to hold a display of decorative glassware. Installed behind the shelves is a decorative lighting system (see page 219).

Below the stained glass panes and the decorative shelving is a section with adjustable wooden shelves capable of holding several dozen bottles. They are covered by 4 matching Brazilian rosewood plywood doors. The entire back bar front surface is covered with matching and continuous grain Weldwood Brazilian rosewood plywood only pleasantly interrupted by the vertical feature strips.

RIGHT-SIDE UNIT: In the lower section of this end of the installation are 5 drawers, 4 of which are for silverware, utensils, and small bar items. In the last one (on top) a continuous cartridge tape unit and two spare cartridges are stored. All drawers slide on full extension slides (No. 329).

In the top of each of the 2 solid door compartments to the left and right of the stained glass doors are small cutouts in the back bar top for 8-inch loudspeakers that are installed inside to face the acoustical ceiling. These reproduce sound both softly and clearly. The source of the music is the Autostereo cartridge tape unit which is part of the cycle controlled by the electronic brain (see page 207). Above the sink, at the very end of the right-side unit, is a 12-inch-high compartment with a removable front panel which is hardly noticeable. This inconspicuous niche can be used for a number of things.

The design for this division of the back bar was guided primarily by practical considerations. The compartments for the refrigerator and the ice maker determined the height of the bottom section, and the 9½-inch distance from the ceiling to the top of the structure established the height of the stained glass panes and adjacent rosewood plywood doors, and the cornice which, besides covering the cones of the two speakers, served a number of other functions.

*Lighting:* Behind the 6½-inch cornice across the top of the back bar, a group of 12 No. 1383–20W–12–16V autobulbs were mounted in twist sockets. (The 3-inch clearance space left between the top edge of the cornice and the ceiling is adequate for reaching in to replace bulbs.) These bulbs operate on 12 volts and must therefore be connected to a transformer that converts 110 volts to 12. Connected to the Luxtrol motorized dimmer, as part of the overall program, these bulbs create a very interesting lightline against the black ceiling.

To the extreme left, slightly to the right of the left speaker, and just behind the cornice and the indirect lighting, is a charcoal air purifier filter. Also part of the overall electronic cycle, it turns on automatically when any light is switched on.

ILLUMINATING THE GLASS DISPLAY AREA: In order to achieve well-distributed lighting behind the stained glass panels and to prevent the bulb lines from showing through the diffused glass, a 6-inch-deep boxlike unit the same size as the glass section of the back bar was installed on the back wall portion leading to the garage. This unit, lined with aluminum foil, con-

tains all-deluxe warm white fluorescent tubes. To change the tubes, all one has to do is to lift up the 6-inch-deep lighting container in the garage. To cover the lighting tubes, a frame at the rear of the back bar contains a special three-dimensional opaque glass ³⁄₁₆ inch thick. It was mounted in 3 equal panes against this frame and fastened with clips in the back. This glass was over 3 inches away from the bulbs and of such finish that it diffused the light evenly. The outside light box (which was felt-lined on the contacting edges to keep the glass from breaking) is actually a part of the 2-x-6 garage wall framing, and when closed it slides right into the cut-out of the partition wall. Three 10-inch heavy-duty strap hinges hold the box, which can be lifted up and safely supported to change bulbs.

Because of their width (more than 49 inches), the six 40-watt deluxe warm white fluorescent bulbs (with remotely located dimmer ballasts to avoid the usual humming sound) are staggered horizontally. When the 2 center stained glass doors are opened, an illuminated display of glassware is dramatically exposed. When the doors are closed, the stained glass panels are shown to fullest advantage. In fact, because of this carefully planned back lighting and the glassware on the shelves which reflect the light unevenly in many directions, the stained glass received the most ideal illumination.

Because the lighting had to be installed so that it would not interfere with the glass storage area as noted above, it made for easy access through the back of the partition wall (which bordered on the garage). The same successful experience was apparent by having all valves (refrigeration, ice maker) and the main shut-off valve for this area in the garage. In fact, removable panels allowed free access from the garage.

In the House of Ideas, the kitchen, the pantry, and the bar had many sophisticated appliances and gadgets which would require some servicing at times. To avoid having repairmen come into the house more than absolutely necessary, these three areas were located and built against the garage partitions (see page 13). Here is how the back bar situation was solved: A 5-x-3-foot opening was framed out in the 2-x-6-foot partition structure and a top-hung trap door was mounted. Made into a frame of 2-x-6s like the rest of the wall, but hollow, this door could be properly insulated with thin aluminum pads, covered on the garage side with 2 layers of plywood, and be safely locked. The placement of the bar in this area (as mentioned before) made it possible to mount all the shutoff valves for hot and cold water, the electric master switch for this area, and even the automatic Luxtrol dimmers and other emergency items on the garage side of the wall, neatly installed, precisely labeled, and, very important, easily accessible.

MULTISOURCE LIGHTING: The important multisource lighting connected to automatic Luxtrol dimmers creates a concert of hues and shadows which are constantly changing once a button is pushed. These motorized dimmers are connected to an electronic brain system (a network placed in the same electronic container used for the Living Wall, as well as the entire environment in the Living Area, page 14).

By providing versatile overall coverage with multisource lighting, all on automatic dimmers, using both electric poles of the dimmers, we achieved a balanced change of action, two different actions from one motor. This was driven by the same slow speed as the opening of the entrance door panels (Figures 8 and 9)—a 50-second total cycle. This illuminates one balanced light source up to 70 percent, while the other source dims down to a mere 30 percent. To use both electric poles of a dimmer one must use a reversible motor. The motors used here for door drive are for motorized dimmers by Luxtrol—SS (Slo-Syn) 150 and 250, depending on the load, were used throughout the house. This, of course, will reverse when closing the bar, and unless bypassed by another switch independent of the electronic program, will shut off all lights, music, etc., 20 seconds after the bar is closed.

To properly balance the light sources when the bar is open, all indirect lighting, such as the back and front bar cornices and the front bar bottom, will cut down to 30 percent. The round front bar top as well as its indirect light spillage projecting down through the slotted openings in the bottom of the round bar top (plywood) and the stained glass panes in the back bar will illuminate to 70 percent. This highlights the stained glass and subdues the surroundings. All overhead lights and wallwashers also dim along with the others, while the charcoal air purifier, as well as the continuous cartridge tape player, turn on. This not only properly disperses the light, but in combination with the surrounding materials and textures, it creates a very dramatic atmosphere of glowing hues. Since all of the lighting was activated by the motorized dimmers, it was possible to properly create this designed lighting by slowly adjusting the illumination, the dimming, the timing, and the diffusion during the installation. This obviously was not just a matter of adjusting screws or the like, but involved mainly changing mini-sprockets in the timers of the electronic brain. These are available in precision units to perform within fractions of seconds.

The bar's 4 entrance panels (Figures 8 and 9) have 6 translucent, sculptured, hand-poured 9-x-9-inch amber panes in each of the two center panels (made by Loire of Chartres), which, when illuminated, are an impressive sight. Following are the results:

When the button that sends power to the relay system (electronic brain) is pushed, a 150-watt wallwasher (Kliegl) in the ceiling on the inside of the bar room (in the exact center, 18 inches in from the doors) aimed at the glass inserts, turns on at once, washing a rather strong flare of light down the inside of the two center doors. This creates an indescribable glow on the amber glass panes, as the music simultaneously starts receiving it softly on the outside. This is reinforced five seconds later by a group of 4 type R-1030 flush ceiling down lights, each 75 watts (R-30 bulbs); 3 miniature eyeball type wallwashers installed 10 inches from the wall, sending 100-watt strong, rather narrow light streaks down the Brazilian rosewood paneling on the left wall; and a 150-watt wallwasher illuminating the Zeba (antique copper) Faientex mosaic tile wall to the right. This totals up to an approximation of about 100 candle foot power of illumination, which remains intact for about 12 seconds. At that time the center doors are about 2 inches open, the center-front wallwasher is off at once (as the panel begins to move) and all other ceiling lights dim down to 30 percent of overall power, changing at the same speed (starting at 70 percent) as the doors move on. The action of the center case behind the stained glass doors does the same in reverse as it picks up during the motion (starting at 30 percent), and so does the round bar top, which has a series of bulbs installed on the inside of its plywood bottom. The cornices stop at about 60 percent illumination, thus maintaining an even glow. All this takes place in the 59-second cycle, and all at the same speed as the moving doors. This process reverses when the button that closes the doors is pushed.

Such is the dramatic display during the 1 minute of action that includes 10 seconds of delay for seeing the illuminated center doors. Following that time, the bar structure can be seen in several ever-changing shades and hues. Of course, several details of the structure outlines become less noticeable as the lights dim down. This tends to soften the distinct outlines of some structural characteristics, which is desirable for the proper bar mood.

There is a period of perhaps 20 seconds in which one can appreciate the beautiful flow of the integrated bar design with its many different textural entities, before using it and enjoying the service, which is equally efficient, owing to the availability of all the necessary accessories.

To further dramatize the bar through lighting, little bulbs, of the type used in the cornices, were installed on the bar bottom and connected to the cycles of the indirect lighting in the cornices. To protect them in this precarious area, a 3-inch-high cornice strip made of matching wood was mounted in front of the bulbs and was fastened with metal corner angles.

For even further dramatization, an instant cartridge stereo tape unit, placed in the back bar, turns on with the first light and feeds beautiful soft bar music into the two small speakers mounted into the top of the left and right back bar cabinets. At the same time, the charcoal air filter (by Ductless Hood Co.) is activated to keep the air in this small room clean. Finally, when closing the bar electronically by pushing the button, everything reverses automatically and shuts off completely. Check all diagrams carefully to better understand the practical applications.

*Color Scheme:* The tones of the materials used in the bar area were purposely muted: rowan Naugahyde on the scallops, antique copper Faientex mosaic tiles on the wall, flat black ceiling, Barcelona pebblestone flooring (by Amtico), black leather and wrought-iron bar stools (by Woodward), and accents such as the divider strips of ivory inlaid rosewood. All these served to set off the main feature—the *very colorful stained glass panels.* Because dark woods and dark-textured materials lend themselves best to elaborate lighting, the two complement each other very well. The stained glass panels in the back bar reveal the unmatchable artistry by world-famous Gabrielle Loire, of Chartres, France. The motif is "The Best of Paris," which in the sparkling reflection of the rough-cut multicolor glass pieces embedded in ½-inch panels of epoxy inserted in delicate but strong frames of stainless steel, becomes the most magnifying point of interest once the doors to the bar are open. The rest of the lighting is at low level, leaving "The Best of Paris" as the major source of light. The music, combined with the pleasure of seeing these fabulous panes come to life every time you push that button, will make a visit to your bar a delight.

### The Mediterranean Bar

Despite its elegant appearance, the free-standing bar in Figure 13 is really a simple and basic project that the home hobbyist can build. Unlike the Continental Bar, no advanced skills or major preparations are required.

The Mediterranean Bar was part of a basement remodeling job. When the basement walls were furred out with 2-x-4s, the front bar structure became a continuation of the wall structure as the basic skeleton was tied in to the wall studs. The curved sections of the top and bot-

Fig. 13. At the end of a rather long basement area is this bar with an interconnecting door to a small kitchen. This was a perfect solution to problems of size, space, location, and style. Not shown here are the many gadgets such as glass washer, built-in Nutone mixer and ice crusher, good storage, and—most importantly—lighting with infinite possibilities of change from behind the bar.

Fig. 14. Basic frame structure following full-size layout on the floor.

Fig. 15. After application of 1/8-inch hardboard on the inside and ¼-inch fir sheathing on the outside, vertical grain — Accent — random groove walnut paneling was applied on the outside.

Fig. 16. Bar top of ¾-inch Duraply overlapping 6 inches with a 6-inch apron return provides interesting 3-dimensional feeling. The unusual indirect down light glows from behind the apron.

tom plates were cut out of 2-x-12-inch fir planks while 2-x-4-inch fir planks were used for the straight section. The bottom plates were fastened to the concrete floor with steel cut nails. Next, vertical 2-x-4s were toe-nailed to the bottom plate, and the top plate sections were nailed to the verticals (Figure 14). As in the rest of the structures as well as furring, the 2-x-4 studs were mounted 16 inches o.c. By properly marking guidelines to the floor, the assembly became very easy.

For a strong and even surface, it is advisable to cover the frame structure of the bar with ¼-inch fir sheathing. It is also advisable at this point to cover the inside with ⅛-inch hardboard. The sheathing on the outside provides a surface on which to glue and nail ¼-inch prefinished Accent walnut panels matching the surrounding walls (Figure 15). And by marking the center of each vertical stud to the floor in order to locate its position, one can get solid support from the studs by nailing the plywood into them. Then the inside front bar shelves and the counter top are cut from ¾-inch Weldwood Duraply (waterproof and very strong) and installed (Figure 16). The shelves are notched between the studs, which will bring them out flush with the front of the studs. This will enable you to support the shelves with wood strips nailed to the studs below the shelves.

The bar top and apron, as well as the 4-inch trough, are covered with ¾-inch random-colored mosaic tiles which lend the Mediterranean influence. The basic tile comes in pure white; the color inserts are available in a variety of accent colors. To order such tiles, you pick the colors you want and determine the desired percentage of each accent color. One-x-1 or 1-x-2-foot are the type of random sheets ordered and then custom-assembled by the dealer. These are gauzed-backed to hold them together with a proper distance between each tile for grouting. To make sure you know what to order, experiment on 1-x-1-foot paper. It is wise to order a couple of 1-x-1-foot solid color patches in addition to the random sheets. These should be colors of extra strength and quality so that you can add more color accents to the already installed sheets at your discretion.

After the tiles have begun to adhere, about ½ hour after putting them down, it is easier to cut around the individual tiles or any section (with a sharp knife) to separate the tiles from their cloth backing and lift up single tiles here and there. This is a very interesting and creative part of this project. When this bar was built the accent colors used to embellish the creation were orange, silver, and gold. When ordering the assembled tile sheets, these colors were purposely left out. The predominant colors ordered were white (70 percent), blue and Mediterranean green.

Although the simple structure and construction of this bar precluded an extensive front bar installation, several features were installed: 2 built-in Nutone mixer-blender-ice crusher combinations, two 14½-x-16½-inch stainless steel bar sinks, and a single lever American Standard hot and cold water faucet between the sinks. In addition, a commercial glass washer and a stainless steel drainboard were mounted on the long stretch of the bar shelf. To illuminate the work area, a continuous line of 2-foot kitchen counter light fixtures were concealed under the bar top.

The area from the work shelf down to the bottom, which is 6 inches above the floor (mounted on a recessed base), totals nearly 22 inches and is used for beverage storage. This area is divided into compartments separated by sliding doors which vary in size according to the curve in that section and can be locked upward into the shelf with special cylinder locks.

Unlike the front, the back bar was custom-built in a 5-piece sectional set to facilitate transportation and installation. It has a very diversified layout and many functions built into it. An additional splash top and sink comes in handy for big parties.

Just about all the decorative lighting is controlled by Luxtrol WBD manual dimmers so that the light intensity can be preadjusted. The three-way switch system (one switch at the entrance of the entertainment room and another behind the bar) controls the same lights so that once the dimmers are properly set, there is no need to reset them when turning on the lights by switch. This system prevails

Figs. 17, 18. Behind these bi-fold doors is a bar that can roll out nearly 2 feet, providing full service with access to the back bar. This is not just a bar, it is a bar room—as complete as necessary, and out of the way when not in use.

HIDEAWAY BAR
EXPLODED VIEW

Fig. 19.

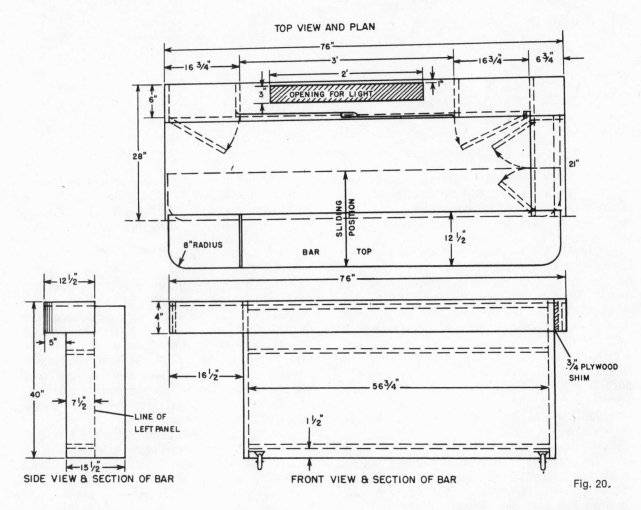

TOP VIEW AND PLAN

SIDE VIEW & SECTION OF BAR    FRONT VIEW & SECTION OF BAR    Fig. 20.

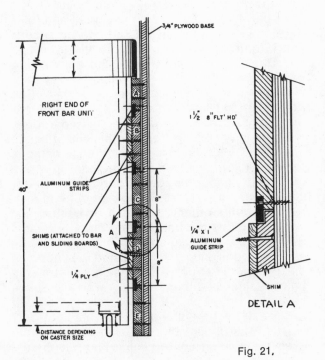

Fig. 21.

throughout the basement area.

A 4-inch glass trough stretches across the inside of the bar top, 1 inch below and parallel to it.

Graceful white bar stools and a specially designed off-white terrazzo floor (by Amtico) provide the finishing touches. It must not be taken for granted that direct and indirect lighting, above, below, and within the back bar and inside the front bar in one way or another enhanced this rather basic installation. This is again a testimonial that while good design is most important, designed lighting is, if done well, that which elevates the already good into an achievement that no other medium has yet been able to attain.

**The Hideaway Bar**

The bar in Figure 18 was built in a very busy family room that was only 10 feet wide. This area was also a playroom used by children. It was, therefore, designed to remain out of sight when not in use. A self-contained unit requiring only 3 feet in depth, this bar is dramatically lighted both directly and indirectly. Because of its beautiful Weldwood walnut plywood and matching plastic laminate of the bar top and apron, it is a striking contrast to the silver-gray Surfwood that covers the rest of the room; the bar is a delightful and unusual visual surprise.

Almost 16 cubic feet of all kinds of storage is concealed either behind touch-latch doors or behind the ¼-inch laminated Acrylite sliding panes. Because the overall depth of the area is only 30 inches, the front bar (14 inches deep) rolls on 4 perfectly aligned fixed-base casters. Although this bar is mounted on the right end with a tongue-and-groove panel device on which it slides out (see Figure 21), heavy-duty Grant slides would function still better. Two right-side, full-extension slides can be mounted parallel to one another at least 26 inches apart.

All the shelving, both wood and glass, is fully adjustable on metal shelf carriers placed in ¼-inch holes and spaced every 1½ inches. The work shelf behind the front bar is plastic covered and includes a small, removable copper dry sink, as well as a Nutone mixer-ice crusher behind the front bar.

The front door enclosure (Figure 17) is activated with Stanley bi-fold hardware: two pairs of door panels each support a third panel which is not connected to the track, and is supported with continuous hinges to the attached pair. Heavy-duty magnetic catches keep these aligned when closed. Made of ¾-inch Novoply, these doors are first installed and tested to make sure they work properly. Then the outer sandblasted fir panels (1¼-inch silver-gray Surfwood) are spot-glued and nailed with ¾-inch No. 16 brads. A three-dimensional surface effect is achieved by building the panels in 3 parts separated by 4-inch recessed bands (painted a sandlewood color), which also continue the same way all across and around the room; very unusual. These panel sections were so mounted as to stay consistently aligned by using temporary tacked-on spacers.

The paneling used on the doors and throughout the family room makes the room seem larger than it is. The dark coral ceiling is further dramatized by indirect fluorescent lighting behind molded plywood cover, especially above the bar.

Though there is much that can be said in praise of this bar, its basic simplicity is perhaps what makes it so interesting. The unusual element of surprise, however, remains its most outstanding feature.

### Suede Bar

The bar in Figures 22 through 24 is part of a room which was originally the living room in a 70-year-old colonial-style home. Because relatives, friends, and business associates were to be entertained here frequently, a rather luxurious setup was called for. But appearance alone was not, and never can be, the most important objective—this bar had to efficiently handle the needs of the large number of people this room could accommodate.

The shape of the front bar is the first consideration. Next is the back bar design which is integrated with the front bar layout. Then comes the arrangement of functional features. Many of these can be purchased commercially, but some, such as the refrigerator in the back bar and the stainless steel drain board in the front bar, had to be custom designed and built. The ice cream fountain was purchased second hand, refurbished and fitted into the front bar.

Despite its heavy weight, the bar itself is cantilevered. Because it stands on stainless steel pipe legs (similar to the Continental Bar, page 208) and because of the strong, perfectly aimed light stream (the wiring is passed through the pipe legs coming from the basement where the power unit is installed) of cold cathode tubing, which is molded to fit the bar top shape especially lighting up, down, and between horizontal structural layers, it appears to be in mid-air—as do the other suspended or freehanging bodies such as the bar top and the arm railing. Stainless steel brackets and supports had to be especially designed and fabricated to support all these separate structured parts only at strategic points. Otherwise there actually was just space between each item. This obviously lends itself to very dramatic lighting. In this bar, not only the top was translucent, but also the lower top over the main structure (which is a 6-inch suspended entity).

The lighting of this bar is even more elaborate than that of the Continental Bar. Here,

Fig. 22.   The Suede Bar. (These photos by Alex Georges.)

Fig. 24.

Fig. 23.

construction involves two layers of illuminated bar tops; the front 6 inches of the bottom layer are illuminated by strong light spilling through the slots cut into the bottom of the top unit. This light spillage is also reflected through the 2-inch space between the armrest and the front edge of the upper bar top. Through this dramatic lighting, an illusion of floating form is created. The back bar top is also illuminated from below, and a light stream coming from the upper cabinet unit directly above it creates a very powerful light concentration in this 16-inch-high area.

Although there are numerous systems of built-in illumination for a bar, most of them provide inadequate coverage. The one perfect way to avoid spottiness in this front bar was to use special custom-molded glass tubes (½ to ⅝ inch diameter). These tubes follow the inside and outside perimeters of each of the areas where lighting is needed. With special adaptation and proper installation they create a cold cathode lighting system which assures even dispersal of very strong illumination. See more about cold cathode lighting in Chapter 14, page 270. It was mandatory to connect these sections to the three dimmer zones: one for the bar top including the lower top and front spillage between; a second for the bottom downlight; the third for the back bar top and the indirect cornice lighting of the back bar. Since the second level top is recessed 6 inches directly below the bar top (in front), the nearest lighting tubes project the light intensity through the glass-shielded recess directly below the top and below the armrest.

Three more dimmers were used for special effects around the bar. One controlled illumination of the stained glass panes and the inside glass (two doors for the drinking glass storage area). Another controlled lighting for all the indirect cross-beam cornices. The final one controlled all the ceiling down lights including the wallwasher fixtures.

No matter how well a lighting system is designed and executed, its success is dependent on the background material. Obviously, a dark (Macassar ebony) background will expose a lighting design better than a light one, but this is especially true when using cold cathode lighting, especially on motorized dimmers.

The fluted front bar and the armrest are done in warm medium-brown plastic suede. The surrounding woods are flitches of hand-matched Macassar ebony veneer made into plywood sheets (by U.S. Plywood). Surface tiles are imported Italian glass ceramics (the same Sarim tile used for the Continental Bar) laminated to ⅝-inch plate glass.

Careful examination of this bar reveals a number of creative structural and design innovations. One of the remarkable achievements is the pair of stained glass back bar feature doors. They were designed by the author for production of an abstract version of the famous seventeenth-century painting by Giambattista and executed by Gabrielle Loire of France. The contrast between one of the darkest woods and the strongest and perfectly dispersed lighting created the most desirable foundation for dramatization. The lighting controls, so sensitively planned, allowed the creation of settings for any occasion or mood.

**Built-in bar in library combination wall**
Because bars do not necessarily have to be units at which one sits or stands, and because it is desirable to conceal the beverages where you are supposed to do your homework, the library is as good a place as any. There in your privacy you can help yourself or be a good host to your guest and give him a night cap as you fold down the bed.

This project is simply a cabinet, built separately with special sliding glass doors and an indirect light inside. Made to fit, it is put inside the unit and fastened to each side and the back.

To further utilize the available space, a slide-out top mounted on full extension slides (Grant 325) and covered with white plastic provides a fine bar top large enough to have a party. In order to conserve the space in this 12-cubic-foot unit, another plastic-covered top, mounted ½ inch above the slide top, provides further storage while not obstructing the bar top. Since there was extra room in the adjacent unit, a 1½-cubic-foot refrigerator was placed right next to the built-in bar. The bonus of this

Fig. 25.  Built-in bar in library, open.

compact feature is that it can be hidden. All one has to do is push the sliding top in and close the folding doors, which are covered with the continuous prefinished Accent-grooved walnut paneling that covers the entire built-in wall at very low cost and without any complications. This is a bar one can well think about and perhaps own someday.

### The Wine Bar

Here is a 6-foot unit which is a front and back bar with proper storage for wine bottles and wine glasses and with a drawer on each end for corkscrews and other accessories. In the center there is a slide-out plastic laminate bar top (like the one in the library). Here again, everything can be covered up when not in use. The

tambour doors provide a different approach, but when you entertain and want to show off a little, the cornice light in the center unit (top-back) lends a touch of elegance to this small and busy unit. Made of walnut plywood throughout, it took only one 4-x-8-foot sheet, ¾ inch thick.

The glass sliding doors are of very fine Belgian glass, but they are small enough not to upset the budget. If you are a wine connoisseur or just like the stuff stored in a unit that will enhance any area, this may well be a solution worth considering.

### Portable bar for formal living

This is a truly unique weekend project for the budget-conscious person who likes to entertain in style. As shown in Figure 27, the

Fig. 26. Wine bar.

structure basically consists of two boxlike structures. The top, which is a multitude of gadgets most men like, is perhaps more practical than a fabricated bar twice this size, and it is attractive too. By a careful observation of the structure one can appreciate that this is not hard to tackle. The main unit is of ¾-inch Novoply (chipboard) covered with warm off-white plastic laminate. The door and lid (except drawer front) are cut out after the unit is assembled and covered with the plastic. There are numerous ways to do this with hand tools or small portable Stanley power tools. After cutting, all edges must be planed. Fit all pieces, leaving enough room for edge banding and clearance for the lids to move freely. The drawer is built

separately and is mounted on Grant #325 full-extension slides. The drawer sides and back are low enough to accommodate a top with as many holes as you can fit, and of the size to take an average bottle. All hardware shown in the diagram is easily available. To contrast this duo-level structure, the bottom was built of ¾-inch walnut plywood.

The casters must be a flat-base nonswivel type. The handle is a ¼-x-1-inch aluminum bar bent in a vise. By following the diagram carefully, perhaps laying it out full size on the back of the ¾-inch Novoply sheet, you may have the time of your life building this bar and sharing it with your family and friends.

Fig. 27.  Portable bar for formal living.

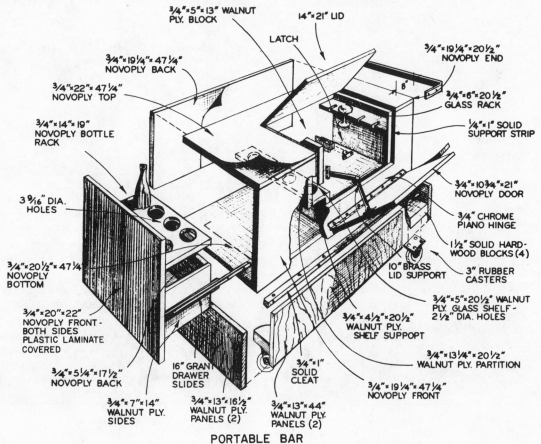

3/4"×5"×13" WALNUT PLY. BLOCK

14"×21" LID

LATCH

3/4"×19 1/4"×20 1/2" NOVOPLY END

3/4"×19 1/4"×47 1/4" NOVOPLY BACK

3/4"×22"×47 1/4" NOVOPLY TOP

3/4"×14"×19" NOVOPLY BOTTLE RACK

3/4"×6"×20 1/2" GLASS RACK

1/4"×1" SOLID SUPPORT STRIP

3/4"×10 3/4"×21" NOVOPLY DOOR

3/4" CHROME PIANO HINGE

1 1/2" SOLID HARD-WOOD BLOCKS (4)

3 9/16" DIA. HOLES

10" BRASS LID SUPPORT

3" RUBBER CASTERS

3/4"×20 1/2"×47 1/4" NOVOPLY BOTTOM

3/4"×5"×20 1/2" WALNUT PLY. GLASS SHELF - 2 1/2" DIA. HOLES

3/4"×20"×22" NOVOPLY FRONT - BOTH SIDES PLASTIC LAMINATE COVERED

3/4"×4 1/2"×20 1/2" WALNUT PLY. SHELF SUPPOPT

3/4"×13 1/4"×20 1/2" WALNUT PLY. PARTITION

3/4"×5 1/4"×17 1/2" NOVOPLY BACK

16" GRANT DRAWER SLIDES

3/4"×1" SOLID CLEAT

3/4"×19 1/4"×47 1/4" NOVOPLY FRONT

3/4"×7"×14" WALNUT PLY. SIDES

3/4"×13"×16 1/2" WALNUT PLY. PANELS (2)

3/4"×13"×44" WALNUT PLY. PANELS (2)

PORTABLE BAR

Fig. 28.

Fig. 1. Suspended patio and Gazebo.

# Chapter 13
# Outdoor Living

The idea for a "patio," or a patch of solid ground in back of the house, first became popular on the West Coast. Homeowners wanted a redwood table and bench set and a couple of chaise longues for use during warm weather. These patios gradually became refined by the use of concrete, flagstone, or simply bricks set into dry sand.

Innovations were more a matter of high-profit sales than of legitimate and constructive improvements. One can well do without enormous and expensive stone barbecues filled with gadgets and overpowering in proportion, monsters which were starting to pop up mostly in lower and middle class homes with the help of FHA home improvement loans. These structures tended to unbalance or overcrowd too-small backyards. This trend, however, did not last too long and gave way to realistic portable metal barbecues well within a budget anyone could afford. Nearly all such units have survived the test of time.

In the colder climates of the Northeast, people had similar inclinations, but the solutions of the Far West were often impractical for the easterner who needed an outdoor setup that could withstand bad weather. Builders in the East often poured 300-to-400-square-foot concrete slabs behind their houses. These areas were big enough for a few chairs, perhaps a table, and, of course, a portable barbecue. Today patio and terrace construction has become more refined. As a home improvement project, it is usually very worthwhile and can be handled in various ways.

## Design

Overall design of the patio should be in keeping with that of the house to which it is attached only if the house design is worth extending and following. If it isn't, the proper approach would be to create an integral plan using the patio structure to enhance the house façade.

City-planning ordinances determine at least part of the planning and physical layout of the patio. Legal boundaries may dictate just about the size it is to be and the structural requirements that are necessary. By considering all the existing restrictions, the overall functional and aesthetic design will have a sound base.

The two features in this chapter are good examples of outdoor construction. While they are completely different from one another, each fulfills its function.

## Poured-concrete and flat terrain patios

For those interested in a poured patio complete with built-ins and storage, the Outdoor Living Center described on page 255 represents such a venture in full detail while revealing some interesting and helpful facts and new techniques.

The building of a patio can become very involved, and the results can be disappointing. Because concrete buckles and cracks frequently, people often ask if there is some kind of guide to avoiding costly traps.

The best thing to do is to always face the facts. It is important to realize that, although the degree of damage can be reduced by a good preparatory job, hard floorlike concrete will eventually crack. To reduce the chance of damage, however, cushion the area beneath the cement with gravel, and then cover this with a double layer of wire mesh (4-inch squares) and at least 2 inches of fine sand above the wire mesh. A minimum of a 4-inch thickness of concrete should be used, carefully mixed in the correct proportions (the mixture varying with the climate) and grooved in 2- to 3-foot squares. This not only creates a pattern, but it also relieves the pressure somewhat, thus reducing the cracking of the floor. Concrete should be poured on a rather cloudy and humid day (not over 65-70 degrees and never in strong summer heat). However, if the project is done in midsummer, concrete should be poured before the sun has gained in strength. Before concrete starts to dry, it should be sprayed with a very fine spray of water and kept moist for a minimum of 72 hours. This will slow the drying of the outside surface, thus curing from the inside out, which will prevent initial cracking and help guard against future cracking. Finally, the slab should be roofed over with either fiberglass panes or louvered wood slats. There are numerous inexpensive and attractive solutions to serve this purpose. If these or any other pro-

Fig. 2. This barbecue is charcoal-fired and shares the same flue with the electrically operated unit inside—all part of the large fireplace structure. For heavy entertainment (which this patio certainly can accommodate), the ledge to the right of young Claudia is available for an additional 10-inch x 5-foot grill, or 14 to 16 more steaks.

Fig. 3. This is a classic illustration of a patio overlapping the side of the house. Besides giving the patio area all possible dimension, it achieved an important aesthetic appearance.

gressive guidelines are followed, a concrete floor will stand up quite well for a fairly long time in just about any climate.

## Flagstone, slate, and brick patios

Installation of flagstone, slate blocks, or even quarry tiles produces beautiful results although it is much more costly than concrete. The same careful preparations are required: gravel or sand and wire mesh with a good mixture of cement and sand. The blocks must be embedded in a minimum thickness of 3 inches of concrete and spaced no less than ⅜ inch apart. Again, installation in hot weather is risky, and watering to keep the area, even the stone, moist for at least 48 hours is imperative. In fact, the best way to insure success is by soaking the stone prior to installation.

If a patio floor of this type is laid on uneven terrain, a dirt fill must be packed down with a heavy machine roller. If the fill is to cover a substantial area and depth, it should be done in two stages and preferably over two seasons. This allows natural settling to take place, thus avoiding future disasters. This may seem somewhat involved and economically unacceptable, but the choice is very important and the results will prove your judgment.

Less permanent installations and low-budget and -labor projects are often done simply by putting down used bricks embedded in sand or fine gravel. This type of patio can survive a couple of years of rough weather and will look presentable and even very rustic, but after a while the blocks tend to rock, making them difficult to walk on, and it is almost impossible to clean them off without washing away the fill. Under an awning and protected from rain, this type of installation may be more durable.

The other feature in this chapter is the revolutionary Suspended Patio built in the House of Ideas. It is recommended primarily for uneven terrains. You may very much enjoy the rugged terrain with its growth of grass and trees, as was the case in the House of Ideas.

For decades, uneven ground conditions have been corrected with landfill—gradually building up the area and packing it down over a considerable period of time. Such jobs are still handled in the same way they were years ago, except for the use of modern equipment. The Suspended Patio is less expensive and more easily constructed than a patio using the fill system and covered with flagstones or slate. The latter would take at least twice as long to build and the heavy equipment necessary to do the job could easily damage the surrounding property. Furthermore, the Suspended Patio can be built to blend with the design of the house, or, as in this case, blending the patio with the house façade in that area, including the integration of existing old trees. This would be difficult to accomplish with the other method.

The general upkeep of the Suspended Patio proved to be simple and inexpensive—in fact, there were almost no maintenance costs. A poured terrace, on the other hand, could eventually demand costly repairs, especially where exposed to harsh winter weather.

There are occasions, however, when this type of structure should not be used. It is not feasible to build a platform on the ground if the terrain is even and level with the house. There must be a minimum of 2½ feet between the ground and the joists supporting the deck, so that the air can circulate and the annual coating of all wood parts with Woodlife preservative is possible. Also, it is necessary to get beneath the platform to clean and rake the crushed gravel, which is put there mainly to prevent weed growth, but which lends a decorative touch as well. From the good-design point of view, a Suspended Patio should be built substantially above the ground.

## Budget considerations

Formulating a budget for building a patio is difficult and may be deceiving because it is almost impossible to predetermine just what factors will be involved. Many building jobs can be closely adjusted to a reasonable budget because there are enough known factors within proven price structures with which to work. But to analyze a job for which most of the price-determining factors are unknown (such as general experience in terrain work) is very difficult. Most contractors are reluctant to tie themselves down to a fixed budget if the job involves much

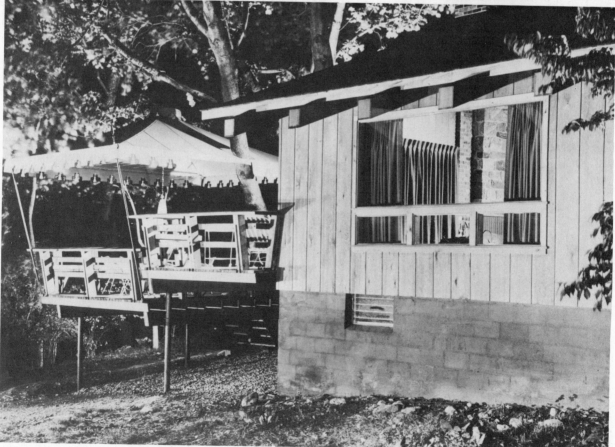

digging, filling and leveling.

Labor costs represent a major part of the expense in any job. An outdoor patio could end up being done on a time and material basis, which is a risky proposition since the contractor will probably cushion his charges generously for his safety.

Those with experience in building and negotiating with contractors should be able to adequately supervise the performance of workmen. At worst, such persons will pay about 15 percent above what they should. Consequently, they are perhaps best able to agree to a time and materials arrangement.

Those who have no idea of the mechanics of labor in the construction field are advised to pay a trustworthy architect or designer for design and supervision. They should also turn over to the supervisor the buying or at least the specifying of all materials and the cost control. For the inexperienced, arriving at a workable budget would be guesswork at best. In any case, it is wise to stay clear of "lopsided proportions." Investing $5,200 in a patio for a $25,000 home that stands on a ⅛-acre lot, especially in a neighborhood where other homes fall in this price range, would be impractical and foolhardy. Within reasonable limits, however, there should be few restrictions on the homeowner's desire to build and enjoy what he wants.

## Suspended Patio

When a concrete slab is not suitable because of uneven or sloping terrain, the patio shown in Figures 1-3 is the ideal solution.

This Suspended Patio in the House of Ideas was built in a colder section of the Eastern Seaboard where the ground is frozen for over a quarter of the year. The building details are, therefore, geared to a very sturdy construction which may not be required in milder climates. The base support, in particular, is under strict code requirements. Different sections of the country have building codes dealing with such specifics as concrete footings (to support the columns). The local building authorities in your area should be consulted prior to planning.

When laying out the patio in relation to the house, it should, if possible, spread across the full width of the back. The steps leading up to it should not extend beyond the house line, and the level of the patio should be 4 inches below the saddle of the lowest door opening onto it. At the end opposite the steps, the platform can extend beyond the house by the same distance as the overhang of the roof. This will give an interesting visual appeal to the sloped-out banister, both from the front and from the side of the house.

Structural tie-in points (frame or concrete, depending on the base and foundation structure of the existing home) should be marked clearly as to where the installation and attachment of the patio to the house is to take place. Follow the construction layout. These points or markers will serve as a reference guide as to where best to anchor supporting bracing when attaching the new addition to the house. A 2-x-12-inch fir plank is fastened to the base of the house 5⅝-inches (net) below the lowest door saddle. This plank must be mounted perfectly parallel with the horizontal structure lines of the house whether or not it is perfectly level. In extreme cases only, adjustments must be made. Sizing up the degree of the problem and applying aesthetic judgment will usually provide a solution. The 2-x-12-inch board and the 2-x-4-inch sections mounted continuously in line to the bottom of the 12-inch support plank must be of the full span of the patio platform, less the stairs at the beginning. If the needed span of the plank exceeds the maximum of a commercially available length, it will be necessary to joint together several planks to meet the required dimensions. However, in such cases, it is advisable to first use as long a span as possible in a single piece and position it so as to get the support from the anchor point nearest the end of the plank and the next support from the next anchor point for the second plank. This obviously will leave a few inches on the end of each plank unsupported, which can be capped off by mounting another piece of 2-x-12, long enough to pass the two anchor points near the join of the two main planks, while at the same time covering the join. The 2-x-4 bottom strip will have to be in that section, mounted to the capping block. Consequently, the floor joists in that portion will be somewhat shorter (the thickness of the second plank, to be exact).

The next step will be to fasten the support plank to the house with spikes, followed by ½-inch-diameter lag bolts and washers, long enough to reach well into the established anchor supports. Then mount a 2-x-4-inch fir piece to the 2-x-12 eight inches below the top edge (7⅝-inches net lumber size), again using spikes. This is the basic support for the 2-x-8-inch fir floor joists. Usually 2-x-6-inch joists would be sufficient for up to a span of about 8 feet, although some builders may stretch it even further. All joists for the floor of this Suspended Patio are 2-x-8 (see Figure 4). The reason for the importance of the 2-x-12 plank anchored to the house is that this is where it all begins. First, starting at the right end of the building, guidemarks indicate the positions where the floor joists are to be toe-nailed to the plank and on top of the 2-x-4 support ledge (16 inches on center). Next, the joists for this platform are cut equally to the same length and the ends opposite those that are mounted against the house are cut back, slanted toward the bottom on a 15-degree angle (see Figure 4). A temporary frame structure to support the 2-x-8 joists level is erected and braced to the ground at a distance of about 6 to 7 feet from the support plank. The top plank of this temporary support is marked like the 2-x-12 plank, and those guidelines are exactly parallel to those of the opposite side planks for the 2-x-8 joists to be aligned at 16 inches on center, starting at the right end of the house. This will enable you to permanently toe-nail the floor joists to the 2-x-12 plank, while at the same time tacking them to the temporary support in line with the guidelines, thus achieving a perfect floor substructure of 2-x-8 joists perpendicular to the house line at 16 inches on center and at right angles to the plank.

With all cross members in place, a fascia plank is temporarily tacked to the slanted front edges of the 2-x-8s, keeping the highest edge even with the top of the joists. Mark each 2-x-8 joist to the inside of the 2-x-8 fascia, then fasten it to the joist permanently with 15 d nails. In case a long stretch cannot be covered with one plank and piecing is required, cut the fascia support pieces so as to have the joints meet in the center of the end edge of a joist. It is advisable at this point to check the entire row of the 2-x-8 joists with an extra-long straightedge to make sure that all top edges in all areas and in all directions are perfectly even. The straightedge may be made of pieces of ¾-inch plywood about 6 to 8 inches wide, using the factory-finished edge for the test.

*General guidelines:* Because it is important to have a straightedge at least twice the width of the area in length for best results, several plywood strips, each 8 feet in length, are joined together by overlapping them about 10 inches and nailing them together from both sides, while aligning them to a chalk snap line or a carefully drawn straight pencil line. To finally check a straightedge, lay the wood strip on its flat side if it is flexible, or set it on the unfinished edge if it is rigid, and look down the entire edge, backing up about 1 foot, moving and tilting your head to bring it into proper focus. Most people close one eye to get what they call an undistorted reading. Surprisingly enough, this system has survived centuries of tests, and even in this age of sophisticated instruments architects, designers, and especially builders use the system of eyeing or sizing up. Even structural wall areas are still judged by this method. Since most of the creative work in the House of Ideas was laid out and built on the spot without working drawings, the drawings and detailed instructions for the Suspended Patio were done after completion for inclusion in this book. However, more intermediate checking than is customary was imperative. Among the necessary tools were a set of assorted straightedges ranging from 6 feet to 16 feet and including 2-foot and 8-foot good quality levels, along with an assortment of squares ranging from an adjustable 4-inch precision square to a reliable homemade ash wood unit, 4-x-6 feet (with a supporting cross brace), which was checked every time before being used for a layout. There were numerous types and sizes of compasses, ranging from 2-inch mini types to an old-fashioned one 2 feet long (in closed position).

These were adequate to work out the problems of any one of the features.

There is, of course, the most basic and useful Trammel point set for large curves and circles. These are clamp-on units (about 2 inches high), with metal points on the bottom and a fastening bolt-head on top. One clamp also has a pencil fastening device which is very useful. This set is one of the most valuable aids for large layouts. The adjustable and removable point set will fit on a ¾-inch thick by 1-inch high (maximum) oak or ash wood strip, which should be treated with a couple of thin layers of good protective finish. In addition to the Stanley locking tape measures ranging from 6 to 12 feet, a set of folding wood measuring rulers and 25-foot and 50-foot Stanley tool precision measuring tapes, there was another very helpful and important device. This patio, with its enormous size, its changing levels, and especially its many points of interest, such as the subtle integration of the huge oak tree into the patio setting, needed more than just a sketch or layout—it needed a heightened imagination projected into the finished product. To do this best, a rather unorthodox method was used.

The device was the viewer on top of the wide-angle camera which photographed most of the House of Ideas, whose theme was created by focusing in on all features, and sometimes actually photographing work-in-progress. As in motion picture photography, the camera moves in on the action, picking up points of interest as planned in the script. However, it seldom turns when it retreats; it keeps moving toward new and more dramatic points of view. This statement would have to be qualified in that some scripts will, by their nature, not call for innovative set design. Yet there is no doubt that most people have been spellbound at some time by a magnificently designed film set—even when the story and dialogue were not exceptional. True interior design and decorating can, and in fact should, be executed on the basic principles used for movie sets—starting with the "script," which is the dream of what you seek in the finished product.

This system proved successful, in general, in the search for new horizons in creative design, and met the challenging task of building and reshaping partial structures, as well as realizing complex new innovations. Even before the creation of the Suspended Patio, studies from all angles, using the camera as the principal "eye" and guide, became the most valuable means of formulating the shape and even the detail of the support. The cantilevered characteristic of the patio structure, the bi-level decks, and the special Gazebo which was actually built around an old and exceptionally healthy tree called for an imaginative approach. The tree was a challenge in itself. The process of trimming, reshaping, and supporting the branches was a typical case in which the camera eye was invaluable. There is no better way to envision the continuity and harmony of the whole; the drawing board cannot achieve this. (More on the creative study method in Chapter 14, "How to properly lay out an area prior to remodeling," page 266).

ABOUT THE CONSTRUCTION: While the patio is a great challenge to the creative imagination, one must not overlook the realistic consequences that follow the design (as in any feature), even if the creative endeavor was a success. As a matter of record, more beautiful features are harder to detail and build than are stereotype projects. While the technical specifications of the Suspended Patio are basic, there are always problems to solve, such as sound construction and procedures obviating the need for complicated equipment and much physical help. Most important is to build a structure that is safe, and effortless to maintain; this was achieved here. Even though this is a web of weight-bearing members and units, with subsupports, concrete bases, lally columns, joists, floor slats, railings, benches, stairs, nuts and bolts, etc., its sequential building and assembly program will enable the ambitious non-professional to accomplish it.

We have described the initial stages and the structural frame assembly of the main deck. While the construction of the lower platform is basically the same as that of the large one, there is still the main structure to be built. Even though the procedure may appear roundabout, it still was built that way successfully, and surprisingly easily. Therefore, except for minor changes to further improve the construction

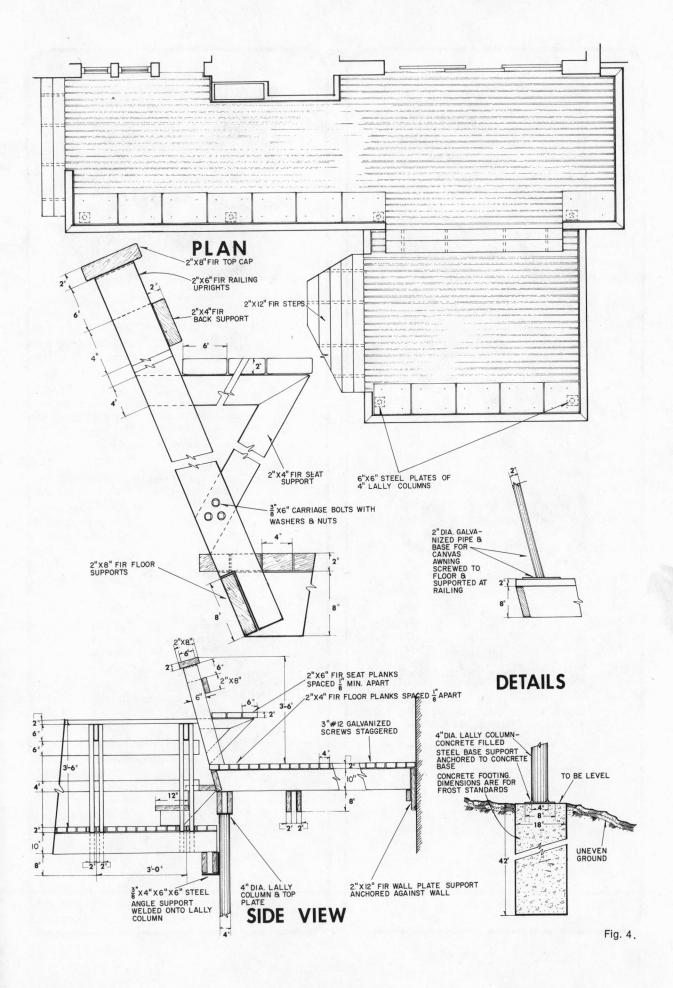

**PLAN**

2"X8" FIR TOP CAP

2"X6" FIR RAILING UPRIGHTS

2"X4" FIR BACK SUPPORT

2"X12" FIR STEPS

2"X4" FIR SEAT SUPPORT

$\frac{3}{8}$"X6" CARRIAGE BOLTS WITH WASHERS & NUTS

6"X6" STEEL PLATES OF 4" LALLY COLUMNS

2"X8" FIR FLOOR SUPPORTS

2" DIA. GALVANIZED PIPE & BASE FOR CANVAS AWNING SCREWED TO FLOOR & SUPPORTED AT RAILING

**DETAILS**

2"X6" FIR SEAT PLANKS SPACED $\frac{1}{8}$" MIN. APART

2"X4" FIR FLOOR PLANKS SPACED $\frac{1}{8}$" APART

3"#12 GALVANIZED SCREWS STAGGERED

4"DIA. LALLY COLUMN— CONCRETE FILLED

STEEL BASE SUPPORT ANCHORED TO CONCRETE BASE

CONCRETE FOOTING. DIMENSIONS ARE FOR FROST STANDARDS

TO BE LEVEL

UNEVEN GROUND

42"

$\frac{3}{8}$"X4"X6"X6" STEEL ANGLE SUPPORT WELDED ONTO LALLY COLUMN

4" DIA. LALLY COLUMN & TOP PLATE

2"X12" FIR WALL PLATE SUPPORT ANCHORED AGAINST WALL

**SIDE VIEW**

Fig. 4.

Fig. 5. This is the portion of the patio where the main upper level leads with two steps to the lower Gazebo platform. Looking beyond are the steps from the Gazebo to the ground. This view shows the concrete-filled steel pipe lally columns (4-inch diameter) supporting the two platforms in this area. These support the double layers of 2 x 10 girders which in turn support the 2 x 6 joists.

Fig. 6. Close-up of same area as Figure 5. Note the corner supports that are welded on to these particular lally columns because they extend beyond this level to support the girder of the upper structure also shown.

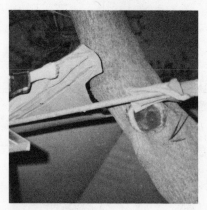

Fig. 7. Installation of canvas roof for the Gazebo.

To save most of a 400-year-old maple tree, several branches had to be cut off to clear the new built-on. Those branches that remained were trimmed and interconnected with ½-inch steel rods. This made the remaining tree a monument to the patio area. However, the patio stairs in that area had to be built around the tree as was the canvas top.

To make the canvas fit properly, a cardboard pattern had to be taken and transferred to the canvas. A couple of inches around the bark for clearance took care of shifting and tree expansion.

Fig. 8. Nothing was directly attached to the tree; only insulated cable was bracketed to it with special insulated clips to install concealed down lights.

Fig. 9. Note how the ends of the hole do not quite meet. This was done to allow room for stretching.

Fig. 10. Lacing the canvas to the top-pitch structure pipes, as done here, and lacing in all other areas is the same, except that this is the last fastening operation. Reinforced ring holes provided and installed by the manufacturer are put in a zig-zag pattern (every 5 inches) to a double-layer reinforced canvas support strip, wide enough so as to surround the pipe, and sewed to the inside of the top following the layout of the pipe structure when properly assembled. This is perhaps best seen in Figure 11. Note also the additional round top frame. This is decoratively covered separately in order to allow up-current, especially wind pressure, to escape rather than to pull the structure out. The junction is mounted in the center for the Heifetz globe light.

Fig. 11. This denotes the precise opening slot for the typical slanted corner support. The upper extension of the pipe will receive the spear head. The bottom plate support is important; this is where the pipe structure is secured through the support sleeve into the pipe. Note also the shape of the border scallops, which are edge-bound with a dark accent color canvas border about ⅜-inch wide.

Fig. 12. Inserting and fastening the spear heads is done last. When taking the top down (usually once a year), the spearheads must be removed first.

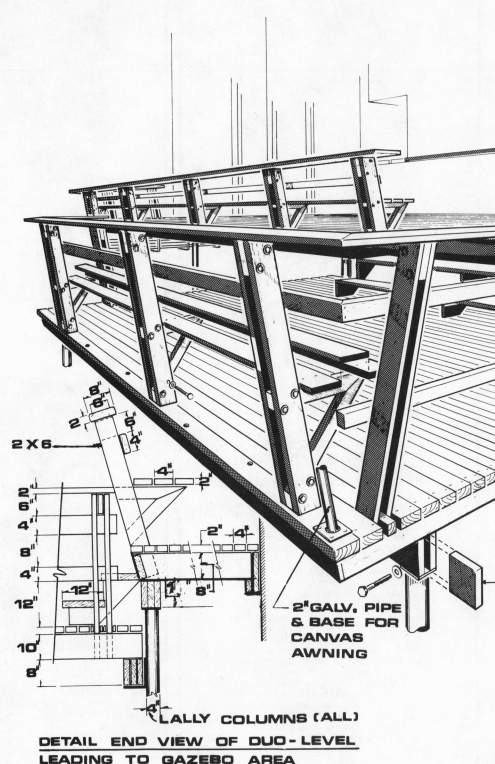

2 X 6

8"
6"
2"
6"
4"

4"
2"

2"
6"
4"

8"
4"

12"
12"

2"  4"

2"
8"

10"

8"

4"

2"GALV. PIPE
& BASE FOR
CANVAS
AWNING

4" LALLY COLUMNS (ALL)

## DETAIL END VIEW OF DUO-LEVEL
## LEADING TO GAZEBO AREA

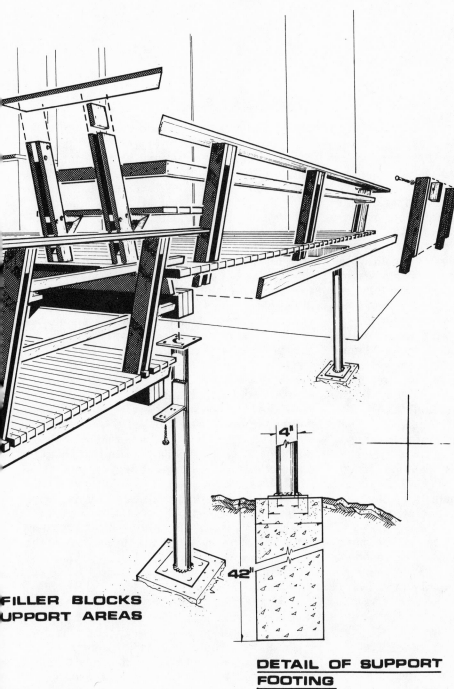

FILLER BLOCKS
UPPORT AREAS

4"

42"

**DETAIL OF SUPPORT
FOOTING**

**SUSPENDED   PATIO**
**EXPLODED   VIEW**

Fig. 13.

method, this is the best solution.

INSTALLING GIRDERS: A girder is any strong or principal member on which the weight of a floor or partition is supported. It is either made of a single piece of lumber, or built up in several paltes, often very large, depending on the weight and stress of the supported construction. In special weight-bearing cases, girders are made of steel, usually calculated by an engineer to support the weight as well as the stress. There was no need for steel girders in this Patio. As shown in the detail of Figures 5, 6 and 13, the girders supporting the platform structures of the Suspended Patio levels were made up of double 2-x-10s with 2-x-10-x-12-inch blocks sandwiched between them evenly every 4 feet and at all ends, using carriage bolts, washers, and nuts in these areas. This makes the girders thicker, giving them more surface for resting and mounting the lally column support plates (see Figure 6). The girder supporting the main platform is placed even with the bottom slant of the front fascia. This girder spreads from the right end, also flush with the fascia at that end, returns, extending the left end of the main (top) platform by 10 inches, thus supporting one step on one end of it.

At this time it is necessary to first mark the locations of the lally columns (evenly) which in this case were 8 feet apart, thus utilizing the 2-x-10-x-12-inch block, mounted every 4 feet. Run a plumb line from the center to the ground at all support areas. Next, with white chalk mark the outline (18 x 18 inches) from the excavation of the footing. After this girder is fitted, it is put in place and is supported vertically with 2-x-4 or 2-x-6 planks (temporarily), avoiding the areas where the footings for the lally columns are marked. The next girder is the one that supports the lower level at the higher platform side. This girder is flush on each end but is recessed so as to leave a space between it and the girder supporting the upper level (by 1 inch). This is to create a clearance for the lally column at each end of the lower platform which supports the large girder at these areas with the top plate, while at the same time supporting the girder of the lower platform (see

Figure 5). Parallel to this girder is another on the outside of the lower (Gazebo) platform, which supports the platform at the front fascia, ranging from end to end where it is flush. While the girders are firmly but temporarily supported, further preparation for the permanent supports, vertical and otherwise, proceeds. It is very important to constantly check the entire structure, insuring that it is straight and square until permanently secured.

VERTICAL SUPPORT: At this time we have a smaller lower platform support frame, beneath the large upper one, which checks out perfectly fiush on the top framing and is also square and level. However, it is supported by temporary support girders which are held in position vertically with planks wedged to the ground. The permanent phase of this structure will commence and the construction will be complete when the installation of the lally columns eliminates the temporary supports. A lally column is a heavy-guage steel pipe, generally 4 inches in diameter. It is filled with concrete and capped off on both ends with a 6-x-6-inch (½ inch thick) steel plate, with a ½-inch hole in each corner. This type of support is as strong as necessary for this type of construction and is also economical. The only drawback is that, due to the type of construction involving the production of this column, one must, as we are doing, first erect the substructure to determine the exact size needed. Quite often, as in this feature where the terrain is substantially uneven, it requires several columns of varied sizes. Here, the lally columns were equally spaced and mounted about 8 feet apart. In addition, as shown in Figures 4, 5 and 13, two of the lally columns were special because they had to support the girders for the main deck as well as for the lower (Gazebo) deck. This, as shown, was accomplished by welding a ¾-x-6-x-6-x-3-inch-wide steel angle to each of the two columns, with two ½-inch holes bored through each top of the braces.

In order for all these details to be correct, it was imperative to have the entire structure properly installed and temporarily but firmly supported. Avoid blocking the areas where the foundations to support the lally columns are outlined for excavation. And before digging the footing holes and filling them with concrete, consult local building authorities. When the concrete of the footing holes is pored and while the concrete is still fresh, drop a plumb line again from the pre-marked center point of the vertical support area (6-x-6-inch lally column mounting end-plate) on the bottom of the girder and transpose it to the concrete footing which is flush with the surrounding ground but has been finished off to be level. The fabricator of the lally columns (usually a lumber yard or building supply store) will supply and weld on a typical 6-x-6 steel plate used to cap off each end of the columns. The fabricator will also include the two ½-inch thicknesses of the end-cap mounting plates to the given dimension of each lally column. This will also contain the four ½-inch holes in the corners, necessary for fastening the welded-on cap-mounting plates. Specify that the ½-inch holes be slightly larger, to accommodate the ½-inch lag bolts without difficulty. Also, at the time of ordering the lally columns, acquire a sample 6-x-6-inch mounting plate, including the four holes for marking purposes, requesting that all mounting cap-plates be identical. Place the sample plate on the leveled footing tops, lining it up with the plumb mark, and scribe the ½-inch corner holes to the soft concrete. Carefully bore the holes (using a narrow screwdriver or similar handtool) at each mark to insert a ½-x-6-inch bolt upside down, solidly packing each bolt into the footing, leaving 2 inches of thread extending. Check again for accuracy by carefully placing the steel plate in position. First clean (using a small, hard bristle brush) and then cover each thread generously with ordinary Vaseline for protection, and continue the same operation on all concrete footings. Make sure that all bolts are solidly packed with concrete and are perfectly straight. Keep all concrete damp for at least 48 hours.

FINAL PREPARATION: While waiting for the lally columns, there are the 2-x-4s covering the decks to be prepared, the slanted banister supports to be built and fitted, and the angular seat supports to be made. Have all necessary parts ready when needed. After preparation of all parts, and while they are handy, apply a generous coat of Woodlife preservative (a liquid to protect any lumber exposed to the elements, by U.S. Plywood) on all surfaces and especially the edges of all parts. Do not do any work on the structure itself until all lally columns are installed and the entire structure is satisfactory. No further parts must be added to the structure until completion of the installation of all lally columns and the removal of the temporary supports. The concrete footings must be firm.

FINAL PHASE: The deck floors consist of kiln-dry 2-x-4 fir slats, carefully selected, straight and without loose knots or cracks, fastened to the joists with 8d galvanized finishing nails. Box nails are placed between the 2-x-4s during the nailing as spacers to insure consistent space (approximately $\frac{3}{16}$ inch). The 2-x-4s must be carefully forced together while nailing them to maintain a perfectly straight alignment, especially where continuous pieces are joined to meet required lengths. In such cases, due to the extreme length of this Suspended Patio, the joints of the many 2-x-4 slats were so arranged as to retain an organized and harmonious arrangement. Besides the necessity to join two pieces in the exact center of the support below, and to fasten each separately near the joint, the arrangements of the joints are symmetrically alternated. This will establish or use several areas where each fourth slat joins depending on the length of the slats. Never should one joint be too close to another, nor is it aesthetically desirable to have joints uncontrolled. After all the boards are nailed properly, a special dual pilot countersink drill-bit in your ¼-inch portable electric drill is used to bore holes for 2½-inch No. 12 galvanized flathead wood screws next to each nail. This system assures a sturdy, tight floor and should be used throughout. The spacer nails can now be removed.

All other cuts and assemblies are shown in the diagrams. Lumber for the rail top-plates is 2-x-8. The slanted upright supports are of 2-x-6-inch fir (sandwiched together with spacer blocks, much as on the girders). Seats are 2-x-6s spaced ¼ inch apart. The spacer blocks

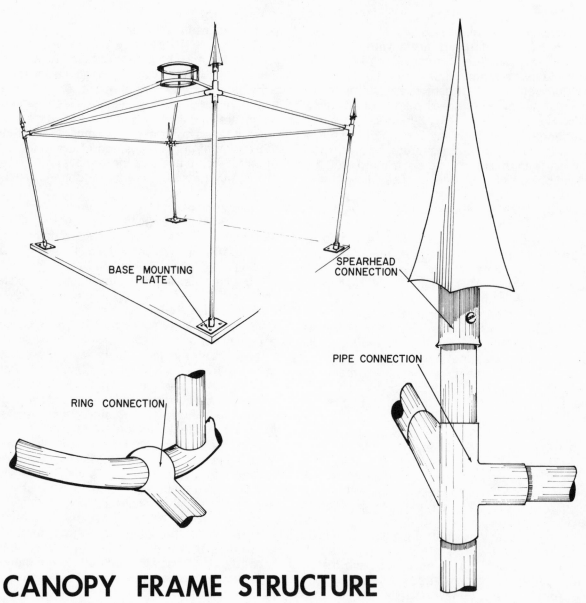

# CANOPY FRAME STRUCTURE

Fig. 14.

between the upright supports on top as shown in the diagram are 6 inches long.

For the stairs, the cutout end stringers are of 2-x-12s. The treads are two 2-x-6s spaced ¼ inch apart. If steps are wider than 3 feet, a center stringer is required; if they are as wide as 8 feet, two intermediate stringers will be needed.

All the lumber for this Suspended Patio is selected straight and clear fir (not ordinary construction fir). After lumber is cut to size, it should be inspected to make sure that all slivers have been eliminated and all coarse parts sanded. All edges must be rounded before installation.

Before any piece is mounted, and again after the entire construction is completed, a heavy coat of Woodlife (preservative) should be applied to all surfaces and ends. (This treatment should be repeated after completion and once a year thereafter.) Woodlife is a powerful preservative liquid making the wood waterproof after several applications. This will protect the wood from insects, as well as from cracking, splintering, and warping, no matter how inclement the weather conditions. To give the lumber an aged appearance, mix one small tube of lamp black into each gallon of Woodlife. The patio will become increasingly attractive as the wood mellows and takes on a more rustic appearance.

### The Gazebo

To create a dramatic solution for the Gazebo, slanted spearlike pipe supports were inserted and secured in support sleeves mounted on each corner of the lower platform. As shown in Figure 14, the vertical slanted spear supports and crossbars for the Gazebo are made of 2-inch galvanized pipe. The tarpaulin, which should be removed every winter, is made of canvas, the tassels of carved wood. The 4 horizontal pipes and the 4 slanted roof pipes sustaining the round air-pressure escape gable-end were all supported by multiple couplings holding all 2-inch galvanized pipes in place securely with set-screws, or as in this case, square-head screw-bolts with sharp ends, heading into smaller pilot holes in the pipes to get a good grip, were tapped into the sleeves. Once all pipes are properly connected and secured, the desired shape of the Gazebo falls into place. The spearheads are mounted after the canvas tarp is installed. The double ring structure on the very top is decoratively embellished to conceal its practical function. If strong winds capable of lifting the entire unit out of the socket should strike, the 30-inch round vent on top may well save the Gazebo. Because of the complexity of this canvas tarp and its installation, it is mandatory to have it made, installed, and removed by professionals.

Cushions for the seats are made of foam rubber covered with orange Naugahyde. Pressure air vent holes are sewn into the edges.

Although this patio has two levels, this type of construction lends itself very well to alterations and additions. Furthermore, once the basic and important structural tie-in work is complete, this is a perfect project for the home craftsman who wants to try his hand at something not too demanding.

The wall of the house can be paneled with exterior grade Early American cedar plywood, which can also be treated similarly to the Patio structure, an economical way to achieve a new look as well as happier summers.

### Outdoor Living Center

The Outdoor Living Center in Figures 16 through 18 was designed to prolong the patio season in a home on Long Island, New York. A weatherproof, open-air area was achieved by shielding the area from the wind and rain and, in some places, from the sun. Because it is partially enclosed, the patio offers some privacy as well.

Built-ins are most important to this Outdoor Living Center. A stereo, TV, intercom, telephone (all removable except the intercom), handsome bar, and well-organized storage are all at hand (Figures 17 and 18), eliminating tiresome trips into the house when entertaining or just relaxing. An interesting lighting arrangement and beautiful color scheme add to the effect. The project is done with waterproof materials throughout and finished with outdoor enamels that can simply be hosed down when they become soiled.

The split-level house onto which the Outdoor Living Center was to be built already had a small concrete patio at the rear connected by a louvered door to the family room (Figure 15). This patio would be enlarged and roofed in, and a unit containing built-ins would be incorporated into a wall at one end.

*Patio:* First the area was measured and outlined with stakes and string. Cement blocks were placed in the corners where the main vertical supports of the roof structure were planned (Figure 19).

Before any concrete work was done, the roof was built. A support for the roof was fastened to the house at the proper level. Main support posts and beams were assembled on the ground.

Figs. 15,16. Outdoor Living Center created a new and better house.

A trench was then dug following the string outline of the patio; soil from the trench was piled outside the line. A form of 2-x-6 boards was built all around it, with several layers of ¼-inch plywood used to form rounded corners. The form was held in place with stakes driven into the ground, and the soil was piled against the boards for additional support. The parts of the vertical support pillars which were to be covered by the concrete were coated on the bottom with Creosote (preservative), and spikes were driven partway into them below the patio level line in all directions to better secure them in the concrete. Sectional guide strips were placed in the larger areas 7 to 8 feet apart; 2-x-6 boards were again used for this purpose. The sectional guide strips divide a large area into smaller sections. This helps to control the concrete, especially when the material is running short, while the temperature rises. It also comes in handy when there is insufficient help. However, if all goes well, the guide strip will serve to even up the surface more easily. When everything is ready for the next section, the 2-x-6 guide board can be removed before concrete is poured for the next area, or it can remain to serve as a troweling guide and be removed just before the concrete sets—cover the narrow trough created by the strip with some concrete and trowel it smooth. After gravel and sand were spread to fill in the lower areas, wire mesh was placed and embedded in a 2-inch layer of sand, making the entire area even and ready for cement. A final check was made to insure that all posts were plumb, and that everything was straight, level, and square. Then the concrete was poured and troweled smooth. Planters were built in one section (Figure 21). These helped create an interesting divider and focal point.

BUILT-INS: The concrete surface was kept moist for a couple of days, allowing it to dry from within. After the concrete had thoroughly hardened, work was begun on the built-in cabinets. The design was outlined on the concrete surface; 2-x-4 fir plates were nailed with steel-cut nails to the concrete floor, even with the right edge of the roof line, keeping it flush with the right end of the concrete slab. All studs were mounted 16 inches on center. (See Fig-

Fig. 17. View of all functional built-ins from the outside. Left: intercom-stereo, room for portable TV on slide-out platform, telephone nook, storage for records. Center: bar unit. Right: garden and general maintenance tool storage. Bar unit slides out as an automatic switch clicks on lights inside the cabinet. All other sections are individually covered by folding door sets.

Fig. 18. View from inside reveals solid and translucent roof, providing an interesting combination.

ures 20, 22, 23). Weldwood texture 1-11 exterior fir paneling was used to cover the outside of the wall (Figure 25). Inside, partitions of the cabinets were of ¾-inch waterproof Duraply. Duraply provides the strong support needed for the slide-mounted bar and top cabinet, as well as the cabinetry of the TV-stereo section. Also, Duraply comes with a laminated paper cover on both sides, which lends itself well for painting. This requires much less paint than the usual surfaces. This interior cabinet structure was painted a solid color. On the parts of the built-in, such as the storage units, Weldwood texture 1-11 was used. Woodlife with a drop of dark stain served well to create a rustic appearance for pleasing contrast.

Rafters are cut to fit, and the outside rafters are placed into position first. These are carefully

Fig. 19. Layout of new concrete base is staked out.

Fig. 20. After completion of the main structure, framing plates are nailed flush with outside of slab.

Fig. 21. Good surrounding was achieved by brick planters.

Fig. 22. Studs are mounted to enclose the right end of the patio, thus framing the built-ins.

Fig. 23. To create the top support of the built-ins, a cross strip is fastened to the studs.

Fig. 24. This is the structure which was partitioned. The inside (shown) is for the music center; the other side is for exterior gardening tool storage.

Fig. 25. Texture 1-11 (exterior fir paneling) is applied to the studded structure on the outside of the built-in section.

Fig. 28. Each cross member is covered with a matching corrugated rubber sealer to support and shield the plastic sheets.

Fig. 26. Installation of corrugated plastic sheets, starting at the bottom end.

Fig. 29. Special extruded aluminum flashing (matching the plastic of the top) is mounted against siding of house with caulking for waterproofing.

Fig. 27. Half round wood strips are mounted on rafters between layers where two sheets join the overlap.

Fig. 30. Special exterior fluorescent lighting fixtures are mounted to house wall.

Fig. 31. To create an interesting effect, a 12-inch soffit mounted in front of the lighting dispersed the illumination up and down.

Fig. 32. Close-up of Grant heavy-duty folding door track and carriers (being adjusted). These support the heavy folding doors at the built-ins.

Fig. 33. To continue the effect of the interior wood panel treatment, the flat ¾-inch Duraply folding doors were covered with ¼-x-8-inch strips of the same material, applied with glue (spotted) and nails.

Fig. 34. Finished row of doors.

Fig. 35. A complete music center, with stereo, remote speaker control, slide-out TV platform, intercom, and telephone jack, and nearly all are removable.

Fig. 36. Sliding bar pushed back into its enclosure.

Fig. 37. Sliding bar section pulled out.

Fig. 38. This is the far right built-in for storage of lawn mower and other garden tools.

Fig. 39. This is the only exterior storage enclosure, also for garden and maintenance equipment.

Fig. 40.

squared with the house and the front supports, and measured to make certain that they are parallel to one another. Then they are permanently nailed. The remaining rafters are also nailed in place, and cross-spacers are mounted between them. Next, the 2-x-4 plates outlining the built-ins are nailed to the slab with steelcut nails, as outlined before.

As the roof is a combination of different designs, textures and materials, grooved Duraply (waterproof plywood) sheets were used to cover the roof where it was to be solid; corrugated plastic was used for translucent areas. To insure a tight and lasting installation of the plastic sheets, corrugated rubber strips were nailed to all spacers (Figure 28) and half-round wood strips were nailed to rafters where the shape of the corrugated plastic would fall onto them, matching and sealing these joints. It is helpful to apply the appropriate adhesive on these and all other joints.

The plastic sheets were installed, working from the lower front up, with a 4-inch overlap between sheets, as well as beyond the front fascia, and an overlap of one corrugation (or flute) at each joining edge. Special galvanized nails with rubber packing on them were used with plastic cement wherever the sheets touched a framing member or the special corrugated rubber strips on the horizontal cross members, and also where two sheets overlapped. Caulking was used extensively, especially against the house where matching aluminum flashing made a waterproof joint where the plastic roofing sheets met the house wall (Figure 29).

The entire house wall in the patio area was furred out with 1-x-2 strips to which ⅝-inch-thick Duraply panels were mounted, snug to the rafter support strip at the top. Next, special exterior type fluorescent tubes were installed across the entire wall 16 inches below the rafters, and shielded by a 12-inch-high Duraply soffit. This created an indirect light, spilling illumination up and down (Figures 30 and 31). Folding doors, held together with full-length solid brass hinges, were finished off by gluing and nailing ¼-inch Duraply to the ¾-inch Duraply doors (Figure 33). The bi-fold doors were divided so as to cover three separate built-ins. (Grant Series 1000 heavy-duty folding door hardware was used.) Flush ring pulls of brass were attached to the doors. Both the upper and lower bar cases were mounted on slides especially made to handle their considerable weight, including the additional leverage and weight when the units are pulled out and in use, which in the case of the lower bar unit could easily reach some 500 pounds. (These heavy-duty industrial slides were made by Grant Pulley especially for this feature). An alternative method to use for the lower cabinet would be to mount it on four heavy-duty non-swivel rubber casters.

The lower bar consists of two basic sections. The front section has three drawers on one side and a compartment with an adjustable shelf and two small doors on the other (Figure 37). The rear section houses the sink, the Nutone built-in mixer and all flexible pipes and wiring (Figure 36). The bar has running water which is supplied from behind the built-in, and is connected through a rubber hose, as is the drain, which leads to a planter bed against the new Patio wall.

The breadboard-type slide-out top, supported on guide strips inside, is simply a Duraply board, placed beneath the top through a cutout. The lower bar unit is covered with plastic laminate.

The back bar unit is of the same width as the bar top. It was mounted to the bottom bar case with metal straps holding it in back and with screws through the bottom in front.

The accomplished distribution of the various built-ins, as shown, can be changed and adjusted to suit the owner's particular needs. The most important part of this outdoor center is that it makes summers longer and pleasanter.

The first built-in unit (Figure 35) is the music center. It is equipped with a swivel-top slide-out platform for the TV, stereo inside the cabinet (removable), and intercom and control for exterior weather-proof University speakers, which were mounted remote, above and behind the built-in units, so as to create broad and refined sound.

Fig. 1. Creating the House of Id

# Chapter 14
# What to Know When Building

In summing up this fabulous transformation of a deteriorated property and succeeding in the fulfillment of a near miracle, one must examine all events in order to record the basic and historical knowledge learned from it and using it as a guideline.

The preceding chapters gave a broad spectrum of an ideal room-by-room analysis aimed at the most favorable and functional living conditions. To achieve this task, a nearly 100-year-old house was chosen so as to create the most advanced and attractive results under the most adverse conditions. Thus, an ancient New England colonial house without adequate plumbing, with inadequate electricity (and installed only to cover a small area), a sagging porch, a swamplike basement, and an attic that would frighten even Superman, especially when the bats decided to exercise, was what would become the "House of Ideas."

It is quite obvious that sheer guts or even extreme talent alone were not responsible for the solutions required. It was a matter of careful and tireless study, and research of projective attempts covering every conceivable approach in keeping with the technological breakthroughs in other fields. Finally a work list was created that represented the useless characteristics of the old house, while at the same time establishing a study of locations for temporary and permanent supports. Of course, besides the installation of the temporary supports at this time, not much other work in the way of physical changes requiring legal clearance was attempted, in order to avoid any local code violations. A very basic plan was created, first to show all partitions—especially the bearing ones—as near perfect as possible, as this was to be the only existing plan of the old house (the original plan was not available). While measuring as accurately as possible, it became frighteningly apparent that most walls were neither straight, parallel nor perpendicular, nor were the heights consistent. In fact, some floors were so slanted that an extended stay in such a room was enough to make one seasick. But there was one good point in the midst of all that mess: the ceilings were, in nearly all areas, over 9 feet high.

By the way, the main floor was supported with tree stumps, odd pieces of lumber, or poles wedged between 2-or-3-inch blocks layered on top of one another on the muddy basement floor. These vertical supports were forced onto 2-x-8-inch pieces above, no more than 4 feet in length (put on edge), used as cross girders, if you care to call them that—mostly in different directions and supported on each end with one of those stumps. This was the only means of supporting the floor joists, and actually most of the entire house. The sight was frightening, considering that this is what held up the three-story, towered structure. The peripheral base consisted of field stones barely holding together, let alone forming a supporting base for this house.

It remains a mystery why on earth this "scare" (as labeled by *The New York Times* in an article on this project) was never condemned. Due to the nature of this property and the attitude of the people living in the adjacent area of this small community, the purchase of the house, plus 1.9 acres of beautiful land, created an aura of suspicion. You see, this house had been on the market over two years—nobody would touch it with a ten-foot pole.

Neighbors asked, "Who on earth is going to live there?" or "Are we in for surprises?" Well, they sure were.

With enough experience at hand, it was not too difficult to project a master plan. What the first "clean-up" step ultimately accomplished was improvement of the stability of the old structure by removal of all unnecessary weight bearers, such as the tower and the porch surrounding nearly two-thirds of the house, to leave a box-like structure.

No matter how engaging the "dream" and how well it was backed up technically (even the building inspector, himself a knowledgeable engineer, was happy with it), it looked like there was just not going to be a "House of the Future" (its first name), and certainly not the removal of the landmark tower. In this very old, tradition-bound section in the exclusive outskirts of Westport, Connecticut, nostalgia rather than progress covered the landscape and influenced the architecture of nearly all the houses.

The author had been made fully aware of past Building and Zoning Commission rulings, which sometimes appeared arbitrary—perhaps reflections of the "Town Fathers'" rather conformist "clapboard" tastes. These traditional attitudes toward "architectural control" initially seemed a dampener to the creative thrust.

But time was of the essence, and the author had to search for an acceptable compromise in terms of the neighborhood, and solutions in terms of the House of Ideas itself that would not depart extremely from the overall innovative concept that was to become an optimum achievement in creative design.

The season was Spring.

Two months had been lost, mostly on nonconstructive, time-consuming exercises, and summer was nearing, leaving little time to reconstruct the exterior and have the house covered properly in time for the cold Connecticut winter. Considering that there was much to be done, and done well, the clock was ticking away.

Actual construction could not take place under any condition before approval was granted by the Building Department. This required issuing to them plans providing for all changes and additions. The well-researched needs included: bringing in a completely new power pole for the required electricity; a new supply line for water; a rather costly septic system (this community had no public sewerage); a 1,000 gallon oil tank in the ground; an emergency gasoline supply tank (for stand-by power), also in the ground; a water supply system for exterior use at the house periphery only; the projected telephone setup, including provision for phone-vision; and even the new shape of the driveway. These were only the more basic and outstanding concerns, and each and every one had to have certified specifications by *bona fide* authorities drawn up on them. And, as pointed out before, the design of the exterior facade had to be submitted for approval as well. The only relatively free hand the author had was with the rear facade and back patio area, which was well camouflaged by the abundance of beautiful trees and foliage, and which was oriented in such a way as to provide complete privacy.

At this point, and after a building permit had finally been obtained, the plans were finalized. They outlined only the necessary exterior and interior changes. Because all subsequent procedures more than met structural support requirements, the efforts to create, rather than just to build, began to flourish.

Because this project from the outset was planned for publication, notes of important phases were recorded and completed only after extended and successful tests. The same system was applied to the execution of all working drawings. These, too, were finalized after completion of the project and thorough testing and use. Some of the more complex features are reflected in the instructive dialogue and details of this book, adjustments derived from experimentation to improve methods necessary for realizing the desired results.

The following is an accumulation of knowledge gained through extensive research, and its application is vital when undertaking a project of this magnitude.

## How to properly lay out an area prior to remodeling

Whether building a new structure or remodeling an old room, the measure of success largely depends upon its preparation.

The further back we search into the history of design, the more we will find that drawings and plans of structural projects were more detailed and were also drawn to larger scale than the way we see them today. This surely must have had much influence upon the ultimate success and accuracy of the project.

The assistance of good measuring devices for the interpretation of measurement conversions and the present training in the schools is helpful to those who do mechanical drafting. While a larger scale is accurate and safe, $\frac{1}{8}$-inch scales were widely used for too long a period on the commercial scene. Sometimes a heavier pencil line could represent nearly 4 to 6 inches in full size. Even in the most commonly used scale of $\frac{1}{4}$-inch to 1-foot proportion we cannot realistically judge a proper room division and the application of structural and/or decorative changes.

Very few people, including professionals, can fully envision a major change realistically from a plan or drawing of too small a scale.

Only a full-size representation of objects can transform theory into a realistically projected vision of proportion within an area. But to get full-size prints other than for small details is impossible; consequently, we are forced to find a workable compromise.

While many changes and new techniques were introduced to the field of structural design, the use of a full-size layout for testing proper proportions has not, nor will it ever, change.

With the exceptions of clear, simple, and obvious structural shapes, creative designs are nearly always laid out full size on the job site and in the particular area of construction by this author. While such layouts do not always represent all-detailed planning, they do sufficiently mark a perfect outline for even the layman to understand and use for final decisions.

Before making changes of living quarters, we must first properly visualize what these changes really represent within the available area and in proportion to existing structures.

The technique of properly projecting a design idea into realistic representative shapes and forms is invaluable, and can save future mistakes and often costly disappointments. However, this is not the final solution to creating a successful change of any area.

This author, by working for Hollywood film studios, has learned a very successful technique applicable to the creation and solution of proper space design and the distribution of meaningful structures and objects. Say, for instance, we have a given problem which involves the addition of certain structural changes of visual importance, such as the bed headboard in the Lavish Bedroom in this book. The most important task is to place them at the best advantage to the eye; "The first impression is the most important" holds true here especially.

When designing for motion picture sets, one must please millions of different people.

Each plan has a superimposed guide key showing the camera aim and angle during the different scenes, while using the same set. The camera lens is always the human eye and everything is covered and fully arranged in accordance with this fact.

Even when choreographers create a certain scene during rehearsals, they look through a special eyepiece which represents the camera lens and shows nearly exactly what the camera will pick up. The choreographer will even move about the way he envisions the camera will during the production.

When designing the House of Ideas, this author followed very much the techniques of designing and decorating for movie sets. This was done in nearly all room settings with exceptions only where it was absolutely impossible. But there is a puzzling void in this theory. Why does a single high structure appear wider at the top, instead of narrower, as it should according to the theory of vanishing points? The answer is the optical illusion. At what point, where and how, is not determined. Therefore, good creative designers will make allowances for this by adjusting the perspective to justify these visual distortions.

This author found the camera technique most suitable for capturing the dramatic distortions which so vitally influence the creative projection in pursuit of highly successful solutions.

When dealing with several interconnected doorless areas, as in the House of Ideas, it becomes even more important to capture consecutive points of interest to achieve an uninterrupted visual flow, while changing the physical structure of each area ever so subtly to integrate them all harmoniously.

Starting at the main double door entrance into the foyer, the first thing the eye falls upon is the dramatic staircase suspended from the extremely high ceiling. This is followed by the large multi-functional living area. There, the amber glass panes inserted in the floor-to-ceiling teak bar enclosure are visible to the right, and the "living wall" can be seen to the left. While this 7½-foot-high ceiling extends only 12 feet, it creates a powerful shield against what is yet to come. Entering the area covered by the low ceiling and advancing further into the living area, one is suddenly taken by surprise. The area opens in all directions, upward toward the high cedar-textured cathedral ceiling with its dramatic details, the heavy beams and thin light lines spilling against the top. The enormous living area serves a multitude of functions, incorporating the Living Kitchen in its very midst. The many changing forms and the application of different materials, textures, and colors, illuminated by projective and sharp vertical light patterns, magically draw one's visual path through one area into another. The pleasant music and the automatically changing light patterns in concert with a room in motion —drapes and walls opening to reveal new areas—keep one wondering what will happen next.

This system, in various degrees, proved extremely helpful in the creation of the House of Ideas. As in the case of the suspended Patio, it was the most suitable aid for finding a number of determining guidepoints or areas of maximum interest which in progression (rather than predetermination by design) developed successful results.

Using the wide-angle camera or only the viewer as an instrument of composing creative innovations when designing an area, especially when rebuilding, one sees it as the photograph will ultimately produce it. This is what this project required. But most importantly, the process of moving into and through the areas will also bring the objects into clear focus, uninterjected by the many deterring factors which disturb such results when just looking without this aid. The phenomenon is the reality that any area from an ordinary room to a large multi-shaped area, and in that order, expanding the degree, cannot be seen in its proper symmetry as it would be designed or rendered, no matter how well. Any area will appear distorted to the naked eye; the larger the area, the more accentuated the distortion. Of course, the vantage point of what the observed area offers in exposures or characteristics out of the ordinary will exaggerate this fact. A good way to exemplify such a phenom-

enon is a related visual distortion prevalent when one stands in the midst of skyscrapers. The symmetric rule is that two parallel lines will meet as they disappear into visual infinity, the vanishing point. As an example, look at a stretch of railroad tracks. This same visual theory should be used as a guide for design. The visual results are sometimes good and sometimes lacking what we call "a touch of dramatic reality." To achieve better results on a drawing, we must distort here and there (some call it "cheating a little") in order to achieve a dramatic illustration.

Now, back to the skyscrapers. The theory of parallel lines converging as they depart from our vantage point stands true no matter which direction these lines go. There is distortion as you look up at several high buildings encircling you. It seems as if each becomes wider toward the top, as if to close the sky.

To create this legend-like achievement, the camera, on a rolling tripod, replaced the pencil much of the time. It is perhaps best defined by stating that there is a world filled with infinite creative ideas, even within the once crumbling walls of what was destined to become a House of Ideas. To witness this marvelous manifestation, all one had to do was to keep on looking in order to see. This is the requisite that separates the "definition" from the actual proof—this is the difference between design and creation.

As lighting is one of the most important aids for decorative designing, the basic flow of illumination was initiated opposite the entrance of an area in nearly all of these features.

Lighting in the House of Ideas was so laid out that when entering an area it would almost physically guide one in the proper direction. As one moved, the perimeter light spillage would change. This was not achieved by physically switching on different circuits, but merely by the way the ceiling or wall structure, as well as the illumination within, changed from one level to another. This, with the help of using proper lighting fixtures set closer to the wall than even the manufacturer suggests, changed the luminous characteristics completely. In fact, by installing Kliegl pin-spot fixtures about

16 inches, or even as little as 8 inches on center, from the wall and about 4 feet apart, a multitone, nearly three-dimensional, indescribable experience was created, even though the actual wall surface was of flat monotone finish.

Another way of achieving a successful dramatic effect is by using three-dimensional materials or objects—preferably unusual wall structures and textures such as the fireplace wall in the Family Living Area.

Even without this animation, the integration is magnificent and remains undiminished. It would be almost impossible to single out any one creative element, as this is a fusion of sensitively coordinated functions and materials —an inspired composition whose main ingredient had to be love.

When designing the Lavish Bedroom, it was physically impossible to properly install the dynamic headboard and bed structure on the facing wall, even though it would have been visually desirable. Because of this, the antique mirror covering an important section of the facing wall now reflects this dramatic structure on a diffused level, rather than a direct reflection produced by a clear mirror which may tend to be stark.

There are, no doubt, other aspects contributing to a sound layout. One safe way to start any building venture is to first project one's dream onto a sketch and then transfer it to a larger scale drawing.

Before any final decisions are made, a full-size plan of leading features in the planned area will prove to be most helpful.

## Lighting

Lighting is the most versatile means of creating a decorative, dramatic impact for any surface or area. Its functions are unlimited. Obtaining optimum use from it depends on creative imagination. The House of Ideas is a good example of means available today, either commercially by using a certain type of fixture, or by installing some sort of special effect as has been done in the beams shown in the Living Area's cathedral ceiling. With creative lighting you can make music sound better; you can cut down the extent of your tension, if any; you can put yourself in a special mood, if you so desire; you can create color; you can actually bring out a three-dimensional feeling in a straight wall.

If lighting is applied properly, you can achieve various colors and shades without color bulbs, just having basic colors in your decor and using the right fixtures and bulbs in the right place. Of course, working with dark backgrounds is best. The decor of the House of Ideas is such that, under ordinary lighting, it might be lacking the desirable color impact that people are consciously aiming for. Colors used throughout the house blend from area to area and from room to room, and are, with a few exceptions, based upon the basic earth colors because they were considered to be most adaptable for the projected environment. In other words, because this house was not built for one family, but as a guidance for millions of people and perhaps generations to come, a median had to be applied, as far as color was concerned, to satisfy the many rather than the few. Therefore, earth colors were used, such as browns, beiges, terra cotta, antique gold, matte chrome—stainless steel—pewter, and some black, all in various shades and color combinations harmonious with each other. Also, glazes in semitransparent colors dramatically correlated and softened some selected areas. This is the basic substance of the color scheme. Glossy surfaces were avoided, where possible.

With the use of spot bulbs in condensed fixtures, such as the Emerson R-1030, hues of one color in any area, especially the floor (area rugs, carpets, and the three-dimensional pebblestone vinyl), created a breathtaking multicolor situation. This was even further dramatized by special pin-light wallwasher fixtures. While, especially in the main living area, several circuits of different individual luminous experiences were individually controlled by automatic Luxtrol dimmers, they were created to function independently. Each lighting pattern had its own projected functions that were sufficient to enhance the entire area. Together, all lighting formed a pattern of luminous exposure which with dimmer control was magnificent for large entertaining. The flush ceiling (R-1) downlights used for the traffic areas were used with spot bulbs. With that, the floor was illuminated by 3-foot-diameter round spots about 14 inches apart in a series, equally spaced, resulting, especially in larger areas like long hallways, in a dramatic effect while serving its purpose well.

The reason for this multi setup, besides attaining a spectacular decorative achievement, was to separate different areas and functions of the large living area through light concentration and actual selection of any intended activity. Ordinarily, few homes lack the basic wiring or areas necessary to do what was done in this case with the House of Ideas, even under less ostentatious conditions. Even so, all that most people need is a little imagination and perhaps a few fixtures, properly selected and installed, with the right type of bulbs to create lighting rather than just to illuminate, consequently enhancing their decor. We found that if your general lighting is adequate and can be separately controlled, your decorative and mood lighting is best achieved by using spot fixtures and spot bulbs, especially near feature walls. Their aid and precise function can thus be better controlled.

Cold cathode lighting was used to illuminate the several levels of the Suede Bar. This type of electric installation is advantageous, but costly in comparison to other sources or types of similar lighting. The Suede Bar is the most luxurious bar in Chapter 12. Its shape and complex construction were truly a designer's dream, especially since the budget was not curtailed.

Lighting, as usual, played an important part in the creative projection; consequently, it was an invaluable part of the ultimate success of this feature.

The basic idea was to achieve the appearance of a floating top and armrest (railing), as well as to create the illusion that the large, curved bar was floating in mid-air unsupported. This required, primarily and most importantly, a lighting system that would assist in achieving such a visual illusion. As discussed throughout this book, lighting can be, and often is, the most important single factor which can work visual miracles. Cold cathode light-

ing, while not commonly known, was selected because of its inherent characteristics, making it the only suitable solution for this task.

The following are the characteristics that are mandatory to create this demanding and unusual effect:

1. The primary requirement was a high luminous intensity.
2. The lighting had to be instant-starting.
3. There had to be an even (uninterrupted) illumination in spite of the curved shape of the bar or junctions.
4. There had to be consistent illumination (no flickering).
5. The lighting had to be controllable by dimmers.
6. It had to be safe in the area of use.
7. It had to have exchangeable or removable luminous elements.

While these 7 points refer only to the lighting itself, there were several highly technical requirements, among which was a transformer installed in the basement, well isolated and securely and protectively covered. This transformer converted high voltage (much as your TV set does) into 110 volts to stabilize the electric power fed into the luminous elements. This obviously is a job for a highly qualified electrician. However, we will attempt to describe this type of lighting system because it is unusual. It has outstanding advantages and it achieved an unusual function successfully. Without the unique illumination, a beautiful creation such as this Suede Bar would have failed in its dramatic perfection. The very successful solution attained through lighting alone set an important precedent for this author. There are substitutes, to be sure, as there are substitutes for nearly all products we use. But they are what they are properly called—just substitutes.

Cold cathode, as mentioned before, has an extreme stable light intensity. The high power source was reduced by the transformer to a normal scale by invisible mercury-produced wave lengths within the glass tubes (not similar to the ordinary wire structure of a light bulb). In fact, the basic type of this illumination is comparable to the source used for ultraviolet energy (bactericidal) used for destroying mold, yeast, virus bacteria, etc. Cold cathode basically functions by the electrode which emits electrons (negative ions) and toward which positive ions (electrodes) move and collect in a voltaic cell —in this case, a glass vacuum tube capped off on the ends. For evenly dispersed illumination within the top as well as at the bottom of the bar, the glass tubing used for the lighting was custom-bent to specially-made matching patterns using ½-inch- and ⅝-inch-diameter tubes.

For the required illumination, tests revealed that the proper coverage would be derived by installing a continuous stretch on the inside (about 3 inches from the end enclosure) and another stretch for the outside curve, the same way. Because it was necessary to have the glass tubes made in sections, primarily to exchange faulty sections (due to leakage or accidental cracks), the tube layout was very important. By cutting down on joints (which create light-voids) while coping with the curves (whose tubes would be harder to remove), an actual plan was drawn showing the opening (slots) on the bottom of the main top as well as in other areas. This determines the different section sizes one can live with. After this is established and laid out, the voids and other possible deficiencies are compensated by a center row, which also is placed in sections (staggered) to overlap any voids. Again, one must consistently consider the ability to replace any portion of the center section. Also, to further improve an even light dispersion, the inside of all areas where the tubing was enclosed was laminated with heavy aluminum foil. True, it took some replacement of faulty tubes and some sealers, as well as a bit of electric adjusting, especially with the use of motorized Luxtrol dimmers. Sometimes it was frustrating and, in fact, it barely made the grand opening at Christmas. But was it worth it? The owner-client claimed, after nearly 6 years of rather extensive use, "It's magic—whatever it's called. It transforms one into a different world in which no one thinks back, but enjoys every minute of it. By the way, there was never any defect in all the years—what a joy!"

In the House of Ideas, in order to add the completed touch of imagination to lighting, the superior dimmers—manual and remote—were automatic and motorized in concert. These, with a well-planned layout, enabled us to control the light strength to balance all sources properly. This left practically nothing to be improved upon, in order to meet any desired lighting. While the basic installation and the equipment cost (a one-time investment) may be more than usually exacted, a well-designed, sophisticated lighting system will save money in the long run, even in electricity consumption.

**Wood finishing**

Finishing is a process of staining wood and applying a cover or final finish (or variety thereof). While staining is not always a desired or necessary operation, the final finishing is. If for no other reason, the final finish will not only enhance but also protect the wood for some time (depending on type and quality).

In the past few years, much has been accomplished in the wood finish industry. Today, the environmental protection agencies have become aware of the harmful effects of some products, and consequently have set forth stringent rules for the manufacturers of such products. Since much of the finishing in our homes is done as a do-it-yourself project, control of the chemical substances that are used is certainly a good idea. In fact, leading finishing product firms have said that due to the necessity for making their products safe and acceptable, they found better ways with better products, with simpler applications. With the right product, and adhering to the manufacturers' instructions, even the most inexperienced amateur can do a professional job.

However, there are some important points to observe:
1. The finish you finally apply will be as good as the surface to which it is applied—a blemishless one—well sanded if not smooth when purchased (such as unfinished wood paneling).
2. Make sure, when purchasing finishing material, to specify interior or exterior use, indicating whether an area of interior panel-

ing or cabinet is exposed to sunlight or not.

3. Try to apply a finish that will not merely cover the top of the wood surface for a little while—only to fade or peel off in time—but that will penetrate the wood fiber, thus accentuating the natural wood grain and creating a tough and easy-to-maintain surface.

4. Before buying, be sure to check out future maintenance contingencies. There are products which will require very little, if any, maintenance.

5. Always make sure (as in cases of paneling and hardwood trim) that the product you buy will match both types of wood. If not, get proper instructions on how to best achieve the results you want.

6. Because of the availability of a broad variety of prefinished wall paneling (such as that used in the House of Ideas), and the fact that cabinetry, doors, and trim are available in unfinished material (especially where ¾-inch plywood is used for cabinets when the walls are covered with the same type of wood, but prefinished), a careful match or blend should be made. Matching the materials to those given the most exposure is best done by taking a sample of the prefinished product to the store. Never work with paper samples.

7. Finally, in order to get the most for your money with the least effort and risk, consult your dealer where you buy most of your primary products (like paneling or plywood), or call the nearest plywood producing branch for guidance. You may find that your finishing problems have newer and better solutions. No one would know better than the people who make these plywood products. Also consider matching colored nails, Weldwood Blend Sticks (to cover nail holes and blemishes), and of course panel adhesive by the same manufacturer), which will reduce the use of nails considerably while permitting better installation.

For protective finishes such as that used for the Suspended Patio, see Chapter 13—Woodlife, for instance, is an outstanding product. It has survived the test of time—many hard winters, rainy falls and springs, and direct hot sun.

Considering all these points, it may be advisable to engage professional painters or wood finishers to do the job properly. Much cost is involved in the material and labor prior to finishing, but the finish may well make the difference between success and failure—and that cost is only a small percentage of your investment for the overall project.

In all cases, make sure that the product you buy has the proper protective approvals. This is for your safety, as well as an insurance on your investment.

## Ecology

In general, the cheapest way all around to supply heat and air conditioning in your home is to run sheet metal (mostly uninsulated) ducts from your heater, wherever it is installed, branching (optional) air conditioning into the same duct. Because it is feasible to run ducts as high up as possible, you will find the register grill always near or against the ceiling of your room if you have what is called forced air heating. The air conditioning is usually extra and window units are used very often.

As heat rises and cool air drops, this forced air system is principally wrong. People who have this system in their homes know that in cold weather their feet are cold. And in order to warm up the room, the burner will have to work constantly and the blower will grind away while you barely feel comfortable sitting down. While standing up or walking around, especially if you are tall, you will feel uncomfortably hot. The heat sits up there in the upper 2 to 3 feet of the room. While all that mechanical labor continues, after a while your oxygen is replaced increasingly by hot dirty air, and at a fuel cost way out of proportion. All this while you can't help but hear the noise of the blower and that hollow, tunnel-like sound of air forced through the sheet metal duct. You will probably end up opening a window to get some fresh air into the house (especially after prolonged use), and when you have new fresh air in the area, you will close the window and start all over again. Now, if you connect an air conditioner unit to the existing duct, using it of course on a hot day, you had better stay away from the register grille area or else you will be exposed to too much direct cold air, which may not be healthy. While the location of the forced air is ideal for cooling, it is, if used with the blower installed for the heating, much too severe to be comfortable directly under or near it. Here again we are exposed to that tunnel-like sound. Of course, in most cases people have window air conditioners installed, so the experience is known to most, and for the combined investment one can have the right system.

Surely, by insulating your exterior walls and ceilings well, you can cut the cost of heating and cooling considerably while at the same time dampening the noise in your home. One way to make a forced air heating system less annoying, while at the same time cutting down on fuel, is to wrap the duct wherever possible and accessible with heavy cloth-covered insulation. If you live in a cold climate, wrap the ducts specially heavily in areas like the garage, through which they usually pass.

The most ideal installation ever experienced was the one in the House of Ideas. Perhaps the most ecologically perfect one ever devised, it was engineered by American Standard's best. The project also involved different products created by others. It was an experience which proved that with proper planning and the selection of an overall concept we may still have, at least in our homes, a desirable atmosphere.

Hydronic was first put to test in the House of Ideas by the Heating and Cooling Council of America.

American Standard provided all the equipment, engineering and supervision of installation. The Heating and Cooling Council of America provided much-needed guidance and additional help in the do's and don't's.

Hydronic is perhaps best explained by pointing to a better distribution of heating and cooling through special valves and pumps at the production source and an overall preparation of the end, or leads, to the output source at the living end—such as the convector, the pipe or duct that leads to it. Especially in hydronic cooling, we not only had to insulate the ducts on the outside with a special fiber skin covered fiberglass insulation, but the same was done during the fabrication of the ducts, on the entire inside. This helped contain the cool air with a minimum loss while in transit, while at the same time eliminating any sound that is common with ordinary air conditioning. It just disperses the cool air evenly on top and lets it fall however gently, cooling the room evenly.

In the heating setup, perhaps the most noteworthy factor was the quick dispersion of hot water to the radiator or base panel strips. This was also achieved by subtle reduction of pipes on the route and the extremely good retention of heat by the cast iron of the base convector.

*Heating:* Because heat rises, the unit was installed on the floor against exterior walls primarily. The convectors were 12-inch-high cast-iron base strips with built-in copper tubing (2 parallel), which created a circulating hot water motion activated by a pump-circulation motor next to the oil burner. The advantage of cast iron is that it retains the heat, thus cutting down on the need for constant water rotation or excessive use of the pump motor—all of which is completely noiseless. Due to the large size of the house, the system was divided into four independent zones, each with its own thermostat. Due to the sliding glass doors and the many thermo glass panes, mostly on the north wall of the rather large living area (the north wall is the coldest area to which any house is exposed), it was impossible to install heat-based convectors in these areas. Consequently, the heating engineers, in order to achieve the proper heating requirements, had to resort to other means. In order to compensate for that lack, two small blower units were built below each speaker of the Living Wall in the entertainment center. On very cold days, five to ten minutes maximum in the morning only did the job. Because heat rises, you could lie on the floor or stand up; you would never know the sources of your comfort, just feel good.

In heating or cooling a home, the success of achieving desired temperatures and retaining mechanisms at a lower cost depends on how well your home is insulated. It also depends on how well your doors and windows interlock and seal, and on the attention given to drawing the drapes or shades to block out the sun.

*Cooling:* Cold air sinks, so the cooling ducts were installed in attic spaces or above shallow ceiling supports. But they were always routed to reach the register grill up high using the shortest and most direct route possible. Where high ceilings or large areas demanded more cold air pressure, it was achieved by coupling the ducts with narrower sections, thus creating more concentrated pressure in those areas. However, in such cases, especially where the cathedral ceiling provided more height, the registers that produced the boosted pressure were installed a couple of feet higher to avoid direct draft. The factor which really separated the excellent from the adequate was the way the ducts were built. First of all, they were lined on the inside with ⅜-inch quilted fiberglass matting. This was done during the fabrication. The sheet metal, of regulation thickness, was wrapped again on the exterior with the same fiberglass material, only a bit thicker. The ducts were firmly supported with custom-bent brackets to fit each location properly and in short intervals to prevent vibrations. The 3 cold air generators (one for each zone) were mounted in the most remote area outside the house and were concealed by shrubbery. This hydronic cooling system further consisted of dual flexible copper tubing for continuous circulation which was filled with concentrated freon (the same substance used in ordinary refrigerators). The ends of each pair of pipes were sealed and broke open only when properly screwed into the sockets of the compressor and booster units. The length, which can vary considerably (a broad variety is available from American Standard), was the correct one to reach the blower units installed remotely in different attic areas without coiling or kinking, thus reducing the freon flow. To get the tubes to their destination in the house, they were first led into basement or crawl space through a hole in the foundation (which was later sealed), then mounted to the floor framing with special clips in the precise area where they could be best routed to the upper areas. The blower units were mounted on a platform consisting of two ¾-inch pieces of plywood sandwiched together with a ¼-inch sheet of rubber cushion between and a 1-inch rubber mat on top, directly under the blower unit. The entire assembly in all three cases was solidly anchored to a frame mounted to the ceiling joists, and, with further brackets, to the rafters.

This very important installation made any vibrations caused by the fan or distribution units virtually impossible. The inside ends of the pipes were connected, the main sleeve of each duct lead fastened, and for precaution a safety power switch was installed in each area next to the electric outlet. A pair of thin bell wires were connected to the control box on each unit and fished down behind the wall of each of the three thermostat locations and reconnected to the stats. Each stat was set to a desired temperature. The stats and the control center automatically regulated the proper supply. To cut down on any possible sound coming from the drive units, the attics or crawl spaces were insulated with Owens-Corning fiberglass pads (press-on) not only between the roof rafters but also on top of all ceilings. In addition, before paneling, all walls were covered with fiberglass pads between the studs and also covered with ½-inch sound-deadening boards. Beneath the floors, in the basement, fiberglass pads were mounted between the floor joists. The result of all this was that on the hottest day, when all three units were going, sometimes even all together, you could not hear a sound nor detect the source of the filtered cold air softly dropping down. The most phenomenal experience was, when after a hard day in the office and over an hour's train ride in often poorly air-conditioned cars, you came home, took off your coat and stretched out on the carpeted floor in the master bedroom. This was heaven. You could not hear a sound, even if the children played, or the television blasted only 20 to 30 feet away. You could hear only your spine cracking and tingling until you were totally relaxed. The quiet and pure air made you wonder, "Why can't everybody enjoy life like this in their homes?" One thing is sure: if they don't enjoy their homes to the fullest, they are surely investing in the wrong thing. Once you experience the reality of achieving ecological perfection where you live, as did this author, you will retain faith and hope that someday, maybe soon, the term ecology will have a purpose everywhere and for everyone.

### The new energy challenge

When Thomas Edison invented the light bulb, he first fabricated a pear-shaped vacuum glass housing which contained a wire filament. This eventually became the first operable light bulb. Obviously, many attempts preceded this invention, and the many refinements which succeeded were most importantly in the variation of the filaments for the emission of greater light intensity.

The many variations of lighting devices that followed the first Edison principles, such as fluorescent tubes, neon tubes, mercury tubes and tubes with mercury and phosphoric gases, have all aimed toward broader and stronger illumination.

The ever-increasing number and types of lighting systems certainly have allowed us to expand our illuminative needs, and have afforded us creative lighting almost without limitation. Now a paramount requirement has abruptly come to our attention: to find illumination and even heating with considerably lower power consumption.

It is a known fact that some of the giants in the plywood and plaster board manufacturing industry have, at one time or another, achieved tangible success in utilizing their material for the additional application of heating. There is no reason why phosphoric ingredients, which have been used on clock numerals since their earliest development and are now used to fill lighting tubes for brighter light emission, cannot become a part of the material applied to our walls and ceilings.

While much research has been done and more will be needed to expand such theories and make them workable, the idea of achieving a much-needed departure from highly electricity-consuming devices is much closer to reality than perhaps the desperate hope of getting enough fuel to illuminate and heat our cities, offices and homes by present methods.

# Acknowledgments

The Author wishes to thank the following individuals and companies for their cooperation and advice, as well as for supplying some of the materials for the House of Ideas.

TONY ANTOVILLE, board chairman, U. S. Plywood Corporation. NATALIE MARCUS, design director of Amtico. GABRIELLE LOIRE, France, world renowned in the arts of stained glass applications. FREDERIC STRAUB, the nation's leading expert in kitchen appliances. MARTHA TURI, a most ingenious innovator in the field of plastics. SIDNEY HEIFETZ, an artist whose medium is stainless steel. ALFRED S. NELSON, president, The Superior Electric Company, inventor of the Luxtrol dimmer and many other related devices found in theaters throughout the world. ANDRE RAHMER, an ex-Scotland Yard officer, who helped formulate a variety of security plans. LAWRENCE J. EPSTEIN, Chief Coordinator of British Industry Wharfdale Speaker Division, consultant for sound system equipment, one of the pioneers of component high fidelity in this country, a co-founder of the Institute of High Fidelity. STANLEY GOLDSTEIN, engineer and electronics expert, who was of immeasurable help in assisting the author to achieve many unusual effects.

U.S. PLYWOOD CORPORATION, New York, N.Y. Exterior siding, interior paneling, veneers, doors, Flexwood, and all plywood, wood preservatives, glues, adhesives, etc. THE STANLEY WORKS, New Britain, Conn. Special hardware, hinges, sliding hardware, drapery hardware and motors, all portable power tools, etc. AMERICAN STANDARD, New York, N.Y. Hydronic heating and cooling system and engineering, special kitchen fixtures and sinks, bathroom fixtures. ALLIED CHEMICAL CORP., Acrylan Fiber Division, New York, N.Y. Carpets, drapes, headboard, unholstered bed trim, bedspread. ALLIED CHEMICAL CORP., Barrett and General Building Supply Division, New York, N.Y. Roofing, sound-deadening boards, plaster wall boards, basement and base-wall waterproofing, protective driveway coating. HEIFETZ METAL CRAFTS, INC., Wood-Ridge, N.J. Stainless steel suspension system for staircase, hoods, and stainless steel trims, and supports for kitchen-barbecue, bar. EASTMAN KODAK CO., Accessories Department, Rochester, N.Y. Movie and slide projectors, special lenses, portable remote controls, programmer for sound injection and automatic movement, dissolver, film cutting and editing equipment for the Living Wall. CREATIONS IN PLASTIC BY MARTHA TURI, New York, N.Y. Design and handcrafting of plexiglass enclosure for sunken tub. Coordination of plastic stair fabrication. JUST PLASTICS, INC., New York, N.Y. Fabrication of plastic steps and all other plexiglass features. U.S. RUBBER CORP., New York, N.Y. Koylon mattresses, cushions for patio, upholstery material for Continental and Suede bars, and Naugahyde. ROCKWELL MFG. CORP., Delta Power Tool Division, Pittsburgh, Pa. Power tools for the Dream Workshop. GRANT PULLEY AND HARDWARE CORP., West Nyack, N.Y. Drawer and special heavy-duty (custom) slides, sliding hardware for mechanized walls for Continental Bar and Living Wall projection theater, all hardware for Outdoor Living Center. THE SUPERIOR ELECTRIC CO., Bristol, Conn. Dimmers (Luxtrol), automatic and motorized, remote controlled motors—reversible S.S. (slow syn) 150 and 250 for combination dimming and door drive for Continental Bar and Living Wall, TV elevator, etc. AMTICO, American Biltrite Rubber Co., Trenton, N.J. All vinyl floors. OWENS-CORNING FIBERGLAS CORP., Toledo, Ohio. Fiberglass insulation for entire house and luminous ceilings in laundry, power control room, and projection room. RUSSWIN DIV. OF EMHART CORP., Architectural Department, R. D. Lemay, New Britain, Conn. Custom architectural services, locks, latches and door stops. Special hardware for custom wood windows. EMERSON ELECTRIC CO., St. Louis, Mo. Rittenhouse hi-fi intercom system, special exhaust fans, recessed electric wall heaters for bathrooms, flush ceiling light fixtures; also combination bathroom ceiling heater-exhaust and blower fan-lights, exterior lanterns. BRIDGEPORT BRASS CO., Bridgeport, Conn. Copper pipes and coils for snow melting system. KEYSTONE SHOWER DOOR CO., INC., Southampton, Pa. Specially designed and fabricated shower and tub enclosures for bathrooms. CABIN CRAFTS, INC., Dalton, Ga.—New York, N.Y. Special area rugs, blending carpet for staircase. BRITISH INDUSTRIES CO., Port Washington, N.Y. Record players and stereo speaker systems for major custom units, especially the Living Wall. ISABEL SCOTT FABRICS CORP., New York, N.Y. All drapery fabrics for main living area and some of the children's rooms. THE MAGNAVOX CO., New York, N.Y. Remote TVs (color sets only in Living Wall and master bedroom elevator). Remote controlled Astro-Stereo combination console in Master Bedroom. MARBLE INTERNATIONAL, LTD., New York, N.Y. Italian imported travertine marble with sealed pores, for entire Mediterranean-style Master Bath. Sarim venetian ceramic glass tile for Continental and Suede Bars. AMERICAN DRAPERY & CARPET CO., INC., New York, N.Y. Labor and installation of all drapes. HERMAN MILLER, INC., Zeeland, Mich.—New York, N.Y. Furniture, adjustable shelving and desk system in Teenage Boy's Room. AMERICAN CHAIN & CABLE CO., INC., Hazard Wire Rope Division, Wilkes-Barre, Pa. Stainless steel wire rope for staircase suspension. REVCO, INC., Deerfield, Mich. Built-in refrigerators, freezers, and ice makers. SPEED QUEEN ATLANTIC CO., INC., Long Island City, N.Y. Hobart Kitchen-Aid dishwasher, Toastmaster food warmer, Speed Queen washer and dryer for Deluxe Laundry and Pantry. KOHLER CO., Kohler, Wisc. Generator for standby electricity. A. MARCHAND, INC., New York, N.Y. Conceal-All built-in accessories for bathrooms, kitchens, and pantries. LATEX FOAM RUBBER COUNCIL OF AMERICA, New York, N.Y. Latex foam rubber items. AUTOMATIC SWITCH CO., Florham Park, N.J. Automatic switch control for standby power generator. LIQUIDOMETER CORP., Long Island City, N.Y. Levelometer for generator fuel tank and for 1,000-gallon oil tank with remote gauge. THE MOSAIC TILE CO., Cleveland, Ohio. Decorative ceramic walls, kitchen counter and soffits, and floor tiles. LEE L. WOODWARD SONS, INC., Owosso, Mich. (Factory) BERNARD FINKELSTEIN ASSOCIATES, New York, N.Y. Wrought-iron furniture for Suspended Patio and Continental Bar. THE SABA CORP. W. GERMANY. Remote control TV projector, stereo, and tape recorder for Living Wall projection room. LINE ELECTRIC CO., Division of Industrial Timer Corp., Orange, N.J. Electronic timer and relay system (electronic brain) for Living Wall and Continental Bar as well as entire environmental programming of Living Area. MANESCO, INC., Manhasset, L.I., N.Y. Special equipment for Living Kitchen barbecue, Deluxe Laundry and Pantry, fans and ductless Charco air purifiers, etc. SWANSON MFG. CO., INC., Owosso, Mich. Portable ironing board, built-in toaster, can opener, paper dispenser and roof exhaust fan for Living Kitchen. RISING & NELSON SLATE CO., INC., West Pawlett, Vt. Vermont colored slate for all exterior walls and cover of entire house base. COMMITTEE OF STAINLESS STEEL PRODUCERS, AMERICAN IRON & STEEL INSTITUTE, New York, N.Y. Stainless steel for counter seat suspensions and brackets for Living Kitchen, footrest and support brackets, etc. for Continental Bar. LOIRE IMPORTS, INC. FRANCE, Division of Société d'Exportation d'Art Religieux, Pierre Masin de Miroval, Pres., Paris 8, France and New York, N.Y. Stained glass doors for Continental Bar and Suede Bar back units, hand-poured 9-x-9-inch amber glass panes inserted into the sliding enclosures of Continental Bar. DONALD SEIP CO., Swedish Wood Floors, Greenwich, Conn. Imported vinyl coated, random planked oak hardwood floors for downstairs children's bedrooms and library. AMERICAN TUBES & CONTROLS, INC., West Warwick, R. I. Plumbing pipe supports, special controls, pumps and other equipment for the plumbing of the heating system. MURRAY MFG. CORP., Brooklyn, N.Y. Electric circuit breaker switch panels. THE CROMAR CO., Williamsport, Pa. Mosaic wood parquet floors for the entire upstairs. EDWARDS CO., INC., Norwalk, Conn. Fire alarm and smoke detector systems. H. P. PRODUCTS, INC., Louisville, Ohio. Built-in vacuum cleaner system. TACO, INC., Cranston, R. I. Heating circulator motors and snow melting pumps and special controls. JERROLD ELECTRONICS CORP., Philadelphia, Pa. Complete AM-FM-antenna system including a booster amplifier and multi-wall receptacles. HART & COOLEY MFG. CO., Holland, Mich. Registers and special grilles for air-cooling system. JOHNSON RUBBER CO., Flooring Accessories Division, Middlefield, Ohio. Rubber treads, risers and entire covering of staircase leading to basement. SAMUAL STAMPING & ENAMELING CO., Chattanooga, Tenn. Viscount-Suburban double wall oven with special ventilating system (Living Kitchen). PORTLAND WILLIAMETTE CO., Portland, Ore. Accessories and screens for fireplaces. JOHN BOYLE & CO., INC., New York, N.Y. Awning fabrication for gazebo of Suspended Patio. TORK TIME CONTROLS, INC., Mount Vernon, N.Y. Security timers for automatic light control, automatic garage door closing with interconnected area lighting controls. DESIGN-TECHNICS, New York, N.Y. Ceramic fixtures over dining table, lamp in Family Living Room and all ceramic planter containers. I. V. CHAIR CORP., New York, N.Y. Suspended kitchen counter chairs (Living Kitchen). HOMELITE, DIV. OF TEXTRON, INC., Portchester, N.Y. Motorized cart with all necessary interchangeable lawn maintenance equipment including snow-plow. KNAPE & VOGT MFG. CO., Grand Rapids, Mich. Special storage hardware for Man's Closet and Deluxe Laundry and Storage in basement. TELEPRO INDUSTRIES, INC., New York, N.Y. Rear projection engineering. THE BILCO CO., New Haven, Conn. Exterior basement steel door structure. MOBILE GLASS CO., Greenvale, L.I., N.Y. Fabrication and installation of all exterior insulated window panes (1 inch thick), also antique-type mirrors and special glass work. REMCON, Division of Pyramid Instrument Corp., Lynbrook, L.I., N.Y. Low voltage lighting system. THE HEIFETZ CO., New York, N.Y. Special lighting fixture for the gazebo of Suspended Patio. NATIONAL CONCRETE CORP., Long Island City, N.Y. Decorative exterior concrete blocks. WINCO INC., Houston, Tex. Hardware for Ease-Down cabinets. THERMASOL CORP., New York, N.Y. Steam bath equipment for bathrooms. FIELDCREST CORP., New York, N.Y. Special fashion accessories for beds and baths. BETTER HEATING AND COOLING COUNCIL OF AMERICA, New York, N.Y. NATIONAL ASSOCIATION OF HOME IMPROVEMENT & REMODELING CONTRACTORS, New York, N.Y.